Say It Well

Say It Well

FIND YOUR VOICE
SPEAK YOUR MIND
INSPIRE ANY AUDIENCE

Terry Szuplat

WHITE HOUSE SPEECHWRITER
FOR BARACK OBAMA

HARPER
BUSINESS

An Imprint of HarperCollinsPublishers

HarperCollins books may be purchased for educational, business, or sales promotional use. For information, please email the Special Markets Department at SPsales@harpercollins.com.

FIRST EDITION

Designed by Bonni Leon-Berman

Library of Congress Cataloging-in-Publication Data
Names: Szuplat, Terry, author.
Title: Say it well : find your voice, speak your mind, inspire any audience / Terry Szuplat.
Description: First edition. | New York, NY : HarperCollins Publishers, 2024. | Includes bibliographical references and index.
Identifiers: LCCN 2024002920 (print) | LCCN 2024002921 (ebook) | ISBN 9780063337718 (hardcover) | ISBN 9780063337725 (ebook)
Subjects: LCSH: Public speaking—Handbooks, manuals, etc. | Speechwriting—Handbooks, manuals, etc.
Classification: LCC PN4129.15 .S98 2024 (print) | LCC PN4129.15 (ebook) | DDC 808.5/1–dc23/eng/20240609
LC record available at https://lccn.loc.gov/2024002920
LC ebook record available at https://lccn.loc.gov/2024002921

24 25 26 27 28 LBC 7 6 5 4 3

For Mary, Jack, and Claire

. . . let me think clearly and brightly;

let me live, love and say it well in good sentences,

let me someday see who I am . . .

—SYLVIA PLATH

Contents

Introduction: The Way We Talk   xi

YOU GOT THIS

Chapter 1:   Love Your Sacred Story   3

Chapter 2:   Say What Only You Can Say   22

Chapter 3:   What a Speech Really Is   40

Chapter 4:   The 50–25–25 Rule   55

THE BEGINNING

Chapter 5:   Have 'em at Hello   81

Chapter 6:   Be a Uniter   99

Chapter 7:   Appeal to Values   118

THE MIDDLE

Chapter 8:   Speak from Your Heart . . . and to Theirs   139

Chapter 9:   Talk Like a Human   163

Chapter 10: Make It Sing   179

THE END

Chapter 11: Tell the Truth   199

Chapter 12: Turn Your Words into Deeds   220

Chapter 13: The Only Way to End a Speech   238

SHOWTIME

Chapter 14:   Make It Better   259

Chapter 15:   Stand and Deliver   277

Epilogue: After the Applause   299

Acknowledgments   305

Notes   309

Index   321

Introduction

The Way We Talk

I was shaking.

It was almost time for me to speak, and I could feel my heart starting to race. I shifted anxiously in my seat, desperately thinking of ways to escape.

I don't have to do this.
I'll just smile and politely decline. "No thanks. Not tonight. Maybe another time."
Disaster averted.
Dignity preserved.

But it was too late.

"And now," a voice announced, "give it up for Terry!"

Every eye in the room was on me. I started to talk into the microphone, but I sensed my voice trembling. Then I thought about the audience hearing my voice trembling, which only made my voice tremble more. I tried to hold the pages of my speech steady, but my hands were shaking. I thought about the audience seeing my hands shaking, which only made them shake more.

For a moment, I felt like I was out of my body—floating above, looking down on myself as I stammered and quivered. My mouth was moving, but the only sound I heard was the Voice of Doubt in my head:

They can see that you're nervous.
You're going to screw up and embarrass yourself.
Please, just let this be over.

The way I was stressing out, you'd think I was delivering a major address to a huge audience. Far from it. I was in a karaoke bar with my coworkers—fellow staffers at the White House, where I was a speechwriter for President Barack Obama. We were on a work trip in Yokohama, Japan, and after a week of grueling international travel, we'd gone out for the night to unwind. I knew the audience. They were my friends. I spoke from my seat and didn't even have to stand up.

In fact, I wasn't even delivering a speech (or doing karaoke) at all. It was a silly little skit I'd written about Obama and other world leaders scrambling to pull the world economy out of a ditch like a wrecked car—a fun parody of a story Obama loved to tell back home on the campaign trail. In other words, it was no big deal. It didn't matter whether I nailed it or flopped, which made my nerves all the more frustrating.

Why was this happening?

In my gut, I knew. Even though I've been a professional speechwriter for nearly my entire adult life, for most of that time I'd been uncomfortable with public speaking myself. I was a speech*writer* who couldn't seem to hack it as a speech *giver*.

It's not like I avoided public speaking altogether. I could usually handle talking to a small group or giving a eulogy at a family funeral. And sometimes I wasn't half bad. Most of the time, though, just the idea of speaking in front of a group of people left me wracked with anxiety. So, for most of my life, I largely stayed where I felt safe— behind the scenes, writing speeches for others.

But I paid a price.

I spent so many years helping President Obama and other leaders speak in *their* voice that, over time, I lost my own. I coached speakers on how to tell *their* stories, but the idea of sharing mine could be nauseating. I was able to draft remarks for Obama, who, even his critics agree, is one of the world's great speakers, but I struggled with a meaningless skit.

Somehow, I made it through that night at the bar, though it's mostly a blur. My coworkers laughed and applauded. But walking back to our hotel through the empty streets of a city far from home, I felt helpless.

All I could do, it seemed, was hope that my fear of public speaking might fade over time.

It didn't.

When Obama's presidency was over, I left the White House and tried putting myself out there more—doing interviews and speaking to small classes of college students. Sometimes I was fine. Other times, not so much.

During one live TV interview, I tensed up, started stumbling over my words, and then just stopped talking altogether. I froze. Mercifully, the interviewer ended the segment, and I darted out of the studio, embarrassed.

Another time, on a conference call with a group of young foreign policy activists, my mouth dried up in the middle of my presentation, sending me into a full-on coughing spasm. The host put me on mute while I lunged for a glass of water and tried to collect myself.

At an intimate dinner with colleagues, everyone around the table took turns giving toasts and then looked at me to offer one as well. But I couldn't summon the courage. I just sat there, looking down at my plate. After a few seconds of awkward silence, the conversation moved on, and I spent the rest of the evening replaying my party foul in my mind.

Clearly, I wasn't meant to be a public speaker. Or a private speaker.

As time went on, I tried to avoid it as much as possible. If some-one invited me to talk to their group about working at the White House, I made up an excuse about why I couldn't. At dinners, I watched silently as others delivered toasts that got everyone raising their glasses. For me, it just felt safer not to speak.

Then, one day, an unexpected phone call forced me to face my fears.

"Hello, this is Antti Mustakallio," said the voice on the other end of the line, in a crisp Nordic accent. He said he was one of the very few speechwriters in Finland.

"So, I hear you give a lot of speeches about giving speeches?" he asked.

"Oh, absolutely," I said, mustering as much false confidence as I could. "I love it."

Antti wanted me to come to a conference later that year in his hometown of Hämeenlinna. A few hundred miles from the Artic Circle. In November.

"I would like you to deliver a keynote speech about how to de-liver a speech. It will be onstage with an audience of three hundred people."

I almost hung up. Antti kept talking, but I wasn't really listening. The scenes of my past failures flashed through my mind.

"I'll think about it," I told him, with no intention of thinking about it.

But then, in the days that followed . . . I began to think about it. I was now in my late forties. I was being given a great opportunity, which I'd miss if I let my fears continue to control me. How many more experiences would I pass up—and later come to regret? Was I going to hide from public speaking for the rest of my life? Plus, what's the worst that could happen? If I flopped, no one back home would know. It would be in Finland. In November.

Maybe I *could* do this. Maybe this time could be different. Maybe

I could try to remember the lessons I'd learned as a speechwriter, including for President Obama, and use them to develop and deliver a speech for myself.

Fortunately, I had plenty of lessons to draw on.

I was fortunate to write for Barack Obama across all eight years of his presidency. It was the most exhilarating and uplifting—and at times exhausting and terrifying—experience of my professional life. I learned from him every day as he connected with audiences around the world, which I witnessed up close while joining him on trips to more than forty countries.

In Kenya, flying with Obama aboard the presidential helicopter, Marine One, I looked down and saw the streets of Nairobi filled with people ecstatic over his return to his father's country, some with handmade signs that read "Welcome home!"

In Vietnam, where throngs of people lined the streets of Ho Chi Minh City to get a glimpse of his motorcade, the crowd—perhaps thinking they'd seen Obama—broke through the police line and chased me and other staff into a hotel.

The crush of the crowd was so strong in Tanzania that our staff bus got separated from the motorcade and hit a telephone pole, which smashed one of the bus' windows and sent shattered glass across the laps of frightened staff.

Moments like that could be nerve-racking. But they were also revealing. With the power of his words and story of his life, Obama tapped into something universal: ideals, values, and aspirations that transcend boundaries of race, religion, country, and culture. And *how* he connected with his audiences—including people who didn't necessarily agree with his politics—can offer lessons for us all.

When I started writing this book, a speechwriter I'd worked with at the White House joked, "What? You're going to give away all our secrets?!"

Well, yeah.

And why not?

Yes, speechwriters are supposed to be ghosts—heard but not seen. And for more than twenty-five years, that was me: behind the scenes, largely invisible, penning the words in private that a president, members of Congress, executives, activists, and celebrities spoke in public. But why should these leaders be the only ones to benefit from these skills?

The art of public speaking is a skill we *all* need—now more than ever.

It's been two decades since a presidential speechwriter offered a book of advice on public speaking. Since then, the world has changed. A new generation of young people—diverse, restless, hopeful—are raising their voices, demanding to be heard. We're finally beginning to talk more openly about systemic issues that for too long were swept under the rug. Everyone—whether you're an elected official, a business executive, or a school principal—is now expected to speak to world events and complex issues of race, religion, and individual rights.

At the same time, raging political and social debates have turned language into a battlefield where words are wielded like weapons. Some people seem oblivious to how language from a bygone era, especially around race, can inflict pain on communities that historically have been marginalized. Other people can sometimes be quick to shame or condemn well-intentioned family, friends, or colleagues who struggle to keep pace with the rapidly evolving vocabulary around identity, sex, and gender.

From what I can tell, most people feel caught between the front lines—trapped in a rhetorical no-man's land—not wanting to fall back on the coarse language of a cruel past, but unsure how to move forward without misstepping and setting off a linguistic land mine that can destroy their relationships, career, or reputation.

We've lost, it seems, the ability to communicate with one another.

Too many leaders seem more intent on scoring rhetorical points against their opponents than engaging in the dialogue that democracy needs in order to function. Too many speakers seem more eager to drown out those with different views than to practice the persuasion that brings more people to their cause. Our airways and communities are flooded with misinformation and cruelty—vitriol that undermines the trust, understanding, and shared sense of purpose that we need to live and work together.

The way we talk has to change.

I worry, though, that, just when we need it the most, the art of public speaking often seems more complicated and intimidating than it needs to be. Too many books on rhetoric have overlooked the voices of women, people of color, and historically marginalized communities. Some books on public speaking can make your head spin with obscure words from ancient Greece and Rome. But I'm here to tell you that you don't need to know what *chiasmus* is to be a great speaker. One thing Obama never told us was "You know, this is a good speech, but what it really needs is more chiasmus."*

All the while, technology continues to transform how we talk to one another. For the first time in history, every one of us has a megaphone—our smartphones, social media, and Zoom—that allows us to instantly share our voice with the world, with all the power and peril that it brings. With the rise of artificial intelligence, chatbots are revolutionizing how we learn, create, and communicate—with untold benefits and dangers. This may be the

---

* Chiasmus is a rhetorical device in which a phrase mirrors a previous phrase in reverse, like when President John F. Kennedy said, "Ask not what your country can do for you—ask what you can do for your country." And yes, sometimes Obama used it, like when he said, "My job is not to represent Washington to you, but to represent you to Washington." More often, though, Obama's rhetoric was rooted in direct and straightforward language, which reflected his belief not in the power of leaders to inspire their people, but in the power of the people to inspire their leaders. (See what I did there?)

first book on public speaking in the age of AI, and I'll offer some thoughts on how we might harness this technology to sharpen our voice without losing the humanity that's at the heart of all great communication.

In short, the art of public speaking needs an upgrade—a new guide for our diverse and changing world, with practical tools for the presentations, pitches, talks, toasts, and tributes that we give in our daily lives.

I hope this book can be that guide for you.

But before we dive in, I have a confession: I never read a book about public speaking or took a class on rhetoric before I became a speechwriter. Every lesson I'll share in the chapters that follow I learned by doing. This is the book I wish I'd had when I started out on my own journey.

I'll take you behind the scenes at the White House—into the Oval Office and aboard Air Force One—and share never-before-heard insights from President Obama on his approach to public speaking both as a candidate and as president. You'll hear, for the first time in his own words, how he became the speaker who burst onto the world stage with his unforgettable speech at the 2004 Democratic convention in Boston. "We all have weaknesses in how we communicate with people," he told me once as he reflected on his evolution as a speaker in the years before the convention. "There were definitely some habits of mine that weren't particularly useful, which I had to learn to correct."

This book also includes insights from many of the speechwriters who wrote for President Obama and First Lady Michelle Obama. That's because even as I worked on hundreds of speeches in my windowless office in the basement of the West Wing (with mice scurrying through the ceiling), I was just one member of an extraordinary team. You'll see how we did it, but even more important, the mistakes we made (more than once, I thought I might lose my job), how we learned from them, and how you can apply these lessons to become a better speaker yourself.

You'll hear from some of the world's leading scholars, psychologists, and neuroscientists whose research shows why these lessons are so effective. Yes, public speaking is an art. But since leaving the White House, I've tried to understand the science of speaking—evidence-based approaches that can help us all communicate better.

Finally, even as we can learn from a gifted orator like Obama, I believe we can also learn by listening to one another. I'll introduce you to people from all walks of life who have used the lessons in this book—without even realizing it and without the help of a professional speechwriter—to deliver remarkable speeches, many of which went viral and inspired people around the world. Just about all their speeches, and every one of Obama's, are on the internet. As you read, I encourage you to take breaks, put this book down, find these speeches online, and enjoy them the way they were meant to be experienced. *Watch* them. *Listen* to them. *Feel* the connection between the speaker and the audience.

As you do, you'll see why the lessons in this book can work for you too—no matter who you are or to whom you're speaking. Whether you give speeches for a living or are trying to summon the courage to speak for the very first time. Whether you're giving a toast, delivering a presentation at work, raising your voice for change, or running for office to deliver that change yourself. In fact, these lessons can help you be a more effective communicator in all sorts of situations—from a job interview to a difficult conversation with family, friends, or coworkers.

As you begin to apply these lessons in your own life, I hope that, together, we can also learn how to speak to one another—our families, neighbors, coworkers, and fellow citizens—with a greater sense of understanding and mutual respect. Most of us say that we want our public discourse to be more civil, but we don't seem to know how to get there. I've been fortunate to work with and learn from leaders, including President Obama, who have tried to forge a better path. This book shares those lessons as well—because if our diverse democracy is going to endure, we need to find a way to speak to one another with civility, empathy, and honesty.

So, yeah, there's a lot going on when we stand up and speak our mind in front of other people. It can be intimidating. Believe me, I know. But here's the first secret I want you to remember: you already have everything you need to succeed, including something powerful no one else has—your own unique voice.

That was the lesson from a visit Obama made to the small town of Greenwood, South Carolina, during his first presidential campaign. He'd been on the road nonstop. It was raining. He was wet, a little cranky, and there were only about twenty people in the room.

Then, just as he was getting ready to speak, a voice called out from the audience.

"Fired up!"

"Fired up!" the people yelled back.

"Ready to go!" the voice shouted.

"Ready to go!" the people yelled back.

Obama didn't know what was happening.

On it went, until Obama and everyone in the room was . . . well, fired up and ready to go.

The voice that energized the room that day belonged to Edith Childs, a local councilwoman and civil rights advocate, and for the rest of Obama's presidency her chant became a rallying cry. He loved to tell the story, especially at the end of big rallies—how a single person, a Black woman in her late fifties in a small, rural town, had inspired everyone around her.

"It just goes to show you how one voice can change a room," Obama would say, his voice growing stronger. "And if it can change a room, it can change a city! And if it can change a city, it can change a state! And if it can change a state, it can change a nation! And if it can change a nation, it can change the world!"

But how?

How do we *find* our voice? How do we speak up for what we be-lieve? What do we say? And how do we say it so that we're inspiring the people around us to work together for the future we want? That's what this book is all about.

So . . .

Fired up?

Ready to go?

Let's do this.

You Got This

(Really)

CHAPTER 1

Love Your Sacred Story

Perhaps everything that frightens us
is, in its deepest essence, something
helpless that wants our love.

—Rainer Maria Rilke

The first step of giving any good speech or presentation—and where I think many of us struggle—is believing that we can. It's having the confidence that our voice matters and that we deserve to be heard. Too often, we *don't* believe it. We reject ourselves—we stay in the shadows and don't speak up—to protect ourselves from possibly being rejected by others.

As I debated whether to give the speech in Finland, I realized that this is what I'd been doing for so long.

I hadn't always been anxious about public speaking. Growing up in Falmouth, Massachusetts—a seaside town on Cape Cod with gray-shingled houses and a quaint main street where you always run into a friend—my parents and public school teachers always encouraged me to use my voice. And I enjoyed it.

I gave my first "speech" in the fourth grade, dressing up as President John F. Kennedy for a book report. I said something like

"Ask not what your classroom can do for you, ask what you can do for your classroom!" (Cute, but zero points for originality.) I entered a speech contest at the local VFW, read scripts on camera for our high school's weekly TV news program, and, as president of our student government, presided over assemblies of hundreds of students.

Then I headed off to college in Washington, D.C., and I didn't give another speech for decades.

What happened?

The same thing that happens to a lot of people—maybe even you.

~

A fear of public speaking is one of the most common phobias in the world. Many of us, according to some surveys, fear it more than snakes, more than flying on a plane—more, I suspect, than snakes on a plane. I have a friend who, for years, dry heaved before every presentation he gave. As a speechwriter, I've worked with world-famous actors and actresses, some of whom have appeared naked on-screen, and they *still* get nervous when speaking to a live audience (with their clothes on). Toastmasters International, which helps people become better speakers, has members in nearly 150 countries. To struggle with public speaking, it seems, is to be human.

To find out why, I reached out to Boston University's Center for Anxiety and Related Disorders, which put me in touch with Dr. Ellen Hendriksen. She's a clinical psychologist who treats people with social anxiety, including paralyzing fears of public speaking. "We're all social animals," Dr. Hendriksen explained to me. "We all need to feel safety, love, and belonging." Fears of being rejected by an audience, she said, may be rooted in our ancient survival instincts. "Rejection used to be fatal. If you were kicked out of your family or your tribe, you'd be cast to the wolves. You could literally die." Today, "*social* rejection can feel like a fast track to death."*

My own anxieties around public speaking as an adult started to make more sense.

Back home as a kid, I felt the safety, love, and belonging that Dr. Hendriksen described. Even in Washington, I was blessed with friendships and opportunities that should have bolstered my confidence. I worked on my first speech for a president, Bill Clinton, when I was a college intern at the White House.** I got my first speechwriting job a few years later, at the Pentagon, and went on to become the chief speechwriter for the secretary of defense. I fell in love with and married an extraordinary woman, Mary Abdella—smart, witty, loving, and my best friend. We had two beautiful children, Jack and Claire, who, when I'd work on speeches in my home office, would wiggle their tiny fingers under the door to get my attention and slide in notes ("Wen r u dun?").

Life was good.

A few months after President Obama took office, when I was thirty-six years old, I became one of his foreign policy speechwriters, and I'll never forget the day I met him for the first time. It was during a speechwriters' meeting in the West Wing office of David Axelrod, one of the president's close advisers. Obama had been in office only a few months, and I'd worked on his first address to a military commencement, at the Naval Academy.

---

* Some researchers think there might even be a genetic basis for our anxieties around public speaking. The genetic testing company 23andMe says that it identified "more than 800 genetic markers associated with a fear of public speaking." Dr. Alisa Lehman, a biologist at the company, told me that some of us "may be genetically predisposed to having a fear of public speaking." As I write this, 23andMe hasn't yet broken down the data, but perhaps future research may reveal who among us, based on our genetics, may be more likely to have these fears.
** I still have the president's schedule from that day, framed and hanging on my wall: "The Trip of the President to Kiev, Ukraine, May 11, 1995: Embassy Meet and Greet, U.S. Embassy gymnasium, Remarks: Terry Szuplat." As a twenty-two-year-old kid, I had to pinch myself, especially as a Ukrainian American.

"Where's the new guy?" Obama asked, popping into Axe's office as he tossed around a football. "Nice job on the speech," he said, shaking my hand.

I felt like I was on top of the world.

And yet, the more time I spent in Washington—a town obsessed with pedigree, power, and wealth—the more I sometimes felt like I just didn't measure up.

Privileged family background? Not us Szuplats. My father's Ukrainian parents worked in a labor camp in Nazi Germany during World War II. When my dad, Stach, was a child, they emigrated to America and settled in the factory town of Amsterdam, New York. After a childhood spent partly on food stamps, he joined the Navy, and fell in love with and married my mum, Peggy, the eldest daughter of a large Irish Catholic family in Boston, who worked as a secretary.

Wealth? We didn't have any. As young newlyweds, my parents lived in a furnished trailer on the outskirts of my dad's hometown. After I was born, we lived in a small second-floor apartment in Roslindale, then a working-class section of Boston. My dad was a plumber's apprentice, and my parents lived paycheck to paycheck. By Fridays, he recalled years later, "we had just enough money for a six-pack of beer and pizza."

When Dad got a new job, we moved to Falmouth, down on Cape Cod, which, despite its reputation as a summer playground for the rich and famous, is home to proud year-rounders who work hard to get by and raise their families. Like anywhere, Falmouth had its inequalities too. "West Falmouth is old money," people joked to my mum back in the 1970s when we arrived, "North Falmouth is new money, and East Falmouth is no money."

We settled in East Falmouth. We lived on a two-mile-long boulevard of hundreds of houses, then mostly summer cottage rentals, and every morning Dad started his old Chevy Bel Air with the twist of a screwdriver. As my two younger sisters and I neared college, Dad took on extra plumbing jobs, and Mum went to work as a lunch lady at my high school, a night-school secretary, and, later, at the town library.

With a patchwork of Pell Grants, work-study jobs, and scholarships—and some money I'd saved from mowing lawns and a job at the Dollar Store—I was lucky to attend a great school, American University in Washington, D.C. The professors were world-class, and I was given life-changing opportunities—internships in the White House, the U.S. Senate, and, during a semester abroad, the British Parliament.

And yet, at just about every point in my career, it seemed like so many of the people I worked with had gone to the Ivy Leagues. In many ways, Washington can feel like a small town run by alumni of the country's most elite schools. It's often only a matter of time in any conversation before someone asks where you went to college, or graduate school (I didn't). And when you answer, you can almost feel yourself being sized up, assigned to your place in the hierarchy.

Truth be told, speechwriting was, at first, something of a fall-back. In college, I dreamed of becoming a lawyer and imagined myself arguing history-making cases before the Supreme Court. But a funny/not-so-funny thing happened on the way to law school. I didn't get in. Anywhere. (I've never been that good at standardized tests and my LSAT scores were . . . how might a lawyer say it . . . suboptimal.)

As I studied to retake the LSAT, I got the speechwriting job at the Pentagon, enjoyed it, and started having a different dream—maybe, just maybe, I could someday write speeches for a president and help tell America's story to the world. And my dream came true.

Despite all that, I did what so many of us do. Instead of being confident in who I *was*, I too often focused on what I *wasn't*. I hid it well. But in the recesses of my mind, there was always someone who was more deserving than me, more experienced, more qualified, or more credentialed.

That was my story—at least the story I often told myself.

To buck me up, my sister Erica, a talented artist on Cape Cod, sent me a book, *The War of Art*, by the author and screenwriter Steven Pressfield. He talks about the barriers to confidence and creativity and warns against defining ourselves in comparison to others. A person who "defines himself by his place in a pecking order," he wrote, will "evaluate his happiness/success/achievement by his rank within the hierarchy."

I'd been doing exactly that, I realized, for most of my professional life. Which meant the Voice of Doubt was always there, and it was at its most insistent on those few occasions when I tried to stand up and talk in front of other people.

You're out of your league.
You're going to mess up.
They're going to judge you.

I was still hearing that voice as I tried to decide whether to give the speech in Finland. Fortunately, I also found myself remembering another voice—President Obama's, and how he had told me about his own early struggles, both with his identity and as a speaker, and how he had worked to get better.

"I JUST STARTED FREEZING UP"

In 1981, students at Occidental College in Los Angeles held a rally against South Africa's brutal apartheid policy of racial segregation. Obama, then a nineteen-year-old sophomore, was the first speaker. He managed to get out only a few sentences, however, before two students rushed up, pretending to be South African security forces, and dragged him away—a bit of political theater to highlight the oppression of anti-apartheid activists.

"The whole thing was a farce," he explained years later, and his "one-minute oration" was "the biggest farce of all."[1]

"That's the last time you will ever hear another speech out of me," he told a friend. "I've got no business speaking for Black folks."

Decades later, I asked Obama what he meant. His struggles with his racial identity—with a white mother from Kansas and a Black father from Kenya, and having been largely raised by his white grandparents—were "part of" the reason for how he felt at the rally, he told me. More, though, it was rooted in larger doubts about his place in the world and whether his voice could make a difference.

"I think the starting point for effective speaking, for me at least, and for most people who I find persuasive," he said, "is do they have a sense of who they are and what they believe?" At the rally on campus that day, he recalled, "I was a callow youth who was trying to sort out who I was and what I believed. I was nineteen years old, thinking, 'Do I deserve to be in the spotlight? Do I have something specific to say about this topic when I'm still trying to sort out who am I and what I represent?'" The rally had given him a chance to raise his voice. But looking back on his younger self, he said, "I wasn't ready yet."

After college, Obama sometimes had the opposite problem—not a lack of confidence, but perhaps too much. For several years, he worked as a community organizer with churches on Chicago's South Side. "At that point, I was accustomed to speaking in front of people," he told me. "I was not naturally inclined to be nervous"—until one day when his swagger proved to be his undoing. It was a story I'd never heard.

"I remember it vividly," Obama said. He was twenty-four years old, in a high-rise in downtown Chicago, making a fundraising pitch to a conference room full of philanthropists. "I was feeling pretty cocky," he remembered. "I had not written down my remarks. I felt like I could go into any room and just sort of wing it, which was a bad mistake."

He started his presentation. "There are a bunch of people in suits," he recalled. "I'm looking a little raggedy and a little out of place. About four or five minutes into my presentation, I just started freezing up. I lost my train of thought."

"Why?" I asked.

"I was in an unfamiliar setting with unfamiliar people and one in which there were some stakes involved"—the money he needed to sustain his community organizing.

"I was terrible," he said. "I felt a little bit of flop sweat and hemmed and hawed, and got stuck, and was not particularly coherent."

I asked if he remembered how it had felt.

"You erase it from your mind," he joked at first. Then he turned more pensive.

"You feel," he said, pausing to find the words, "stupid and embarrassed."

So how did Obama get better?

There were four places, he told me, that shaped "the strands of my public-speaking style."

"EVERYBODY HAS A SACRED STORY"

After freezing up in that conference room, Obama continued working as a community organizer, which brought him to the first place where he learned to be a more effective speaker—church basements.

"Sometimes, I'd only have twelve people there," he said. "But step by step, speaking to bigger audiences gave me a baseline level of comfort in communicating to folks." As he did, he learned one of the most important lessons of communication—listening before you talk.

His remarks in those basements "were presentations, but they were also conversations" with residents and leaders from the neighborhoods, he recalled. "The best speakers are in a conversation with their audience. They're not talking *at* an audience. They're speaking *with* an audience"—and that includes listening to what's important to the people you're communicating with.

Those conversations, he said, "helped me understand how all of us put together a narrative for ourselves about our lives and what's important to us, where we've come from and where we're going, how that defines our values and what our fears and disappointments are."

"Everybody has a sacred story," he told me, "one that gets to their essential selves. And listening to other people tell their stories helped me understand my own."

As he listened in those church basements, he also learned how to be a better speaker from a second place—the pulpit upstairs. "You know who were good coaches for me?" he said. "All those Black pastors I was in church with. The pastor of a small storefront church who works for the bus company during the day and is there on a Saturday—you watch him tell a story to his little flock of a hundred people. There's a tradition there that is powerful, a particular oral history, a capacity to tell stories. Preachers know how to preach. Just listening and hearing and watching, I soaked a lot of that in." Of all the places where he learned to speak, listening to the pastors of Chicago, he said, "was probably the most valuable."

A few years later, he got his first big chance to show what he'd learned.

He was a twenty-eight-year-old law student at Harvard, and he'd been elected president of the *Law Review*. One of his responsibilities was to speak at the *Law Review*'s annual dinner and introduce that year's honoree—the civil rights icon and congressman John Lewis. "He was one of my childhood heroes," Obama told me. "I wanted to make sure that I did him justice."

"This was the first time I gave a big public speech in front of a large group of people that I did not know, in a setting that mattered to me, on a subject that I cared about. I took a lot of time to think through what I wanted to say. I wrote out the speech. I memorized the speech. And then I delivered the speech"—brief remarks, perhaps five to seven minutes, to a few hundred people.

To the best of his memory, Obama spoke about the importance of the rule of law and paid tribute to the lawyers, professors, and students who uphold it. As the first African American elected president of the *Law Review*, he touched on his own journey. And he delivered a heartfelt tribute to Lewis, who had endured brutal beatings and jailings for daring to stand up for civil rights—sacrifices that made Obama's own presence at that podium possible. And it seemed to work.

"It was the first time I felt like 'I've got the audience, I'm moving them, I'm telling a story that resonates with them,'" Obama said. It all came together—"the material, the moment, the delivery.'"

Obama was starting to find his voice. Over the next decade, he worked to refine it, including in the third place where he learned to speak in front of an audience: the classroom. Even as he served in the Illinois State Senate, he taught classes at the University of Chicago Law School, delivering lectures on constitutional law, civil rights, and voting rights. "I'm getting up in front of a classroom of

---

* Obama's speech at the dinner seems to have been lost to history. He told me he doesn't have a copy of his remarks, and representatives from the *Law Review* told me they have no record of any of the speeches from that night.

students and thinking, 'I'm not going to screw this up,'" he recalled. "It's where I learned to feel comfortable being in a dialogue with people for long stretches of time."

That dialogue continued in the fourth place where Obama learned how to communicate better: his early political campaigns. He spoke to voters at town halls and churches, gave speeches in the Senate chamber in Springfield, and ran for Congress in 2000—the only election he ever lost. "When I first started running for Congress," he said, "I had a tendency in some settings, including debates and impromptu remarks, of not telling stories, but rather listing off talking points, factoids, and policy. I was too abstract, too wonkish, and, as a consequence, too long-winded. I just didn't have enough reps"—enough times doing it. "I still needed to learn how to make effective, impromptu speeches to larger groups of strangers in a high-pressure situation."

Four years later—and with a lot more reps under his belt—he drew on all the lessons he'd learned as he prepared for what would be, to that point, the highest-pressure moment of his life.

As a volunteer speechwriter at the 2004 Democratic convention in Boston, I'd heard rumors that the keynote speaker—a state senator from Illinois I'd never heard of—was going to be good. So I made sure I was down on the convention floor when it was time, surrounded by a sea of delegates in red, white, and blue.

Barack Obama took the stage—smiling, clapping, waving to the crowd—adjusted the mic, and began to speak, introducing himself to those of us in the hall and millions watching at home.

My father was a foreign student, born and raised in a small village in Kenya. He grew up herding goats, went to school in a tin-roof shack. . . . While studying [in America], my father met my mother. She was born in a town on the other side of the

world, in Kansas. . . . They would give me an African name,
Barack, or "blessed," believing that in a tolerant America your
name is no barrier to success.

All around me, the crowd roared.

"I stand here today, grateful for the diversity of my heritage,"
he continued. "I stand here knowing that my story is part of the
larger American story, that I owe a debt to all of those who came
before me, and that, in no other country on earth, is my story even
possible."

I didn't realize it at the time, but over the next sixteen minutes,
it was all there—every lesson about public speaking that Obama
had learned over the years. He told the stories of the people he'd
listened to back home in Illinois. At certain moments, he spoke
with the rhythm of the preachers he'd heard at the pulpit. He
didn't speak *at* those of us in the audience, but *with* us—a
dialogue, a conversation. Instead of ticking off wonkish talking
points and factoids, he told a bigger story—his voice rising as he
neared the end of his speech—about who we were as a country,
our values, where we came from, and where we're going:

> *Yet even as we speak, there are those who are preparing to*
> *divide us. . . . Well, I say to them tonight, there's not a liberal*
> *America and a conservative America; there's the United States*
> *of America. There's not a black America and white America*
> *and Latino America and Asian America; there's the United*
> *States of America.*

I'd never heard anyone speak like this—someone who so un-
abashedly saw our diversity as a people not as a weakness to be
exploited for political gain, but as a strength to be celebrated and
nurtured; someone who didn't just give voice to that diversity, but

who embodied it, calling himself "a skinny kid with a funny name who believes that America has a place for him too."

"There's no question," his adviser David Axelrod told me years later, that "Obama couldn't have given that speech if he hadn't thought deeply about his own identity over many years. He knew who he was, and he understood how his story shaped him."

He was an effective speaker because *he knew who he was.*

I thought about Obama's journey as I tried to decide whether to give the speech in Finland. And the more I reflected on Obama's growth as a speaker—how he'd struggled at first and worked to improve—the more I began to think that maybe I could get better too.

I also found inspiration in someone I'd seen on TV—a boy named Brayden.

"YOUR IMPERFECTIONS ARE YOUR GIFTS"

On a summer day in 2020, thirteen-year-old Brayden Harrington got a phone call he couldn't believe.

He was invited to give a speech. On national television. With millions of people watching.

"I was shocked," he recalled later.

Growing up in the small town of Boscawen, New Hampshire, Brayden was a pretty typical kid. He spent his free time playing catch with his friends or watching the Boston Celtics on TV. At school, he liked English and science and earned good grades.

Speaking to a nationally televised audience would have been nerve-racking for anyone. And Brayden was just a kid. "I still didn't have a lot of confidence in myself," he remembered. For him, there was an added challenge. Brayden has a speech impediment.

In fact, that's how the invitation—from the organizers of that summer's Democratic convention—came about. Months earlier, Brayden had met Joe Biden as he campaigned for president in New Hampshire. Video of their encounter—two people with a stutter bonding over their shared challenge—went viral.

Now, Brayden was torn. He was honored to be invited to speak at such a big event. But he also carried painful memories of stuttering in school and how some kids giggled. "Sometimes, they mocked me." He worried that speaking on national TV would be even worse. "I was scared of what people would think of me."

Over the next few days, Brayden debated what to do. And the more he thought it over, the more he began to think, "I might inspire a lot of people."

He decided to speak.

Over the next few weeks, Brayden and his family worked on his speech, and a speechwriter at the convention helped him edit it. When his little sister, Annabelle, suggested a line—"We all want the world to feel better"—Brayden added it in. He practiced reading it out loud, one day more than twenty times. But as the day of the speech approached, the pressure became too much.

"I just couldn't get the words out," he recalled. "I broke down crying."

Brayden's parents said he didn't have to speak. But he was determined. "I wanted other kids who have a speech impediment like I do to believe in themselves."

The week of the convention—held virtually because of the Covid pandemic—Brayden and his family gathered in his bedroom where a camera was set up to record his speech. His little brother, Camden, goofed around, making faces to help him relax.

Holding his script in his hand, Brayden took a deep breath, sat up straight, and started to speak. Then he started to stutter. He started over. He stuttered again. So he started over again. He took a break, came back, and tried again. It took several tries, but eventually he got it. A few days later, his face was on televisions across the country.

"Hi. My name is Brayden Harrington, and I'm thirteen years old," he began, his braces sparkling as he smiled. Casual in a pink T-shirt, with his desk and schoolbooks behind him, he talked about how he'd met Biden, who had told him they were both "members of the same club."

"We . . ." Brayden said, pausing to take a deep breath, looking down at the speech in his hands. But the next word wouldn't come out.

Brayden looked off camera. He made the *s* sound and closed his eyes, as if to pull the word from his mouth. But still nothing. He took another breath.

Finally, the word arrived.

". . . stutter."

Every few sentences, a word got stuck in his throat. But every time, Brayden pushed through. "We all want the world to feel better," he said, as Annabelle smiled proudly from across the room. "We all *need* the world to feel better."

Brayden's speech was only about two hundred words. He spoke for less than two minutes. But "it was the scariest thing I'd done in my life," he told me when I interviewed him a few years later to learn how he did it. He found the courage to speak, he said, by remembering what his mom always told him: "Your imperfections are your gifts."

Soon, people around the world were giving thanks to Brayden for sharing his gift. His speech went viral. Hashtags spread online, including #BraydenHarrington2044.

"Over the years, I've gotten more comfortable with my speech impediment," he told me. "I don't believe it defines me. I believe you can take something in your life that's maybe bad or that maybe hurts you and turn it around into something good."

"There are a lot of people who don't speak up because they're afraid. But if you have the opportunity, you might as well take the chance. What you have to say matters."

YOUR STORY IS WORTHY

Obama's evolution as a speaker and Brayden's courage in facing his fears hold an important lesson for us all: no one is born a naturally gifted speaker. Public speaking is a skill, and like any skill it can be learned and sharpened—and it starts with the story we tell ourselves about ourselves.

Over time, I tried to better understand and take pride in my story too. Not the one I'd been hearing in my head for so long—the narrative where I defined myself in comparison to others and by what I was not. But, rather, who I *really* am and how my story has shaped me. And if there's any larger story that I can claim to be a part of, it's that with the love and support of the people around us we can always make progress, in our work, our lives, in anything we put our minds to.

It's why I'm grateful beyond measure to my mum and dad, who scrimped and saved and took on extra jobs to lift up our family and made it possible for me and my sisters to get a college education. I'm indebted to patient mentors—including President Obama—who taught me new ways of listening, writing, and communicating. And today I can look back on a journey that I never could have imagined: a kid from a blue-collar family who got to work in the White House and help a president speak to people around the world about the values and hopes that bind us together.

That's my story—the one I finally started to tell myself. It took me many years—longer than it should have—but I found it. And as I considered whether to give that speech in Finland, I began to hear a different voice.

Your story is worthy.
Your voice matters.
You deserve to be on that stage just as much as anyone else.

Love our story—because the feeling of safety, love, and belonging that we all need starts in our own hearts. It's so simple. And yet, so many of us struggle to do it. Our doubts and insecurities, our pain and our traumas, often forged in our youth, warp our sense of self and blind us to the beauty of our own unique life. We buy into hierarchies—real or imagined—that convince us that we're somehow less worthy than others or less deserving of the spotlight.

But as you'll see in the speeches throughout this book, you don't have to come from a wealthy family, the best neighborhood, the most elite schools, or be the most credentialed person in your organization to stand up and give remarks that touch people's hearts and maybe even change their minds.

You just need to believe that you have something to say and that you're the one to say it.

I finally decided to believe in myself too. When it came to public speaking, I was tired of being afraid. It was time to take a chance. I called Antti in Finland and gave him my answer.

"I'll do it."

Over the next few months, I tried to remember all the lessons I'd learned as a speechwriter and use them to prepare my own presentation. In the chapters that follow, I'll share those lessons with you.

The Download

A week or so before President Obama gave a big speech, our gaggle of speechwriters would file into the Oval Office and sink into the light-brown couches with our laptops and notepads balancing on our knees. Obama would usually sit, legs crossed, in his brown leather armchair by the fireplace, with a large painting of George Washington looking down on us.

We had a name for it: the Download. It was the president's chance to tell us what he wanted to accomplish in his speech and what he wanted us to remember as we wrote.

Here's what I hope you remember from this chapter as you develop *your* presentation:

» **No one is born a naturally gifted speaker.** Public speaking is a skill, and, like any skill, you can learn how to do it and how to get better.

» **The first step to giving any good speech or presentation is believing that you can.** It's having the confidence that you have something to say and that you're the person to say it.

» **Ignore the Voice of Doubt in your head.** Everyone has a sacred story, and your story is worthy. Your voice matters. You deserve to be on that stage as much as anyone else.

» **Effective communication starts with the story you tell yourself about yourself.** Before you can speak, you have to know who you are and what you believe. Set aside some time, find a quiet place, and ask yourself these ten questions:

Who am I?
Where do I come from?
What am I working toward?
What's important to me?
What are the values that guide me?
What do I believe?
Why do I do the work I do?

What are my disappointments and fears?
What do I hope to achieve in my life and work?
How are my life and work perhaps an example of a larger
story that can bring people together?

Think deeply about your answers. Write them down. As you go through life—as you achieve some goals and fall short of others, as your hopes and dreams evolve—revisit these questions and update your answers. As you do, I believe you'll begin to find your confidence and voice as a speaker—someone who not only knows your own story, but even loves it and is ready to share it with other people.

CHAPTER 2

Say What Only You Can Say

For, while the tale of how we suffer, and how
we are delighted, and how we may triumph
is never new, it always must be heard.

—James Baldwin

In his second year in office, Barack Obama delivered one of the most unlikely speeches ever given by an American president.

He was visiting Indonesia—where he'd lived for a time as a child with his family—and Indonesians were celebrating his return like a homecoming. The emotional high point of the trip was his speech to several thousand university students in Jakarta. Standing off to the side with other staff, I watched as Obama not only shared his memories of growing up in the city, but did so speaking the language he'd learned as a child, Bahasa Indonesia.

"Terima kasih!" (Thank you!), he began.

"Selamat pagi!" (Good morning!), he said, and the ecstatic audience yelled it back. To which he replied, "Assalamualaikum dan salam sejahtera!" (Peace be upon you and prosperous greetings!)

"Pulang kampung nih!" (I've come home to the village!), he added, to huge cheers.

"Let me begin with a simple statement: Indonesia bagian dari diri saya." (Indonesia is part of me.) The thunderous applause could have blown the roof off the place.

Obama talked about the pedicabs and small taxis he rode in as a kid and the neighborhood he'd lived in, Menteng Dalam, prompting cheers from people in the audience from Menteng Dalam. He recalled buying local food, satay and bakso, from the street vendors and impersonated their calls for customers. "Satay! . . . Bakso!"

"Enak, ya?" (It's delicious, isn't it?), he ad-libbed.

He was just minutes into his speech, and the audience was already in a frenzy. I turned to Ben Rhodes, the president's chief foreign policy speechwriter, who had worked with Obama on the remarks.

"No other president in American history has ever given a speech like this!" I yelled over the cheers.

"And no other president," Ben yelled back, "will ever give a speech like it again!"

~

One of the first things that many of the speakers I work with ask is "What should I say?"

The answer is simple: give the speech that only *you* can give. Personalize it. Tell the stories that only you can tell—especially your own. That's why, as we learned in the previous chapter, knowing your own story—who you are and what you believe—is so important. Because once you know it, you can share it with your audience.

That's what Obama was doing in Jakarta. It's what he did in his convention speech in Boston and in so many other remarks as he shared his own "improbable journey." And it's why, for our team

of speechwriters, every speech became an opportunity to ask ourselves: What could Barack Obama say that no one else could say?

Whenever I worked on a speech, I'd think of all the things that
made Obama who he is. There's his heritage—his Black father from
Kenya; his white mother from Kansas. His faith—he's Christian,
with Muslim ancestors on his father's side; his name is Barack
Hussein Obama. There were the experiences of his youth, growing
up in multicultural Hawaii and in Indonesia. There's his extended
family—cousins, aunts, and uncles around the world—which the
First Lady joked was its own "mini United Nations." He was the
first African American president of the United States.

And then there was his worldview, shaped by his experience as
a Black man in the United States. He spoke of his faith in "the
greatness of America" even as he recognized that our country had
at times fallen short of its founding ideals and that we have to keep
striving to uphold equality for all people. As speechwriters, we wove
all these threads—personal stories that only he could tell—into his
remarks as often as we could.

Now, perhaps you're thinking: *But isn't one of the most basic rules
of public speaking "It's not about you"?* I've always thought that's a
little too simplistic. Yes, of course your presentation shouldn't be
all about you or only what *you* want to talk about. Nobody wants
to listen to a narcissist. (Here's a tip: once you have a draft of your
remarks, count how many times you say "I . . . me . . . my . . .
myself"—and then delete as many as you can.) And yes, you need
to think deeply about your audience and what *they* want to hear
(more on that in chapter 4).

But *you* are the speaker. And often the best speeches are personal speeches. Whether your presentation succeeds—whether you
connect with and inspire your audience—*is* about what *you* bring
to the moment.

WHY IT WORKS

There are several reasons why it's important to say what only you can say.

Your Audience Wants You

Audiences want originality and authenticity. If you've been invited to talk somewhere, it's because someone believes you have something unique to offer. Your audience wants *you*. And if you're *choosing* to stand up and speak—for example, at a community meeting—your audience doesn't want you to repeat what they've already heard from previous speakers. Your audience expects you to offer something different—*your* perspective, what *you* believe, what *you* think needs to be done.

It's Less Scary

Giving the speech that only you can give can take some of the fear out of public speaking. I've seen this with the speakers I work with. When you share unique stories from your own life, you're sharing stories that you know better than anyone else. And the best way to tell these stories is the way *you* want to tell them. They're your memories, your experiences. No one can tell them better than you.

It Will Save You

Grounding your remarks in your own experiences can help you avoid a disaster at the podium. Imagine that you have to give a presentation at work, speak at a town meeting, or deliver a toast or eulogy. You think about what you want to say. You write it down and practice. But when the time comes, you're the last of several speakers. As you sit waiting for your turn, you listen in horror as, one by one, the speakers before you say everything you planned to say. They take the words right out of your mouth. Which means the words in your mouth were not unique. You can't stand out if your remarks sound like everyone else's.

There's an easy way to tell if your speech is a speech that only you can give. Imagine someone else giving it. If another person can stand up and deliver your script and it all still makes perfect sense, then your remarks are generic, not personal. And if you deliver generic remarks, what Abraham Lincoln wrongly predicted about his Gettysburg Address will be true for you—"the world will little note, nor long remember" what you say.

Want to stand out? Be unique.

You'll Be a More Compelling Speaker

I asked Obama once about what he believes makes someone a compelling speaker. "Are they speaking from conviction or experience or some baseline of knowledge?" he answered. "Is there an assurance and authenticity that grows out of them being on solid ground?"

We're at our best when we talk about the people, places, communities, causes, and companies that we know and care about. As a result, we're more relaxed. We smile. Our faces light up—because it feels good to share stories that we know and love. We come across as more confident and credible.

You Will Be Remembered (A Chatbot Won't)

Studies show that audiences are more likely to remember something—a moral, a message, or a lesson—when it's conveyed in a story.[1] And lucky you, you have a story—and stories—that no one else has. There are billions of people on this planet. But no one else has lived your life or walked your path. You are unique; your remarks should be too.

Beware of the Bots

The power of your own story is why I strongly encourage you *not* to rely on artificial intelligence to write your speech or presentation, especially one that should be personal. Yes, chatbots are remarkable. They can synthesize vast amounts of information and help you generate a rough first draft at breathtaking speed.

But remember, chatbots are collators. The content you get from a bot is, by design, *not original*; it's an amalgamation of content that already exists on a particular subject. On its own, a bot doesn't know the life *you* have lived—*your* experiences, *your* values, *your* beliefs. Your audience wants to hear from a human (you), not a robot. They want authenticity, not words generated by algorithms.

Remember, too, that a chatbot is only as good as your prompts. Ask a bot to "Write a 500-word wedding toast to my best friend" and it will regurgitate a generic draft that could be about anybody—because it's about nobody. The bot doesn't know anything about your best friend.

Yes, the more prompts you give the bot—the more details you feed it—the more personal its draft will become. I've heard of some people spending days typing in prompts that run hundreds, even thousands, of words. Here's my thought on that: if you're going to go through all the trouble of telling the bot what to write—and then keep feeding it more prompts to correct what it gets wrong and edit it to your liking—maybe it's better, and even quicker, to just write it yourself.

You'll Inspire Your Audience

If you're appealing to an audience for some kind of support, saying what only you can say is also one of the most effective ways to bring your audience to your cause. Obama made this point during a trip to Vietnam. In a convention hall in Ho Chi Minh City under giant American and Vietnamese flags, he gave brief opening remarks to an audience of young people and then took questions. A young filmmaker with a dash of yellow dye in his hair asked him about the power of stories. This is part of what Obama said:

> One of the things that I've learned about being a leader is sometimes we think people are motivated only by money, or they're only motivated by power, or these very concrete incentives. But people are also inspired by stories. The stories they tell themselves about what's important and about their lives and about their country and about their communities. And . . . in whatever field you're in, whether it's business or politics or nonprofit work, it's worthwhile to listen to other people and ask them questions about the stories that are important to them, because oftentimes you'll find their motivations. And when we come together to do important things, it's usually because we told a good story about why we should be working together.

Great speakers are great storytellers. And the most compelling stories are often our own—who we are, where we come from, why we do the work we do.

As these next few speakers show, it works in every kind of pitch or presentation.

SHARE YOUR MOTIVATION

"Susan Komen was my big sister and my best friend," Nancy Brinker said, pausing to catch her breath as she looked out at a ballroom filled with breast cancer survivors, advocates, and researchers. "And I miss her every day."

Over the next few minutes, Brinker shared how she and her sister had grown up together in Peoria, Illinois. How Susan was the homecoming queen, because "she was universally loved and there was something so essentially kind in her." How Susan had gone off to college, began a modeling career, married her college sweetheart, and raised two beautiful children. And then, how Susan received the awful news no woman ever wants to hear: "You have breast cancer."

Brinker invited her audience into the most intimate moments of Susan's fight for her life. Three years battling breast cancer. Nine surgeries. Three rounds of chemotherapy, which ravaged her body. By her final days, Susan had lost her beautiful brown hair, spent most of her time in bed, and struggled to speak. "She was just thirty-six years old," Brinker said. "She left behind a grieving husband and two little children."

The room was silent, except for the muffled cries of a few people in the audience as they wiped away their tears. I was there, watching from the back, because I'd recently started assisting Brinker with her speeches. In truth, she didn't need my help. She'd been delivering a version of that speech for years, and after sharing the anguish of losing her sister, Brinker pivoted to why she was speaking that day.

"Breast cancer—we have to talk about it," she recalled Susan saying in a whisper on one of her last days. "It has to change . . . so women know . . . so they don't die . . . Promise me, Nanny."

"I promise, Suzy," she replied. "Even if it takes the rest of my life."

Two years after losing her sister, Brinker started a new breast cancer foundation in Susan's honor. She traveled the country and told her story to anyone who would listen, even as she battled breast cancer herself. Over time, her organization, Susan G. Komen for the Cure, sparked a global movement. People everywhere wore pink, Susan's favorite color, and millions ran in the Race for the Cure to raise awareness and money for research and treatment.

By the time I started working with Brinker, about twenty years ago, she'd been giving speeches a lot longer than I'd been writing them. It was the first time I'd worked with a nonprofit. And that's when I made a mistake I'll never forget.

Brinker was getting ready to speak to a medical conference, and the draft of her remarks was too long. I figured the audience of scientists would be more interested in the latest breast cancer research. So I cut the opening story about Susan.

When Brinker got the draft, she called me immediately.

"Where's Susan?"

"The speech is too long," I explained. "I was trying to tighten it up."

She quickly set me straight.

"Susan is our story. It's who we are. It's what sets us apart, even at a medical conference. It's why people want to be a part of our work."

She was right. No one else could tell that story. In a universe of dedicated breast cancer organizations, a promise between two sisters made Komen unique. And it's one of the reasons that the foundation that still bears Susan Komen's name has raised billions of dollars for awareness, treatment, and research and helped to save the lives of countless women.

I never skipped Susan's story again.

When you speak—especially if you're seeking your audience's support for your cause—never miss the chance to share your motivation: *why* this issue or cause means so much to *you*.

SHARE YOUR SPIRIT

A few years ago, I received a call from the founder and CEO of a high-tech firm in Virginia. He was mostly happy with his company, which had grown to seventy-five people in about thirty countries and some $200 million in sales to date. Still, he felt something was missing.

"Our clients like our products," the CEO, whom I'll call John, said. "But I don't think they really know what makes us different. I don't think all our employees have a good understanding of everything we offer either. We need to do a better job, internally and externally, of articulating who we are and what we do."

Over the next several weeks, John immersed me in his company, which builds heavy-duty satellite communications systems for American diplomats and troops around the world. We walked his factory floor (the parts that weren't classified), pored over his marketing materials, and talked with his employees. Then we sat down together in his conference room and I peppered him with questions.

"Why did you start this company?"
"How did you start the company?"
"How did it *feel* to start this company?"
"Were you ever afraid you'd fail?"
"What were the biggest challenges you faced?"
"How did you overcome them?"
"What makes your company different from your competitors?"

As John answered each question, I learned that his company wasn't just another big tech firm launched with a mountain of venture capital from wealthy investors. He had started his business with his wife in their basement using their personal savings and assembling communications gear with their own hands.

It was a classic American success story—entrepreneurs taking risks, working long days, and spending sleepless nights wondering if they were going to make it. What's more, many of his employees were military veterans who were now providing the equipment to help their comrades still in uniform stay safe on the battlefield.

But that wasn't the story John was telling. Here's how he was describing his company at the time: "a consulting firm and systems integrator" that offered "systems management" and "data solutions." It was the same generic story that a hundred other companies could tell—and were telling. Not unique. Not compelling.

Working together, we came up with new ways to talk about their business. Instead of a "consulting firm," he told the story of how he started the company, "founded by a husband-and-wife team . . . a quintessential start-up . . . operating out of our basement . . . with just twenty-five thousand dollars in personal savings," and how "we're still driven by the same entrepreneurial spirit."

Instead of "data solutions," he offered concrete descriptions of his company's services, which he said would "ensure mission success— anytime, anywhere." Instead of referring to his employees as "managers and staff," he beamed with pride as he said that most of them were "proud veterans" who "know that our customers depend on our mission-critical technologies, because our lives once depended on them too." It was a story of family, entrepreneurship, service, and camaraderie.

That was the story John started to tell, and he was amazed at the ripple effect it had across the company. "Our employees had a better understanding of where we came from and how their work fit into a larger mission, which boosted morale. Our managers were able to better articulate to customers what makes us different from other firms." A better story even helped win more business. "I get what you guys are about," John remembers a new client saying, one of several additional customers over the next few years that boosted sales by 50 percent and helped position the company for a successful acquisition.

"As a CEO, you can be pretty good at running your business

financially, but if you can't articulate your story, it can affect your valuation," John said. "Good messaging and good financials go hand in hand."

Telling the story only you can tell can set you apart from the competition no matter what field you're in.

SHARE YOUR JOURNEY

A year after leaving the White House, I was part of the group of Americans, Canadians, and Mexicans who campaigned to bring the 2026 FIFA World Cup to North America. It was, in one sense, a sales pitch with billions of dollars on the line. Our three-country United Bid—with our world-class stadiums and infrastructure—should have been the runaway favorite. But that wasn't the story the world was hearing.

Around the globe, people were recoiling from President Donald Trump's restrictive immigration policies and his description of Central American, Caribbean, and African nations as "shithole countries." Soon, soccer associations were announcing their support for the only other country bidding for the World Cup, Morocco, and some in the media speculated that the United Bid might lose.

Fortunately, we had a better story to tell. We had already decided that our presentation to the FIFA Congress, which would vote on who would host in 2026, would show how the United States, Canada, and Mexico were ready to welcome people from all over the world. And there was no one better to help tell that story than three young, dynamic players—one from each country.

Canada's pick was Alphonso Davies, a seventeen-year-old phenom who played for the Canadian National Team and, at the time, the Vancouver Whitecaps FC. After reading just one news article about him, I understood instantly why the Canadians wanted him to represent their country. Born in a refugee camp in Ghana, Davies had emigrated to Canada with his family, ultimately settling in Edmonton. Alphonso wasn't just a great person to tell the story of the United Bid, he embodied it.

When I got on the phone with Alphonso, though, he didn't have much to say. Maybe he was tired from training. Maybe he was shy. Maybe it was because telling your story is hard, and in his case, it would be even harder: he'd have only sixty seconds to speak. How do you tell the story of your life in only one minute?

Fortunately, there were plenty of interviews online where Alphonso talked about his remarkable journey. When I sent him a first draft, just about every word was something he'd already said himself.

Over the next few weeks, Alphonso rehearsed his remarks between training sessions with the Whitecaps. And his practice paid off. When he took the podium at the FIFA Congress in a Moscow convention center on the eve of the 2018 World Cup—dressed proudly in Canadian red and white—he was perfect.

"Good afternoon. Bonjour," he began. "It's a great honor to speak to you today," he said, placing his right hand over his heart.

> *My name is Alphonso Davies. My parents are from Liberia and fled the civil war. I was born in Ghana, in a refugee camp. It was a hard life. But when I was five years old, a country called Canada welcomed us in, and the boys on the football team made me feel at home. Today, I am seventeen years old. I play for the Men's National Team, and I'm a proud Canadian citizen.*

Alphonso flashed a wide smile full of braces.

> *And my dream is to someday compete in the World Cup, maybe even in my hometown of Edmonton. I've played in matches in*

Canada, Mexico, and the United States. The people of North America have always welcomed me. If given the opportunity, I know they'll welcome you. Thank you.

That was it. Just 135 words. Just 55 seconds. And Alphonso was flawless. As he left the podium, he flashed his bright smile one more time, and the audience broke into applause.

That afternoon, the United Bid won a resounding 134–65 victory. In 2026, the World Cup will return to North America for the first time in decades, in part because a young player born in a refugee camp stood up and told the world a story that only he could tell.

"WE'RE CALLED TO SPEAK OUT"

Sharing your story can be scary. It can be especially harrowing if you're a woman, person of color, immigrant, or member of the LGBTQ community where daring to raise your voice can sometimes invite threats and harassment. "Whenever I speak," a friend who is of South Asian descent confided to me, "I always think twice about whether to reference my identity."

If you're reluctant to put yourself out there, it's not my place to tell you to ignore any risks. You know best how your family, workplace, and community will respond to what you have to say. Before speaking out, look within and decide what's right *for you.*

That's what Michelle Obama did. During her husband's first presidential campaign, millions of Americans were drawn to her strength, authenticity, and candor. Others spewed racist and sexist tropes that she was an "angry Black woman." Her first major speech, at the Democratic convention that summer, gave her the opportunity to show the world who she really was.

"I went to her house on the South Side of Chicago, and we sat in her living room for ninety minutes," remembers Sarah Hurwitz, who went on to serve as Michelle Obama's chief speechwriter during her eight years as First Lady. "She talked about who she was, about growing up on the South Side, about the sacrifices her parents made for her and her brother, and about her commitment to public service. She talked about her husband driving her and their newborn daughter, Malia, home from the hospital, determined to give her something he'd never had—the affirming embrace of a father's love."

"She was telling me her story," Sarah said. "And that's the speech she gave."

Some commentators declared that Michelle Obama had "found her voice." Sarah saw it differently.

"It wasn't that she 'found' her voice. She always had a voice. In that speech, she was just being herself. The world finally saw her for who she really was—a strong, smart, confident woman who was passionate about her family and the progress she wanted to see in our country."

More than a decade later, people across the country were moved again by another strong, smart, confident voice.

~

As she scrolled through her phone, thirteen-year-old Naiara Tamminga couldn't believe what she was seeing. Video showed a traffic stop in her hometown of Grand Rapids, Michigan, ending in horror. A police officer, who is white, struggles to restrain a driver, who is Black—a man later identified as twenty-six-year-old Patrick Lyoya. About two minutes into the encounter, the officer wrestles Lyoya to the ground, pins him face down, and kills him with a bullet to the back of the head.

"I was distraught," said Naiara, who, with a father who is Black and a mother who is white, identifies as biracial. "I'd seen George

Floyd's murder, and so many others, but this was so close to home. I was crying in my room. I was a thirteen-year-old girl, and, at first, I felt helpless. Then it lit a fire under me."

As protests spread across the city, Naiara helped lead a walkout at her school. A few weeks later, she joined protesters and marched down to a meeting of the city commissioners. More than a month had passed since Lyoya's murder, but the officer who pulled the trigger still hadn't been removed from the force or charged with a crime.

Naiara hadn't prepared a speech. But she decided to speak. "I'd never done it before, and I was shaking," she recalls, "but I knew what I had to say was bigger than my nerves."

Standing at the lectern in a gray sweatshirt, her hair pulled back in a ponytail, Naiara didn't hold back. She shared how she'd lost trust in local law enforcement—"I don't see them protecting me"—and in the city commissioners in front of her—"You can identify that there is a problem, but you cannot fix it."

Naiara said she was "absolutely terrified" to live in her community. "I'm expected to go outside and walk my five-year-old little brother. God forbid we look too scary . . . and we get the police called on us." Nearing the end of her remarks, she thought of Patrick Lyoya and the young people protesting with her.

"I don't want to do this," she intoned. "Please, please do not make me sit here and scream another name. Do not sit here and make me beg, and God forbid that name is mine. God forbid that name is any of these people. God forbid."

Emotionally drained, Naiara returned to her seat, assuming her words would never reach anyone beyond the room. But soon after, someone shared her speech online, and it went viral. She was interviewed on the local news, invited on podcasts, and gained tens of thousands of followers on social media.

And then came the hate. "I got a few death threats," she told me when I reached out to her the following year. "Those were difficult to deal with." But when I asked if she'd do it all over again, she didn't hesitate. "A thousand percent, yes."

A few weeks after Naiara's speech, the officer who killed Patrick Lyoya was charged with second-degree murder and fired. "It proved to me that I could help make change," she said. The day the charges were announced, she was at a vigil in Lyoya's honor. "Finally," she said, "there was some sort of justice."

It isn't easy to raise your voice, especially if you come from a community that has been historically marginalized. "It's going to be hard," Naiara said, "some people won't agree with you, but that doesn't really matter. We're called to speak out for what we believe in."

The Download

As you think about what to say in your presentation or speech, think about what makes *you* unique and the stories that only you can tell.

» **If you're in a job interview,** instead of giving generic responses that anyone can give, use each answer to share a specific example—a (short!) story from your work or life that shows you have the skills or experience they're looking for.

» **If you're honoring someone you love or admire**—with a toast, a tribute, or a eulogy—what are two or three (brief!) stories from your relationship that capture their essence as a person? Tell *those* stories.

» **If you're going to speak up at a community meeting** or a rally, why are *you* there? Why do *you* care? Share a story of how this issue impacts you, your family, your community.

» **If you're an advocate**—making your case to donors or trying to recruit volunteers—what's your origin story? Why and how did *you* become involved in this cause? Share the story of someone you know whose life has been touched or saved by your work.

» **If you're an entrepreneur or a business executive**—seeking capital from investors, wooing new customers, or rallying your employees—what's your company's founding story? Why and how did you start the business? What obstacles have you overcome? What are the stories—of your employees, your products, your customers—that set your company apart from the competition?

» **If you're a candidate** asking for someone's vote, what's unique about *your* story? Where your family came from? Your childhood? How did your life experiences shape your outlook · and your policies? What can *you* say that no other candidate can say?

» **If you aspire to be a "thought leader"** in your profession or industry, be warned: giving speeches and sharing your thoughts is not enough. People are recognized as leaders after they achieve something tangible. My recommendation: first do the work. Get results. Make change. Then tell the story of how you did it—and how others can too. *That's* how you become a leader who's admired for your thoughts.

There's another reason why it's so important to tell the stories that only you can tell. It sets you up to give a performance that only you can deliver.

CHAPTER 3

What a Speech Really Is

All the world's a stage.

—Jaques, William Shakespeare's *As You Like It*

One of the first speeches that I ever worked on for President Obama was a near-disaster.

In the years before he took office, cyberattacks against the United States had surged. So in his first weeks as president, Obama ordered a major review of the country's cyber defenses. A few months later, the report was done, and I had to draft the speech where he'd announce his recommendations. I read the report, did my research, and circulated a draft around the White House. But when the speech came back from the policy experts, I was stunned. They had crossed out almost everything I'd written.

My references to "America's digital infrastructure" were replaced with sentences like "cyberspace is the interdependent network of information technology infrastructures, and includes the internet, telecommunications networks, computer systems, and embedded processors and controllers in critical industries."

I'd written, "Just as we do for natural disasters, we have to have plans and resources in place beforehand." Now it read something like "Implementation of this framework will require developing reporting thresholds, adaptable response and recovery plans, and the necessary coordination, information sharing, and incident reporting mechanisms."

Painful.

Someone had literally cut and pasted lines from the report into the speech. And, in their defense, why not? Wasn't the purpose of the speech to unveil the report?

I didn't know what to do. I knew a president isn't supposed to sound like a report. But I was only a few weeks into the job, and I didn't feel I had the seniority to push back against the experts. In a panic, I called Ben Rhodes.

"Don't worry about it," he said as he rushed to his next meeting. "Just write what you think Obama should say."

Of course. What the president should *say*.

Obama would have to stand up and *deliver* every line I drafted. He'd have to *pronounce* every word. And his remarks had to be clear to the people in the audience who were *listening*. Can you imagine being in the audience and *hearing* those sentences from the report? Can you imagine Obama trying to *say* them out loud? It would have been a disaster. We *would* have needed an "incident-reporting mechanism."

So I went back to my desk, ignored most of the edits, and reverted to the language that I wanted to *hear* from the president.

A few days later, Obama delivered his remarks. He joked that to protect ourselves from hackers and cyber criminals "we've had to learn a whole new vocabulary." Still, the words he spoke that day were not copied from a government report. Instead, he used the language of a leader—simple, succinct, and understandable to Americans watching across the country.

A SPEECH IS A PERFORMANCE

Those maddening edits to Obama's cyber speech help answer an important question that every good speaker should consider *before* speaking.

What *is* a speech?

It's helpful, I think, to start with what a speech is *not*.

A speech is not an essay that we write for class, where—knowing we'll be graded and might need to meet a required word count—we write ten sentences where four sentences would do.

A speech is not a white paper, a study in an academic journal, or a report written *by* policy experts *for* policy experts—a treatise filled with statistics, facts, and figures.

A speech is not a press release highlighting a company's new product, a university's new program, or an elected official's new initiative.

A speech is not a news article—a summary of yesterday's events—intended for you to read alone over your morning coffee.

A speech is not a book—a long story, perhaps with complex twists and turns—that you sit with and absorb for days or weeks at a time.

None of these things are speeches. And if we approach a presentation the same way we'd write an essay, press release, news article, or book, then we're setting ourselves up for failure.

The best way to understand what a speech *really* is, I believe, is to think of it as a performance—like a play. "There's a theater to public speaking in a lot of ways," Obama said to me once. Let's count the ways. Like a play . . .

- A speech has a setting—a venue, maybe an auditorium or room, where you'll speak.

- A speech has some sort of staging—maybe even an actual stage or even props to help you make your point. There may be some sort of lighting, maybe a sound system, perhaps a podium, lectern, or a microphone.

- A speech begins with an entrance. You take the stage, approach the podium or mic, and you begin to speak.

- A speech involves some sort of script. Maybe it's a fully written draft that you'll deliver word for word, an outline to guide you, or a few notes scratched out on a piece of paper.

- A speech has an audience. Whether they're in the room or on a Zoom, you'll be looking out at people who've come together to listen, learn, or laugh; to be informed, inspired, or motivated. This, more than anything, is what sets a speech or presentation apart from other forms of communication. A speech is not something that we process in isolation. It's a shared moment—*an experience*—between the living, breathing human who is talking and the living, breathing humans in the audience who are listening.

- A speech is meant to be *heard*. Your audience won't have a copy of your script in their hands. If they don't understand something you say, they can't go back and check what they missed. All your audience can do is watch and listen. Which means every sentence, every word, and every syllable that you utter needs to be absolutely clear—to the ear.

Now, I realize that thinking about a presentation like a performance might at first terrify you. *I was already anxious about giving a speech! Now you want me to perform?!* Which is why some speech coaches say you shouldn't think about public speaking this way. But there's no way around it—speaking in front of a group of people *is*, on some level, a performance. Instead of hiding from the thing that scares us, we should be honest, call it what it is—and embrace it.

In fact, understanding that a speech is a performance can be empowering, even liberating. You see, when we give a presentation, we have a lot more control over the experience than we often realize. That includes a power no one else has—the ability to deliver the performance that only *you* can deliver.

THE ROLE YOU WERE BORN TO PLAY

A speech, like any performance, has a lead—or leads. When you're giving a talk or a presentation, *you* are the lead. Lucky for you, you've been perfectly cast. Because just like the audience wants you to give the speech that only you can give, they want you to *tell it* like only you can tell it.

A few years after leaving the White House, I worked on a speech for the CEO of a major U.S. company. He delivered his remarks and texted me right away.

"It was great! I sounded just like Obama!"

He was thrilled.

I was mortified.

Had I inadvertently plagiarized an old Obama speech? I flipped open my laptop and scanned the speech. But I couldn't find a single sentence that resembled anything Obama had ever said.

What was the CEO talking about?

"The flow, the rhythm, the feel, the way the audience responded," he told me later, "it all just *felt* like an Obama speech."

I breathed a sigh of relief. Because, for a moment, I thought he'd committed one of the most common mistakes that many speakers make—trying to sound like someone else.

I understand the temptation. There's no shortage of public speaking books urging us to model ourselves after the great orators of history. As one of his speechwriters, I certainly had to learn Obama's voice. I'd go online, find one of his speeches, turn the computer screen *off*, and then close my eyes. I'd sit there and just listen to the rhythm of his voice. To the way he delivered a few words, then paused, then delivered a few more. To the even longer pauses when he shifted to a new idea. To the way he might lower his voice, or raise it, at the end of a sentence. To how his voice grew louder as he built to a thundering conclusion. For eight years, that was the voice in my head.

But when it comes to giving speeches *ourselves*, I worry that too many of us have learned the wrong lesson—that we're all supposed to sound like presidents and prime ministers. Even some politicians give in to the temptation. They try to sound, for instance, like Obama. And when the press inevitably notices, it's rarely good ("Candidate Mimics Obama"). When you sound like someone else, it means you're not being authentic. Which undermines your credibility. Which makes it harder for your audience to connect with and believe *you*.

So, yes, I'm a former Obama speechwriter telling you—begging you—*not* to try to sound like Obama. Because the only person on the planet who should sound like Barack Obama is Barack Obama. And the only person in the world who *you* should sound like is you.

At times, even Obama felt pressure to speak in a way that he felt wasn't authentic to who he was. "There were times when my political advisers wanted me to say things in a certain way that might have worked for a more conventional politician. But I didn't want to be a conventional politician," Obama told me. He pointed to his desire to talk about hard, sometimes uncomfortable, truths—for example, around race—even if it cost him some votes. "Maybe that's another lesson," he said. "You have to be yourself."

It's the Golden Rule of Public Speaking—be yourself. Speak in a way that sounds natural *to you*.

Beware of the Bots

The importance of speaking in your own voice is another reason not to rely too much on a chatbot. Ask a bot to "Write a 10-minute speech about climate change," and you'll get back something generic—like the bot-generated speeches that some politicians and preachers have delivered in recent years. After all, the bot doesn't know how *you* actually communicate—not only how you *speak*, but how you *think*: how you approach problems and make your arguments.

As I write this, bots can already finish our emails with the words and phrases we use most often. Maybe, over time, bots will also learn our voice and draft speeches and presentations as if we've dictated them ourselves. Maybe by the time you read this they already do.

But remember: your authentic voice—the unique way that *you* speak—is part of what sets you apart. If you want to stand out from the crowd and be heard, in public speaking and in life, don't give your voice over to a bot.

A SPEECH IS AN EXPERIENCE

Many years after his speech at the 2004 convention, Obama reflected on that night in Boston.

> . . . *There comes a point in the speech where I find my cadence. The crowd quiets rather than roars. It's the kind of moment I'd come to recognize in subsequent years, on certain magic nights. There's a physical feeling, a current of emotion that*

passes back and forth between you and the crowd, as if your lives and theirs are suddenly spliced together, like a movie reel, projecting backward and forward in time, and your voice creeps right up to the edge of cracking, because for an instant, you feel them deeply; you can see them whole. You've tapped into some collective spirit, a thing we all know and wish for—a sense of connection that overrides our differences and replaces them with a giant swell of possibility—and like all things that matter most, you know the moment is fleeting and that soon the spell will be broken.[1]

Think about what Obama is saying here. He's not talking about the words he spoke that night, or even the larger themes of his speech. He's describing the *feeling* between himself and his audience. There, down on the convention floor, I felt it too—because a speech is a communal *experience*. It's true with any kind of presentation, even with a smaller audience.

"I remember when I was teaching law," Obama said to me once. "There'd be some classes where I'm like 'Man, I am nailing this thing.' There's an energy. You can feel an electricity of ideas and emotions and people are locked in. You're communicating to them, but they're also communicating back to you. There are cues being sent back and forth. You can feel it. When that happens, it's remarkable."

Of course, sometimes, instead of electricity, there's a power outage. Even for Obama. "There were times I was teaching, and the kids looked hungry and bored, and I was tired, and it was just flat," he said. "It's like playing basketball. There are times when you're locked in and you're in a zone. And there are times where you're clanking things off the backboard."

This is one of the reasons I've always loved being a speechwriter.

I love helping to create that *experience* between the speaker and their audience. It's why, during so many Obama speeches, I stood off to the side and looked not at Obama (I could watch the video later), but at the audience. I wanted to see how they experienced the speech. When he gave a shout-out to the local football team, did they cheer? When he made his argument, did they listen? When he defended a value that they cherish, did they nod their heads in agreement or, better yet, applaud?

Why is this experience—this "current of emotion"—between a speaker and their audience so powerful? It turns out it's deeply rooted in our brains.

Researchers at Princeton conducted a fascinating series of studies in which speakers spoke to audiences while fMRIs scanned the parts of their brains that process sound and language. At first, everyone's brain waves were different. But as the speakers talked, people's brain waves—the speakers' and the listeners'—began to align.[2] The researchers call this "neural coupling." One of the researchers, Uri Hasson, a professor of psychology and neuroscience at Princeton, explained it to me this way: communication—like a speech—is "a single act that connects and unifies the two brains of the speaker and listener. The more our brain patterns align, the better we understand each other."

Deep down, maybe we've always known this. Think of how we describe a great speaker. She *electrified* her audience. She *clicked* with the crowd. She was *in sync* with the room. Now we know why. If we're doing it right, we really are electrifying the brains of our audience, creating a shared experience and an opportunity for better understanding.

That's what a twenty-nine-year-old graduate student did when he surprised his audience with a speech that electrified millions of people around the world.

"THE PERFORMANCE DRIVES IT HOME"

"I had no excuse not to speak up," Donovan Livingston says. After all, he's the son of a Baptist preacher and a speech pathologist. Growing up in Fayetteville, North Carolina, his parents signed him up for local speaking contests where he recited the speeches of Dr. Martin Luther King, Jr.

Still, Donovan struggled to find his voice. "I was nervous all the time," he recalled.

Then he discovered hip-hop.

"When I heard Nas and Lauryn Hill sing 'If I Ruled the World,' it opened my mind to the idea that, as a Black boy, I could change the world too." With the encouragement of a teacher, he began turning his thoughts into poems and eventually started performing them as a spoken-word poet. "Hip-hop and poetry gave me the chance," he said, "to express my own experience, my own voice, and my own ideas in a way that felt natural to me."

Years later, Donovan was selected to speak during his convocation at Harvard's Graduate School of Education. He knew immediately that he'd give a speech about racial inequalities in education. And he decided to deliver the performance that only he could deliver— one that was "true to my identity as a hip-hop artist."

First, Donovan found a place where he could think, create, and write—the kitchen table in his tiny apartment off campus, as he listened to Chance the Rapper for inspiration. He set out, he said, to write "a narrative that told a story, with characters to bring the story to life, and rhythm to move the story along." He rehearsed— reading his poem aloud in front of the bathroom mirror "maybe a hundred times"—because "I was trying to immerse myself in the experience of performing my poem."

As a performer, Donovan understood that what he wore would

amplify what he said. He knew he couldn't wear his usual gold grill on the bottom row of his teeth. "It's hard," he joked, "to read a poem with a grill!" Still, on the day of his speech he found ways to remain true to himself: cubic zirconia earrings and, atop his black suit, a multicolored kente stole to "represent my pride in being a Black graduate."

Taking the podium, he immediately engaged his audience. "Good afternoon, good afternoon," he said, smiling. "How's everyone doing today?" The crowd was already clapping and cheering. "The illustrious class of 2016," he said, "make some noise!" And they did. He was only moments into his remarks, and he and his audience were already in sync.

Donovan explained that, back in high school, a teacher had threatened to cut off his mic if he delivered a poem at graduation, so he was grateful for the chance to finally "share this piece of myself in my most authentic voice." A spoken-word poem, he said, "insists on participation," so he encouraged the crowd to "snap, clap, throw up your hands, rejoice, celebrate." Over the next five minutes, they did all that, and more, as he immersed himself in the experience of his performance.

Beginning his poem, Donovan said that young Black Americans like him are "a lonely blossom in a briar patch of broken promises"— a "thorn in the side of injustice." As he spoke, he shifted between his feet, his body moving with the rhythm of his words, the audience matching his energy with cheers and hollers of approval.

"At the core, none of us were meant to be common," he declared. "We were born to be comets," sparking more applause. Donovan and the crowd were playing off each other, sharing in—to borrow Obama's words—a "collective spirit."

Already an educator himself, Donovan said, "I teach in hopes of turning content into rocket ships, tribulations into telescopes"— cupping his hands like a telescope—"So a child can see their true potential from right where they stand." And then, his pace quickening, his voice rising, he called on every teacher to do the same.

> *Wake up every child so they know of their celestial potential.*
> *I've been the Black hole in a classroom for far too long;*
> *Absorbing everything, without allowing my light to escape.*
> *But those days are done. I belong among the stars.*
> *And so do you. And so do they.*

The audience erupted in applause, forcing Donovan to stop and wait. Then, he launched into his finale.

> *Together, we can inspire galaxies of greatness*
> *For generations to come.*
> *So, no, no, sky is not the limit.*
> *It is only the beginning.*
> *Lift off.*

As Donovan delivered his last line, he raised his arms toward the sky, a preacher's son lifting his words into the world. In the audience, his mother was in tears, and the audience jumped to their feet in a standing ovation. The next day, one of Donovan's friends showed him his phone. "Bro, you're going viral." Soon, his speech was viewed more than fourteen million times.

Why did Donovan's speech resonate so deeply with so many people around the world? Yes, part of it was the power of his message—that ingrained racial inequities in education cannot be ignored. But the power of his remarks also came from the power of his delivery and *the experience* he created for his audience.

"When I spoke, it wasn't just me up there," Donovan told me when I interviewed him a few years later to learn how he'd done it. "It was all of us. I wasn't pouring my words into an empty vessel. I was pouring them into the audience, and they were pouring them back to me. It was a connection bigger than me, like we were all in something together. The words on paper are valuable, but the performance drives it home."

The Download

Few of us will be able to put on a performance like Donovan. But like him, we should always think deeply about how we want our time in the spotlight to unfold—from beginning to end. This is another reason why seeing a speech as a performance can be so empowering. Consider all the different jobs that go into any performance; when you deliver a speech, *you* are doing all these jobs. Once you realize how much creative control you often have, it gives you all sorts of opportunities to create a less stressful and more enjoyable experience—for you and your audience.

» **Write the script you want.** As the writer, you're in control of your script—what you say and how you say it, how you start and how you finish. You get to create the experience that you want to have with your audience—the mood, the tone, the emotional journey you'll go on together. If someone is introducing you, you might even be able to help shape what they say about you. Many hosts struggle with how to introduce a speaker. Ask if they need ideas. Offer some interesting facts about your life or career—or maybe even a brief draft for them to use. You'll be welcomed to the stage on your terms before you've ever said a word.

» **Take charge.** In most presentations, you're also the director. If you're the leader of the organization where you're speaking, you can decide when and where it takes place, who's invited, who else speaks, and in which order. Even if you're a guest speaker, many hosts will let you shape your portion of the program. Is there a specific person you'd like to introduce you? What do *you* want to speak about? How long do you want to speak? Do you want to take questions from the audience? Do what's most comfortable for you.

» **Add a little spectacle.** Even as you focus on what you want to say, don't forget about what your audience will see. Here, I want to say on behalf of long-suffering audiences everywhere: For the love of God, DO NOT SUBJECT YOUR AUDIENCE TO A SLOW AND PAINFUL DEATH BY POWERPOINT. Your audience came to see and hear a human being—*you*—not endless slides crammed with a blizzard of words. Instead, think of your slides as the background—the scenery that helps set the mood and reinforce your message rather than distracting from it. You might try beautiful photographs of the people and places you're talking about with few, if any, words at all. And what will your audience *hear*? Your voice alone? If logistics allow for it, break up your talk with audio or video clips that liven up your presentation.

» **Design the set.** Sometimes, you can even play the role of set designer. If you're a leader speaking to your organization, think hard about how you want the stage to look, what the backdrop will be, and how the audience will be arranged. Why limit yourself to a bland conference room? Perhaps there's an offsite, a historical building, or a scenic backdrop that better reflects the spirit of your presentation. As a guest speaker, you might have a say in how the stage is arranged. Do you want to use a podium or a handheld mic that allows you to roam? Do you want anyone else onstage with you? If you're speaking by

Zoom, you'll have even more control. Your camera angle, your lighting, your backdrop—it's all up to you.

» **Make your audience part of the show.** A speech doesn't have to be a monologue. Instead of seeing your talk as a performance *for* your audience, think of it as a performance *with* your audience. Like Donovan did, encourage their participation. Ask them questions; have them raise their hands or answer from their seats. Invite them to ask you questions. You'll not only create a more engaging interactive *experience* between you and your audience, you'll take the spotlight—and some of the pressure—off yourself.

» **Share the stage.** Like presidents do at the State of the Union address, shine the spotlight on someone else—a member of your community, employees at your company, a person you're honoring or trying to help. If they're able, ask them to stand or join you onstage; if they can't, ask them to wave from their seat. Invite the audience to join you in saluting them. No offense to your beautiful words, but that shared moment of admiration just might end up being the most moving and memorable part of your remarks.

As you prepare your presentation, there's something else I encourage you to do. Like any good performer, it's crucial to know your role, the audience, and the structure of the story you're going to tell.

CHAPTER 4

The 50–25–25 Rule

If you don't know where you're
going, you might not get there.

—Yogi Berra

President Obama was not pleased. Which is never good. Because at the White House, you work "at the pleasure of the president." And if the president is not pleased today, you could be out of a job tomorrow.

It was a Saturday afternoon, and we'd been summoned back to the White House because Obama was scheduled to deliver a speech the next day on U.S. relations with Israel. I'd been working on the remarks for a week or so and thought the draft was in good shape.

The mood in the Oval Office suggested otherwise. Just about every seat in the room was filled with staff, and Obama seemed annoyed. He turned to me, holding the draft of the speech in his hand.

"It's not your fault, Terry, but this is not what I want to say."

I swallowed hard.

It was kind of him to say it wasn't my fault. But I felt like it was. I felt like I'd let him down. I was also confused. I thought I'd followed the usual process—building the draft on things he'd said before, sharing it with dozens of national security officials, incorporating their edits.

Where had I gone wrong?

Before I tell you, let me back up a bit.

~

I believe that one of the most common mistakes people make when they have to give a presentation is that they rush in and immediately start writing their draft or preparing their slides. I get it. The sooner we start putting words on paper, the less anxious many of us feel.

But do you pile your family into your car and drive off without thinking through where you're going? Sounds like a road trip from hell. It's the same with any sort of presentation. Over the years, I've seen plenty of speakers and speechwriters hit the gas, start writing, cruise along fine for a while, and then, after a few paragraphs or pages, they hit a wall. They're lost. They don't know where they're going.

There's a better way.

I follow what I call the 50–25–25 Rule. I spend roughly 50 percent of my time thinking, researching, and organizing my thoughts; 25 percent of my time writing; and the final 25 percent of my time editing and practicing. It works, no matter how much time you have.

The 50–25–25 Rule in Action

Have to give a presentation in a month? Spend . . .
two weeks thinking, researching, and organizing your thoughts;
one week writing;
one week editing and practicing.

Have to give a speech in a week? Spend . . .
three days thinking, researching, and organizing;
two days writing;
two days editing and practicing.

Just found out that you have to give a dinner toast *tonight*? Spend . . .
one hour thinking, researching, and organizing;
thirty minutes writing;
thirty minutes editing and practicing.

Why does the 50–25–25 Rule work so well? Because the best predictor of whether we'll give a good presentation isn't what we do *at* the podium, it's the *preparation* we put in before we ever get near the podium; it's the work that goes into a speech *before* we ever write a single word. Moreover, I truly believe that the more prepared you are, the less nervous you'll be when it's time to deliver—because you know you're ready.

So, you have to give a speech or presentation? Don't try to prepare anything just yet. Take a breath. Relax. Use the first 50 percent of your time wisely. Here's how I use the first 50 percent of my time—I scope it out, think it out, figure it out, and, then, prepare to write it out.

SCOPE IT OUT

(10 Questions to Ask Before Any Speech)

President Obama once delivered a speech in which he ripped into a Republican budget proposal that could have resulted in major cuts in spending on education and health care. He didn't hold back. He said the plan was a "deeply pessimistic" vision for the country, and that there was "nothing serious" or "anything courageous" about it. Tough stuff.

But there was a problem. The author of the plan, Congressman Paul Ryan of Wisconsin, was sitting in the front row. The president didn't know Ryan was going to be there. Ryan was incensed, feeling he'd been personally attacked, and it added another wrinkle to already difficult budget negotiations. Obama later said that had he known the congressman would be in the audience, he "might have modified some of" the speech. "We made a mistake."[1]

Every speech has a lot of moving parts—the venue, the speaking program, the guest list. It's important to scope out the event and keep track of it all. It's why I believe in trying to have 100% Situational Awareness. Assume nothing. Know everything. Ask *lots* of questions. Because what you don't know *can* hurt you. And the more you know, the more in control you will be.

Here are ten questions I ask before every speech:

1. ***Who is my audience?*** "Know your audience" is one of the most basic rules of public speaking. But to truly know your audience, you have to ask *many* questions:

   • Will someone introduce you? Who are the hosts (organizations and/or individuals)? Because you'll want to thank them—not only for their kind words, but for the work they do, the mission to which they're devoted, and the impact they've made.

   • Will there be any VIPs—especially any partners in your work—who you'd be wise to acknowledge? Make sure to get the correct pronunciation of their names.

   • How *many* people will be in the audience? Less than thirty or forty? Intimate events aren't the place for big, formal speeches; consider turning your script into notes or talking points so you can speak more conversationally.

   • What's the *composition* of the audience? People you know, or strangers? The general public? Experts in their field? A group with a shared purpose—workers in the same industry, employees at a company, members of a nonprofit or a faith community?

- What's their *mood*? Are they optimistic or worried? Energized or dispirited?

- What's their *background*? Young, old? Liberal, conservative, moderate? Urban, suburban, rural? Are they from different backgrounds? What's the racial, religious, or ethnic makeup of your audience?

- What does the audience expect of you? Are they supportive or skeptical of your views? What do they want to hear from you? (If you don't know, ask the organizers.)

2. ***What do we have in common?*** I think of any speech or presentation like a Venn diagram with two circles. On one side, there's you—the speaker—your experiences, interests, beliefs, values, and goals; on the other side are those of your audience. Where they overlap—what you have in common—is where you have the best opportunity to connect with your audience and where your best speech lives. In some cases, there's a lot of overlap and you have a lot in common to talk about:

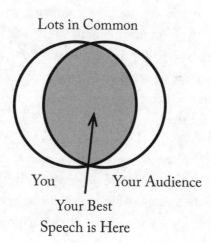

Lots in Common

You   Your Audience

Your Best
Speech is Here

In other cases, you may have less in common with your audience. You'll have to work harder to find things you share with your listeners:

Less in Common

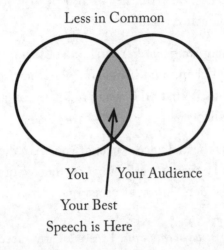

You | Your Audience

Your Best
Speech is Here

No overlap with your audience? I believe there's always *something* you share with your audience—if you look hard enough. (More on this in chapter 7.)

3. ***When*** **is it?** Is there any significance to the date of your presentation—a holiday or important anniversary that you ought to acknowledge? What's the larger context—is there anything going on in the community, company, or country that you should be aware of and perhaps mention? What time of day will you speak? Right *before* a meal? Your audience could be hungry; keep it short. Right *after* a meal? They're full; keep it even shorter. During a reception? Talk too long, and they'll ditch you for the bar.

4. ***What*** **is it?** An annual conference, a special event, a town meeting, a family gathering? *Why* is it happening? What's the *specific purpose* of the event—what are the hosts trying to accomplish and how can your remarks help them achieve it?

5. **Why *me*?** Never assume you know why you've been invited to speak. If you're representing an organization, the host may *not* want you to pitch your company or cause. Maybe they want you to share the lessons you've learned in your work. Maybe you're one of several speakers and the host wants you to focus on a very specific topic. There's only one way to know: ask them what they want you to talk about. It doesn't mean you have to limit yourself to their agenda, but it will help you give the speech that only *you* can give.

6. **Where do I fit in the program?** Ask for the run of show. What happens before or after you talk? Are there any special speakers, presentations, or performances you should acknowledge? Are you the main speaker or one of several? If one of several, will you speak first, in the middle, or last? What will the other speakers be talking about? Perhaps ask to speak early so you can help shape the discussion. If you speak toward the end, your audience may be tired and have less patience for long remarks.

7. ***Where* is it?** As with any performance, you need to know the setting. Does the city or town have any special significance you might mention? What's the venue—an auditorium, your company, city hall, a house of worship? Is the event indoors or outdoors? If outdoors, it could be harder to hear, or the weather might turn nasty. Long remarks don't go over well with an audience when raindrops keep falling on their heads.

8. **What's the staging?** Like any good performer, you need to know your space. Tim Hartz, a White House advance staffer who helped plan hundreds of events for Obama, told me that "we always wanted to make sure the president knew his stage directions—how to enter, where to walk, and his best way to

approach the podium." Will *you* be on a stage? How will you get to the podium? Will you be onstage alone or with others? What's the backdrop behind you? What will you see—to your left, your right, and in front of you? Will your audience be seated or standing? If they're standing, they're going to get antsy, so, again, better to keep it short.

9.   **Will there be a podium?** This is one of the most important questions to ask. If you'll have some sort of podium, you'll have a place to put your remarks or notes—which is essential if you're going to read them word for word. If not, you'll have to hold your script in your hands. Or maybe you don't *want* a podium, which can sometimes act as a barrier between you and your audience. Maybe you prefer to walk about the stage. Will you have to hold a microphone in your hand? If yes, now you're down to one hand, which will make it hard to hold your notes or flip your pages—in which case, don't plan on being able to read your remarks word for word.

10.   **How long should I speak?** Always ask your hosts, especially if you're one speaker among many. With many of us speaking around 150 words per minute, here are a few suggestions for staying within whatever time you're allotted:

Speeches/presentations/keynotes:
15–20 minutes
(2,250–3,000 words)

Eulogies:
5–7 minutes
(750–1,050 words)

Toasts/comments at a public meeting:
3–5 minutes
(450–750 words)

Once you have 100% Situational Awareness about the event and your audience, it's time for the next step—the deep thinking that's necessary to make sure your remarks truly meet the moment.

THINK IT OUT

(Know Your 10 Words)

One of the reasons our Downloads in the Oval Office with President Obama before a speech were so useful was because he often started with the same question: "What's the story we're trying to tell here?" An author before he was a politician, he understood that good speeches are good stories. He wanted to make sure we got the story right—*before* we spent days or weeks writing.

"I can't overemphasize it enough," he told me once, "you have to decide on the purpose of your communication." Sometimes while thinking through a speech, Obama immediately zeroed in on the broad theme he wanted to hit in the speech. "I think the headline we're going for is this . . ." Other times, he'd already thought through his entire argument, including his supporting evidence.

"Point one is this . . . Which leads to point two . . . Which, in turn, leads to point three. And I think point three has several parts . . . Part one is . . ." He'd sometimes talk like this for fifteen or twenty minutes at a time. He already saw the entire speech in his head. "I do tend to think in a rational, orderly way," he told me. "That's the lawyer side of my brain."

"See if that works," he'd tell us, as we'd head back to our desks to see if it worked.

Sitting in the Oval Office that Saturday, seeing Obama frustrated with his remarks about Israel and the Middle East, I realized this is where I'd gone wrong. While I'd followed *most* of our usual process, I never got the Download. We didn't do it for *every* speech, and I hadn't thought I needed it for this one. Obama's policies toward Israel and the Middle East hadn't changed. But something else had.

Days earlier, Obama had delivered a major address as the region convulsed from the popular uprisings of the Arab Spring. In that speech, he spoke about long-standing U.S. policy on the eventual borders of Israel and an independent Palestinian state. Critics misrepresented his comments and tried to portray him as somehow insufficiently supportive of Israel. The next day, the right-wing Israeli prime minister, Benjamin Netanyahu, lectured Obama in the Oval Office in front of the global media. The speech I'd drafted might have worked before that. Not anymore.

That Saturday in the Oval Office, Obama told us that he had worked on the speech late into the night. He didn't want to simply repeat what he had said a few days before about future Israeli-Palestinian borders. He wanted to explain *why* he said it: because reaching a compromise on borders was necessary for the security of Israelis and Palestinians alike. My draft was missing his reasoning, which he wanted the world to understand. By the time we filtered out of the Oval Office, we knew what he wanted to say. The next day, Obama gave the speech he wanted to give.

As you start working on your own presentation, set aside some time to really think through the main message you want to convey. Maybe call a family member, friend, or colleague and talk it out. If you're a leader in an organization and have writers who prepare your drafts, find time on your schedule to sit down with your team. Yes, you're busy. But if the president of the United States could make time in his schedule to think through his remarks with his speechwriters, you can too.

Ask yourself:

- What is the purpose of my presentation? What's the story I'm trying to tell?

- In one sentence—ten words or less—what's the main message I want my audience to remember? Let your ten-word message be your North Star. Print it out. Hang it where you can see it. As you work on your presentation, keep asking yourself, "Am I staying on message?"

- What are the three to four key points (maybe five, but *not* ten!) that support my main message?

Ask a Bot

Struggling to figure out your core message? Consider asking a bot. I still say don't rely on a chatbot to write your presentation. That said, a bot can help you brainstorm. Type in something like:

I am a [your position] at a [your company/organization]. Suggest 10 topics for a [#]-minute speech to an audience of [describe the audience] on the challenges and opportunities facing [the issue/ problem/challenge].

Within seconds, you'll have ten topics. They'll probably be generic and clichéd, but brainstorming has to start somewhere. And since you can keep asking a bot questions, you can flesh out the topics that interest you the most or that are unique to you. You can even ask the bot to suggest an outline. You're on your way—thanks to a robot.

FIGURE IT OUT

(Find the Gold)

I'm often asked "What are the most important skills for being a great speaker?" Here's one skill near the top of the list: you have to be a good researcher. You have to do your homework. This is another reason why Obama credits his years as a professor with helping him become a better speaker. "I learned how preparation can give you confidence," he told me, "because you know your subject matter."

And how do you know your subject matter?

I've always thought of preparing a speech like sifting for gold: you have to sift through a ton of material to find the nuggets—the interesting ideas, surprising quotes, and compelling stories—that you can then sprinkle throughout your remarks so that they shine. It's not easy. Like a nugget of gold, a good story, anecdote, or quote can be hard to find. It needs to be shaped, set, and polished just right. Here are some ways to find the gold that can grab the attention of your audience and illuminate the message of your remarks.

Learn

Before we open our mouths, we ought to open our minds.

As busy as he was, even President Obama took time to make sure he knew what he was talking about, especially before major speeches. While working on his address accepting the Nobel Peace Prize, he read the speeches of wartime presidents and prime ministers and the writings of Gandhi, Martin Luther King, Jr., and the theologian Reinhold Niebuhr—some of whom he referred to in his speech. "It was as if he were having a conversation with everyone who had spoken on the same issues in the past," said Ben Rhodes. "It was almost spiritual."

You're almost never the first person to speak on a topic. Read up on what others have said before you. Learn from them. Join the conversation. Then, offer a voice, and views, all your own.

Listen

Sometimes a week or two before a big speech, Obama would host a meeting in the Roosevelt Room, across the hall from the Oval Office, with scholars, historians, religious leaders, and grassroots advocates from the community he'd be addressing in his speech. For about an hour, he'd listen as his guests shared their thoughts on what he might say in his remarks. As speechwriters, we'd sit in the back and take notes. After a particularly insightful comment from one of his guests, Obama would look over to us and ask, "Did you get that?" Their suggestion almost always ended up in the speech.

"Before you speak," he told me once, "you've got to learn how to listen." Which is why one of the most important attributes of a good speaker is humility. As you think through your remarks, reach out to family, friends, coworkers, and experts in the field. Ask for their ideas. No matter how smart we are (or think we are), we can always learn from others.

Just remember—not everyone will agree. When Obama hosted the Japanese prime minister for a state dinner, we thought it would be a nice touch if he recited a haiku. We shared our draft with two of the world's leading haiku scholars, but they disagreed with each other about whether it met the strict criteria of a haiku. The email exchanges got heated, which was ironic because the haiku was about harmony. We used it anyway—and it was a hit.

It's good to get other opinions. But in the end, trust your gut. It's your speech.

Be Inclusive

While working on a speech that Obama was scheduled to give at a mosque in Baltimore, I realized we had a bit of a challenge: Obama is not Muslim. I'm not either. How were we supposed to make sure his remarks reflected the concerns and hopes of Muslim Americans?

We asked for ideas from Rumana Ahmed—a member of our National Security Council staff, and perhaps the first Muslim American woman to wear the hijab while working in the West Wing—and Rashad Hussain, the president's special envoy to Muslim-majority countries. Rumana, in turn, pulled together a group of about two dozen Muslim Americans from across the government and asked for their input. They shared their pride in their identity, their fears of being the target of hate crimes because of their religion, and their desire to be seen as American as anyone else. When we circulated drafts of the president's remarks, they offered invaluable edits rooted in their lived experience. And when Obama spoke, he channeled their voices.

"As Muslim Americans," he said at the mosque, you worry that "your entire community so often is targeted or blamed for the violent acts of the very few." To any young people who wondered whether there is a place for them in the United States, he said, "You're part of America too. You're not Muslim *or* American. You're Muslim *and* American."

"I welled up with tears," said Ed Tori, a member of the mosque. "The president validated all the feelings we were having as Muslim Americans." Zubair Ansari, another member of the congregation, said, "I felt like the president was talking directly to me."

Want to make sure your presentation reflects what your audience is feeling? Invite members of that community to help you develop and refine your remarks.

Ask Everyone

During one of Obama's trips to Australia, I was in the motorcade finishing his remarks to a few thousand Australian and American troops. But the speech was missing a good opening. Running out of time, I explained my predicament to the burly, middle-aged Australian driving our staff van. He didn't miss a beat.

"No problem, mate. Obama should just say, 'Aussie! Aussie! Aussie!'"

I was confused.

"And then what?" I asked.

"Everyone will yell back, 'Oi! Oi! Oi!'"

"And what does *that* mean?"

"It's hard to explain. But it's a cheer."

I wasn't convinced.

"What if they *don't* say 'Oi! Oi! Oi!'?"

"Trust me, mate, they will."

A short while later, Obama stood in an aircraft hangar with the Australian prime minister and about two thousand military personnel.

"I know that you all have a great Australian cheer," Obama began. "Aussie! Aussie! Aussie!"

"Oi! Oi! Oi!" the crowd roared back.

Obama chuckled, the prime minister smiled, and that warm moment of American-Australian friendship was broadcast across the country—thanks to a driver who probably never imagined he'd help write a speech for a president.

As you think through your remarks, seek out ideas from everyone. Writing a eulogy for your grandmother? Talk to the neighbor who saw her every day. Getting ready to speak to your city council? See what's on the mind of your corner grocer. Preparing a presentation at work about how to make your company more efficient? Ask the receptionist or custodian—they see things every day that executives miss.

Find Quotes That Surprise

Want to brighten up your speech with a quote? This is another opportunity to give remarks that are unique. Suppose you're going to speak about racial justice. You think of the famous quote by Martin Luther King, Jr., hoping that his children would someday be judged not "by the color of their skin but by the content of their character." I don't blame you. It's one of the most beautifully crafted lines ever delivered. Which is both good news and bad news.

The good news: just about everyone knows it.

The bad news: just about everyone knows it.

"In a speech, a good quote isn't familiar," explains Susannah Jacob, who, as an assistant speechwriter, helped us unearth some of the most powerful quotes and stories for Obama's speeches. "A good quote is unexpected. It has a level of depth that surprises the audience and makes them think."

Obama faced this exact challenge when he spoke at the dedication of the Martin Luther King, Jr. Memorial in Washington. What did he do? He *didn't* quote King's "content of their character" line. Instead, he alluded to one of the "uncomfortable truths" to which King gave voice—among them: "There can be no justice without peace, and there can be no peace without justice."

Quote a well-known line if you want to; the only thing you have to fear is fear itself. Just know that your listeners have already heard it a thousand times. You'll miss the chance to say something that sets your remarks apart. Don't be predictable. Be original.

Ask a Bot

A chatbot can help with quotes too. But you have to be specific, for instance, *"Provide 20 quotes from Dr. Martin Luther King, Jr., about the importance of economic justice, and include the source of each quote"* (because, as we'll discuss in chapter 11, good speakers speak the truth, including only using quotes that are real). I guarantee you'll find some quotes you've never heard before that will surprise your audience and make them think.

Look for the Little Things

"Show don't tell" is one of the golden rules of good writing—and good presentations. Great speakers use their words to paint pictures of the people, places, and things that bring their remarks alive. These pictures don't have to be vast masterpieces. Sometimes all you need are small snapshots.

"Help your audience see, hear, and feel the small details that can help you tell a bigger story, which is what every good speech should do," said Stephen Krupin, a speechwriter on our White House team who liked to quote James Joyce: "In the particular is contained the universal."

It's an axiom that Obama followed often. When he marked the fiftieth anniversary of the Vietnam War—looking out at the families of service members who gave their lives—he could have simply said "you loved them." Instead, standing near that long, black wall with the names of the fallen etched in granite, he recited examples of the mementos that families had left at the wall to express their love for their spouses, sons, and daughters: "The baseball bat he swung as a boy. A wedding ring. The photo of the grandchild he never met. The boots he wore, still caked in mud. The medals she earned, still shining."

As you prepare your presentation, think of the images that can help you paint a picture for your audience about the idea you're trying to convey, the person you're honoring, or the story you're trying to tell. And remember, even the smallest pictures can evoke feelings that are universal.

Include Stories That Touch Your Heart

Before he was promoted to full-time presidential speechwriter, Kyle O'Connor was our lead researcher. When a gunman murdered six people and wounded thirteen others in Tucson, Arizona, in 2011, Kyle learned everything he could about each person killed in the shooting, including nine-year-old Christina-Taylor Green. During his research, Kyle learned that Christina was born on September 11, 2001. Then, he found a book about babies born on 9/11, one of whom, remarkably, was Christina. Along with her photo was the author's wish for her life: "I hope you jump in rain puddles."

How do you know if a story will touch the hearts of your audience? Because it touches yours. "The moment I saw it," Kyle remembers, "I knew, 'this is it.' It would bring home the tragedy of what had happened, but also allow the president to make a larger point about the safer world we need to build for our kids."

A few days later at the memorial service, in one of the most emotional moments of his remarks, Obama told Christina's story, paused to keep his composure, and added a wish of his own. "If there are rain puddles in heaven," he said, "Christina is jumping in them today."

WRITE IT OUT

(Don't Wing It)

After all your thinking and research, it's time to turn those ideas in your head into words on paper.

I've heard some speech coaches say that you *shouldn't* write out your remarks or deliver them word for word. That's the worst advice I've ever heard. Sure, it all depends on the situation. You might not want to read from a script if you're trying to offer deeply personal remarks at an intimate gathering of family and friends—although, if your written remarks are personal and intimate, they might be great. Sometimes, all you need is an outline, some bullets, or a few key phrases to keep you on track.

In most cases, though, I strongly recommend that you write out your remarks word for word. Don't try to wing it, like that young community organizer in Chicago who froze up in the middle of his presentation.

"Here's a really good lesson," Obama told me once, laughing as he remembered that day. "Write out what you are going to say. Even if you're not feeling particularly charismatic when you deliver it, you will be able to plow forward simply by reading it. You will not freeze up!"

Writing out your remarks (and not turning the job over to a chatbot) is important for other reasons. If you haven't *written* it out, you haven't really *thought* it out. It's easy to brainstorm and toss ideas around. But writing out your remarks reveals the strengths and weaknesses of your argument and allows you to fill in any holes in your logic—*before* you speak. Also, if you don't write out your presentation now, how can you practice later?

Writing out your remarks is a sign of respect for your audience, which deserves your best. I have a friend who writes out the toasts he gives at family dinners. He outlines, writes, edits, practices, and then—without notes—delivers it as best he can. It's much better than if he had just winged it, and his toasts have become gifts to his family that they cherish.

If you're a leader in an organization, writing out your remarks can be a forcing mechanism for your team. Every business, non-profit, and community has its internal disagreements, which can fester in the absence of clear guidance from the top. That's why many of a president's speeches are aimed not only at the American people, but at the more than four million employees across the federal government, civilian and military—so that everyone understands the president's policies and is, hopefully, pushing in the same direction. If you're a leader getting ready to speak to your organization, write out your remarks so everyone knows *exactly* what you're trying to accomplish.

Writing out your remarks can also help you make a difficult decision. When the U.S. military commander in Afghanistan, General Stanley McChrystal, made disparaging remarks about his civilian leaders, Obama had to decide what to do. He asked for two drafts—one speech dismissing McChrystal, one keeping him. Seeing the two drafts—all the arguments laid out clearly— apparently helped Obama make his decision. The next day, he accepted McChrystal's resignation.

Yes, Writing Is Hard . . .

Writing isn't easy, and it certainly wasn't easy writing for Barack Obama. "I'm a better speechwriter than my speechwriters," he reportedly told a White House aide.[2] It was tough to hear. But it was also true. If you have a favorite Obama speech, chances are he wrote it, or much of it, himself.

Writing out something you want to say is also hard because it involves those essential questions from chapter 1. *Who am I? What do I believe?* Big questions like this can be overwhelming. A lot of folks say that's what "writer's block" really is. It's not that we can't *write*, it's that we don't *believe* we can write—that we don't have anything worth saying, or that we're not up to the job. Again, that relentless Voice of Doubt. It happens to so many of us.

"I had a freak-out every other day," remembers Jon Favreau, Obama's chief speechwriter during his first presidential campaign and his first term. Determined to prove that he was up to the job, Cody Keenan—Obama's chief speechwriter in his second term—ended up in the hospital with hypertension. With me, the stress triggered debilitating migraines; I'd have to close my office door, turn off the lights, lie down on the floor in the dark, and essentially pass out, allowing my brain to reset. Wracked with self-doubt, one member of our team sought counseling. Sarada

Peri—one of the few women of color ever to serve as a White House speechwriter—worried that she had less margin for error than others. "It was terrifying," she said. "I didn't want anyone to think, 'You're not a white bro, you can't handle this.'"

Back when we were at the White House, I don't think we realized just how much many of us were wrestling with our insecurities. "I felt like asking for help," Kyle O'Connor said years later, "would have been admitting that I didn't have what it took to do the job."

. . . But You Can Make It Easier . . .

If you're struggling to prepare a presentation, there are all sorts of things you can do to get your creative juices flowing. And none of them involve writing. Sometimes, your brain just needs a break.

- Listen to some music.

- Move—go for a walk or a run, go to the gym; some of my best ideas come to me when I'm on the treadmill.

- Take a nap, go to bed—while you're sleeping, your brain will keep working; sometimes I wake up and my brain has written out the sentence that I struggled with the night before.

- Take a shower—as the water hits your body, let your mind wander and think and create, what some researchers call "the shower effect."[3]

And if you're telling yourself that you don't have what it takes to get the job done, don't suffer in silence. Reach out to a colleague or a friend. Ask for ideas. Talk it out. Often, you'll see that your remarks are already in your head. And once you talk them out, it's easier to write them down.

. . . And Remember: Your Presentation Only Has Three Parts

My second year in the White House, I was working on an address that Obama would give to the parliament of India. "Don't worry," a White House staffer joked, "the speech will only be seen by one *billion* Indians."

It was not funny.

Or helpful.

The stakes suddenly seemed enormous, and I felt totally inadequate to the task. I was paralyzed. I didn't know where to start, how to structure the speech, or how to end it. Unable to write, I went down a rabbit hole of endless research. For days, the blank pages on my computer screen stared back at me, taunting me.

Finally, I went home, collapsed on my couch, and had the first (and, so far, only) panic attack of my life. I struggled to breathe, my skin crawled, and my chest felt like it was going to explode. "Why is this happening?!" I pleaded to my wife, Mary, as she caressed my forehead, until, emotionally exhausted, I fell into a deep sleep.

In the days that followed, I somehow produced a draft. Maybe it was the fear of failure. Nothing concentrates the mind like a deadline—or the president not being "pleased" with your work. It was also easier to write when I remembered a simple rule:

Good speeches, like so many great plays and performances, can often be boiled down to three acts: a beginning, a middle, and an end.

Sounds too simple to be true, right?

I confess, I didn't quite get it when I first heard it myself. When I joined Obama's team early in his administration, I'd been writing speeches for more than a decade, but I'd never heard anyone talk about speeches this way. Obama and his speechwriters from the campaign would say things like "Make sure the speech holds together—a beginning, a middle, and an end."

I'd nod politely, pretend I understood, and think to myself, *What are they talking about? Of course a speech has a beginning, a middle, and an end. You start speaking, you keep speaking, you stop speaking. Beginning, middle, end!*

Eventually, I realized what Obama meant. A good speech, like any good story, needs a clear structure, a narrative arc—the basic elements of storytelling that we all learn in school: setting, characters, conflict, turning points, climax, resolution. And often, they can fit nicely into the three parts of any speech or presentation—the beginning, the middle, and the end.

How's *that* for an easy structure?

Remembering this, the big India speech I had to write suddenly felt a little less intimidating. My three-act structure went something like this:

- The Beginning (setting, introduction of main characters): the friendship and partnership between Indians and Americans;

- The Middle (the problem): the challenges we face in the world and how India and the United States can work together to meet those challenges;

- The End (the solution/resolution): how—with India and the United States working together—our countries and the world can be more equal, prosperous, and secure.

Suddenly it wasn't so overwhelming. I knew where I was going—because, even though the speech ended up being more than four thousand words, it all came down to three simple parts. And a few weeks later in New Delhi, I sat in the Indian parliament watching Obama deliver his speech to one *billion* Indians.

The Download

Have to give a speech or presentation? Don't rush in. Use your time wisely. Follow the 50–25–25 Rule: spend 50 percent of your time thinking, researching, and organizing your thoughts; 25 percent of your time writing; and the final 25 percent of your time editing and practicing.

With the first 50 percent of your time . . .

» **Scope it out.** Try to have 100% Situational Awareness about the event and your audience. Assume nothing. Know everything. Ask lots of questions.

» **Think it out.** Set aside time to think through and talk out what you want to say. Know the story you want to tell. Boil your message down to ten words or less.

» **Figure it out.** Learn as much as you can about the topic you're speaking about. Learn from history. Listen to family, friends, and colleagues. Look for stories that touch your heart.

» **Prepare to write it out.** Don't wing it. Writing out your presentation word for word is a sign of respect for your audience. And it's easier when you remember that your remarks can be boiled down to three simple parts: a beginning, a middle, and an end.

So let's get writing. And there's no better place to begin than . . . the beginning.

The Beginning

Hook 'em

CHAPTER 5

Have 'em at Hello

Two things remain irretrievable:
time and a first impression.

—Cynthia Ozick

We've all been there. A community meeting. Maybe a conference. Better yet, a high school commencement. The band strikes up "Pomp and Circumstance." The proud graduates march in, decked out in their caps and gowns. There's an electricity in the air. Then, the master of ceremonies begins to speak.

"Principal Smith, Vice Principals Johnson and Brown, Academic Coordinator Jones, Math Department head Garcia, English Department head Miller . . ."

Oh God, you think, *he's listing every leader in the school.*

"Superintendent Davis, Assistant Superintendent Rodriguez, School Board members Anderson, Hernandez, and Nguyen . . ."

Is anyone not going to get acknowledged?

"Distinguished guests, including Mayor Thomas, Deputy Mayor Taylor, City Council members Moore, Jackson, and Martin . . ."

But wait, there's more!

"Friends and supporters from the community, Chamber of Commerce president Katherine White, Rotary Club president Michael Harris, League of Women Voters president Olivia Clark . . ."

The ceremony has barely started, and you're already checking your watch.

Finally, almost as an afterthought, the MC gets to the graduates. A cheer goes up. But it's mostly sweet relief that the acknowledgments are, mercifully, over.

I want to say this as clearly as I can:

This. Is. Not. A. Good. Way. To. Start. A. Speech.

Reciting a long list of acknowledgments is one of the *worst* ways to begin any remarks. It kills whatever vibe you're going for. It's excruciating when *we're* the audience and have to listen to it. So why would we subject our listeners to Death by Acknowledgments when *we're* the speaker? President Obama started one speech by listing nearly every member of Congress in attendance. CNN carried it live—and then cut away. It was just too boring.

Every part of a speech has a purpose. The purpose of your opening is to establish an *emotional* connection with your audience—to forge that all-important first impression. Which means, as a speaker, you should always ask yourself:

What will be *the very first words* out of my mouth?

GREAT WAYS TO START A SPEECH

Say Hello!

The best way to start your remarks is often the easiest. Just say hello. I'm always shocked that more speakers don't do it. It's simple, yet profound. Saying hello is an inherently kind gesture. It's welcoming. It works with just about every form of communication—face-to-face, phone calls, video conferences. It works across cultures and in just about every situation—even a eulogy. That's the universal power of hello.

Why does it work? In one study, researchers found that saying "hello" can cause a listener to perceive the speaker as more trustworthy.[1] When we say "hello" (or "Good morning!" "Good afternoon!" or "Good evening!") we're sending a powerful message: *I'm a friend. You can trust me.* And what happens when we say hello? Deliver it with feeling and enthusiasm—like you're talking to a friend—and your audience will say it right back to you. Instant connection.

Give a Shout-Out to the Home Crowd

If you're talking to an organization you don't belong to, or in a city or town that's not your own, there's another easy way to connect—show the home crowd some love. Think about it. What's the first thing that singers often say at a concert? Or stand-up comedians at a show? "Hello, Los Angeles!" "Hello, New York!" Obama did it all the time: "Hello, Pennsylvania!" "Hello, London!"

Or maybe you're speaking at a meeting, a conference, or a company. "Hello, American Nurses Association!" "Hello, United Steelworkers!" "Hello, Apple!" Or if you're at the University of Florida: "Go Gators!" Again—an instant connection with your audience. You've said only a few words, but already everybody's cheering.

Introduce Yourself

In some cases—like a public meeting—your audience might not know who you are. Or there might be no one to introduce you. You'll have to do it yourself. It sounds boring, but it can be one of the best ways to instantly establish your credibility—on *your* terms.

Think of Brayden Harrington on national TV ("My name is Brayden Harrington, and I'm thirteen years old . . .") and how he immediately talked about his stutter. Naiara started her remarks to her city commissioners in Michigan the same way: "My name is Naiara Tamminga . . . I've lived in Grand Rapids almost my whole life."

This is how a whistleblower from Facebook began her blockbuster testimony before Congress:

> *My name is Frances Haugen. I used to work at Facebook. I joined Facebook because I think Facebook has the potential to bring out the best in us. But I am here today because I believe Facebook's products harm children, stoke division, and weaken our democracy.*

She told you who she is, why you should listen to her, and why she's there ("I believe . . .")—all in just four sentences. More than two thousand years ago, the Greek philosopher Aristotle called this *ethos*—when a speaker tries to persuade an audience by evoking their character or authority—which he called one of the three elements of rhetoric (and which will be one of the very few ancient Greek words that I'll mention in this book, I promise).

Even presidents do it. You've probably noticed that when announcing a military action, they often say something like "As president and commander in chief . . ." We all know they're president and commander in chief. Why say it? They're reminding you of their authority, which they hope will persuade you of the wisdom of their words and their actions.

You can do it too. Start your remarks by reminding your audience why you have the credibility to speak on the issue you're talking about. "As a lifelong member of this community . . ." "As a longtime employee of this organization . . ." "As the CEO of a company committed to clean energy . . ."

A Killer Opening Line (Maybe)

Sometimes, great works grab you with the very first sentence. "It was the best of times, it was the worst of times . . ." (Charles Dickens's

A Tale of Two Cities). "They shoot the white girl first . . ." (Toni Morrison's *Paradise*). "A long time ago in a galaxy far, far away . . ." (every Star Wars movie). "I said a hip-hop, the hippie, the hippie / To the hip, hip-hop and you don't stop . . ." (The Sugarhill Gang's "Rapper's Delight"). Great openings hook us and leave us wanting more.

It can be the same with a speech. On the night of his first victory during the 2008 campaign, in the Iowa caucuses, Obama took the podium and distilled the moment into seven simple words: "They said this day would never come." Adam Frankel, one of Obama's original campaign speechwriters, remembers the line as an encapsulation of Obama's central message. "Every good speech needs to speak to the moment," Adam said. "And that line was a way of addressing perhaps the biggest issue in the campaign and in our country—race—with a light touch, but also with hope and idealism."

Here's another powerful opening line from an Obama speech that a lot of people waited years to hear: "Tonight, I can report to the American people and to the world that the United States has conducted an operation that killed Osama bin Laden, the leader of al Qaeda . . ."

So, yes, if you're able to distill the moment into a great opening line, go for it.

That said, I don't recommend spending too much time trying to come up with the Perfect Opening Line (unless you have an Australian driver to help you). Over the years, I've seen countless speakers and speechwriters bang their heads against the wall trying to come up with a pithy line that they hope will be etched for the ages on monuments and memorials.

But a speech is not a sound bite. Remember, a speech is a story. Which means, if you're obsessed with trying to come up with an unforgettable line, you're doing it backward. The line that most people associate with Obama is "Yes we can!" Still, he never built an entire speech around those three words. And in our meetings in the Oval Office, if he ever sensed that we were too focused on trying to come up with a clever sound bite, he'd quickly remind us, "Don't worry about the lines. Get the story right first, and the lines will follow."

Start with a Story

More than a decade after the attacks of September 11, 2001, Obama joined survivors and families for the dedication of the 9/11 Memorial Museum in New York City. He approached the podium, looked out at his audience, and took them back to that September morning.

> *In those awful moments after the South Tower was hit, some of the injured huddled in the wreckage of the seventy-eighth floor. The fires were spreading. The air was filled with smoke. It was dark, and they could barely see. It seemed as if there was no way out.*

No big windup. Obama just told a story—and not from the beginning. He began in the middle (*in medias res*, "in the midst of things"), at a moment of maximum emotion, pulling his audience in. What's more, instead of sharing lots of moments from that terrible September day, Obama devoted much of his remarks to that single story. He recounted how those injured workers in the South Tower were saved by a young man wearing a red handkerchief against the smoke—Welles Crowther, "the man in the red bandana"—a single person whose heroism and sacrifice embodied what Obama called "the true spirit of 9/11."

If you want to start your remarks with a story, ask yourself: What's the most compelling moment in this story? Start there.

You'll hook your audience immediately, because people always want to know what happens next.

Invoke Scripture

Depending on the event and your audience, quoting from Scripture can be a powerful way to begin your remarks. It can be especially effective in times of tragedy and loss by evoking a source of strength for many people in your audience. It places your remarks—and the moment—in the context of something higher, something sacred.

After a shooting at Fort Hood, Texas, in 2014 took the lives of three soldiers and injured more than a dozen others, Obama's speech at the memorial began with a passage from the Bible: "Love bears all things, believes all things, hopes all things, endures all things. Love never ends."

Still, be mindful. We live in a diverse world. Quoting a biblical passage may resonate deeply with many people in your audience. At the same time, 36 percent of Americans don't identify as Christian, including nearly 30 percent who claim no religious affiliation at all.[2] Quoting from the New Testament, for instance, likely won't resonate as much with the people in your audience who are Jewish, Muslim, or Hindu—another great reason to always know exactly who you're speaking to.

A Better Way to Do Acknowledgments

I've heard some speaking coaches say you shouldn't do acknowledgments at all. *What?*

Acknowledging the people who invited you, your hosts, and your audience is basic courtesy. It shows respect and gratitude. It helps build rapport and trust. *Always* thank your hosts and your audience.

The trick is to do it right—and that means short and sweet.

Every situation is different, but after five or six names, most audiences start to squirm. If you begin your remarks with a pithy opening line, by introducing yourself, or by telling a story, you can save your acknowledgments for a little later and weave them into your remarks.

But even if you do your acknowledgments at the very beginning, there's a nice way to do them. Rather than seeing acknowledgments as a necessary evil, think of them as a way to amplify the story you're telling. Instead of just reading a list of names and titles, turn your acknowledgments into a celebration of your hosts, the work they do, and the spirit that brings you together. Say it with feeling. Chances are, your audience will join in too. This way, a transcript from a commencement ceremony might look something like this:

> *Hello graduates! [Cheers] Welcome to a day four years in the making! [Cheers] Today, we express our gratitude to everyone who has helped you reach this milestone. Thank you, Principal Smith, and all the teachers, faculty, and staff who have guided you! [Cheers] Thank you, Mayor Thomas, Superintendent Davis, and all the leaders who have supported you! [Cheers] Thank you, neighbors from across the community and, most of all, your family and friends who have cheered you on every step of the way! [Cheers]*

Two other pieces of advice when you're thanking people by name: First, be careful not to reinforce old, outdated gender stereotypes. Don't only praise women for their "commitment," "passion," or "empathy." And don't simply compliment men for their "confidence," "determination," and "strength." No gender has a monopoly on any virtue.

Second, never assume the sexual or gender identity of someone you're acknowledging. "I want to thank Parker for his leadership" is a nice compliment—unless Parker goes by "she" or "they." Try to find out how people want to be referred to; it's just basic courtesy. If you don't know, here's an easy way to make sure you're being respectful—just avoid gendered pronouns altogether: "Parker, thank you for your leadership."

Lift Up What They Love

Another great way to connect with your audience right off the bat is to show some love for the things *they* love—what I think of as the Three Fs: firsts, foods, and fans.

Are there any historic firsts they're proud of? On a visit to New Orleans, the audience applauded with pride when Obama commended them for being one of the first cities in the country to make major progress toward ending chronic homelessness among military veterans.

What local foods do they savor? At a Cinco de Mayo party celebrating the contributions of Mexican Americans in the United States, Obama said he was excited about all the tacos, churros, and margaritas arrayed before him, prompting someone in the audience to yell "Tequila!"

Or what teams are they fans of? At an event in San Francisco, he got big cheers when he gave a shout-out to "your NBA champions, the Golden State Warriors!"

Show some respect for the things your audience loves and they'll love you back.

Shock 'em

After giving a speech a few years ago, President Biden was shaking hands with people in the audience. As he worked the crowd, a woman looked him in the eyes and said bluntly, "I'm an American citizen, and my mother is in a concentration camp." It stopped the president in his tracks, giving the woman the chance to introduce herself and make her case.

Her name was Ziba Murat—an American whose family in China, like millions of ethnic Uyghurs, has been brutally oppressed, with more than a million imprisoned in internment camps. She got the attention of the president with just twelve jarring words.

Want to grab your audience's attention? Say something unexpected. Or hit your listeners with a shocking fact or a figure. Giving remarks about economic inequality? Maybe start with this painful reality: "More than a third of Americans don't have enough savings to cover an emergency expense of four hundred dollars."

Pitching investors on a new venture to make food more affordable? Maybe start with this: "Tonight, millions of children in America—the wealthiest nation on Earth—will go to bed without enough food to eat."

Speaking about gun violence? "More Americans have been killed by guns in the last fifty years than in all the wars in American history combined."

Statistics rarely, if ever, change anyone's mind (as we'll discuss in chapter 8). But deployed right at the beginning of your remarks, a stunning statement can hook your audience and make them more likely to listen to the rest of what you have to say.

Speak Their Language (Literally)
If you speak to audiences from different backgrounds, or to groups around the world, consider taking a page from Obama's playbook. Just about everywhere he went, he'd walk up to the podium, flash his wide smile, lean into the microphone, and say hello in words they knew well.

In Mexico: "Hola!"
In Jamaica: "Greetings, Massive!"

In Israel: "Shalom!"

In the Palestinian Territories: "Marhaba!"

In Kenya: "Habari Zenu!"

In Myanmar, formerly known as Burma: "Myanmar Naingan, Mingalaba!"

In South Africa, with its many native languages: "Thobela! Molweni! Sanibona! Dumelang! Ndaa! Reperile!"*

Obama didn't always get every word right. Sometimes he mangled the language a bit and looked to the audience for help. But that made it even better. It was a moment of vulnerability. And every time, the crowd went wild. Saying hello in the local language wasn't just some gimmick. It was a deliberate choice that Obama and those of us who wrote for him made as he traveled the world. Because speaking someone else's language is the ultimate sign of respect.

NO, YOU DON'T NEED A "JOKE"

Of course, there's another great way to connect with your audience—humor. Which is why many speech coaches say you need to "start with a joke."

I disagree.

Let me explain.

Sure, a well-crafted joke can sometimes help you make your point, like when Obama, in a State of the Union address, quipped about excessive bureaucracy. "The Interior Department is in charge of salmon while they're in fresh water, but the Commerce Department handles them when they're in salt water," he said. "I hear it gets even more complicated once they're smoked."

---

* There's a wonderful video that captures many of these moments from Obama's trips. Online, search for: "Obama, Greetings Massive!"

Ba-dum-bump.

But you're not a president with a team of writers at your disposal—and no one expects you to be. You don't have to start your speech with a clever one-liner—because you're not a comedian or a late-night TV host (or a president at the annual White House Correspondents' Dinner, where presidents sound like late-night TV hosts).

You don't have to recycle canned jokes ("A priest, a rabbi, and a minister walk into a bar . . ."); in fact, please don't—it's not the 1950s.

And you don't have to tell a long story that builds up to a witty punch line. Yes, President Ronald Reagan did it all the time and he was great at it. But before he was a politician, he was an actor in movies, including several comedies. He wrote his jokes on index cards and honed them for years.

So relax. As a speaker, you don't have to *tell jokes.* Instead, just add a little humor. What's the difference? "Humor is a means to an end," explains Jon Lovett, who as one of Obama's speechwriters took the lead on several of the president's comedy routines at the White House Correspondents' Dinners. "Humor is a tool to surprise and delight your audience by revealing an unspoken connection. It can be a signal that you have something in common. When people are laughing together, you're delighting in that connection together."

It's why a funny story about a friend or loved one can elicit smiles even at a funeral—because you're delighting in your shared love for the person you're remembering. It's why you shouldn't tell inside jokes, like the best man who, during his wedding toast, turns to the groom and says, "Bruh, remember Cancun?!" and no one else laughs—because, bruh, no one knows what you're talking about.

"You don't have to be hilarious," says David Litt, who spearheaded several of Obama's Correspondents' Dinner speeches in his second term. "You just have to be warm and show some humanity."

Instead of belly laughs, go for chuckles. All you have to do is surprise and delight your audience with a shared connection and a touch of humanity. Here are some easy ways to do it.

Take Yourself Down a Notch

Be self-deprecating. It works for everyone, especially if you're a leader.

Obama sometimes joked that his audience would rather hear a speech from the First Lady. Or that his daughters were tired of listening to him speak. Or that, when it was announced he'd won the Nobel Peace Prize, his daughter Malia was more focused on it being their dog Bo's birthday. It was funny because it was true— and relatable. Few parents are heroes in their own home—even if you're the president.

Surprise Them

When Obama addressed the British Parliament, a solemn occasion if there ever was one, he said this: "I am told that the last three speakers here have been the pope, Her Majesty the Queen, and Nelson Mandela, which is either a very high bar or the beginning of a very funny joke."

Welcoming the Japanese prime minister to the White House, he paid tribute to Japan's many contributions to the world—its innovations, arts, "and, of course, emojis."

Greeting the leaders of the Nordic countries, he thanked them for upholding global security and prosperity—and for inventing "Minecraft, Angry Birds, and Candy Crush."

Hilarious? Not really. But cute. And those quips got chuckles. Sometimes, the easiest way to get a smile and a laugh from your audience is to surprise them with something they don't see coming—even on serious occasions.

Steal from the Best

When Mel Brooks was awarded a Kennedy Center Honor, Obama paid tribute to the legendary comedian at the White House. Brooks served in World War II, Obama said, in the European Theater of Operations, which had "lots of operations" and "very little theater." But then Brooks found success as a comic, which meant, "panic, hysteria, insomnia . . . and years of psychoanalysis."

I wish our speechwriting team had come up with lines like these. In fact, as Obama told his audience, he was quoting Brooks's own jokes back to him. And the crowd ate it up.

There's nothing wrong with cribbing a line from a comedian. They've already road tested it. It's guaranteed to get a laugh. But remember to give credit. When you plagiarize, it's your critics who get the last laugh.

Have Some Pun

Every November, the president of the United States participates in a time-honored—though not necessarily distinguished—tradition: the Thanksgiving turkey pardoning. For Obama, it also became another tradition: "embarrassing my daughters with a corny-copia of dad jokes about turkeys."

It was silly, he admitted, but "no way I'm cutting this habit cold turkey."

He remembered the millions of brave birds who "didn't get to ride the gravy train to freedom." They "proved that they weren't chicken."

And if someone at your Thanksgiving won't let you have any more side dishes, he declared, "I hope you respond with a creed that sums up the spirit of a hungry people, Yes We Cran."

Puns are fun. Your audience gets to solve the wordplay with you—a shared connection. Of course, be careful not to overdo it. And, as always, write it down. Best not to wing it.

Done right, a touch of humor can even help you deal with the most delicate of situations.

Your Humor Should Have a Point

"I was being censored."

That's how Zander Moricz remembers the meeting with his high school principal. Zander was just weeks away from graduation, and, as his senior class president, he was expected to speak at commencement. But his principal at his Osprey, Florida, school was nervous.

Florida had recently passed a law that, among other things, banned "classroom discussion about sexual orientation or gender identity in certain grade levels." But the law was vague, failing to define what kind of "discussion" was prohibited and at which "grade levels." Opponents dubbed it the "Don't Say Gay" law, warning that it would push LGBTQ students back in the closet.

Zander, who is gay, led a walkout at his school to protest the measure and joined a lawsuit to fight it in court. Even though the law wasn't in effect yet, his principal worried that Zander would use his graduation speech to speak out against it.

"My principal said he supported me as a person, but that it 'would not be appropriate' for me to discuss my sexuality, the law, or my activism in my speech," Zander told me when I interviewed him a year later. "And if I did, he said they'd 'cut my mic.'"

Zander tweeted about his dilemma, and some friends and supporters urged him to defy his school and have his mic cut. He was torn. "I wanted to be true to myself," Zander said. "But my classmates and their families had worked toward this day for years, and I didn't want to ruin the celebration."

The days leading up to commencement grew increasingly tense. Angry callers flooded the school's phone lines. Zander received death threats. He stopped attending school and never left home alone. When strangers accosted him at a supermarket, he locked himself in the store bathroom for safety.

On graduation day, Zander took the podium, and a hush fell over the audience.

For the first few minutes, his remarks were like any class president's speech. He celebrated the activities and projects that had brought the class together—how they had weathered remote learning during Covid, and how they had united in protests for racial justice and action on climate change. They had to stand up, Zander said, to the "degradation" of their communities and civil rights.

"That is why I must discuss a very public part of my identity," he said. "This characteristic has probably become the first thing you think of when you think of me as a human being. As you know, I . . ."

Zander removed his graduation cap and touched his mop of brown hair.

". . . have curly hair."

Laughter and applause rippled across the crowd. Everyone knew exactly what he was doing.

"I used to hate my curls," he continued. "I spent mornings and nights embarrassed of them, trying desperately to straighten this part of who I am." He admitted that "having curly hair in Florida is difficult . . . due to the humidity," prompting more laughter. But he eventually found the strength to come out to his gym teacher "because I didn't have other curly-haired people to talk to."

Then Zander got serious. "It's because of the love I've drawn from this community that I came out to my family," he said, placing his hand over his heart as he tried to catch his breath. "Now I'm happy."

He called on his fellow graduates to "use our shared power" to speak up for "the thousands of curly-haired kids" like him who "need a community" of support at school.

Zander wasn't telling "jokes" or delivering zingers. But he was funny. And "the humor had a point," he told me. "By using my curly hair as a metaphor for my identity, I was able to show how ridiculous and dangerous the Florida law is"—all without getting his mic cut. He received a standing ovation, his parents were in tears, and his speech went viral.

Zander and other opponents of the law weren't able to stop Florida's law from going into effect, but they did eventually win an important victory: a legal settlement that clarifies that Florida teachers and students can engage in classroom "discussion" of "'sexual orientation' and 'gender identity.'" Since giving a speech that only he could give—at once funny and fierce—Zander continues to raise his voice for equality. "Society has never changed and become more equal unless we understand why we need to," he told me. "And the most powerful thing any of us can do is share our story with another human being—even if we have to use a little humor to do it."

The Download

As you prepare your remarks, remember that—like any good performance—your opening should grab your audience and quickly forge an emotional connection. Some ways to do it:

» **Have 'em at hello** (or "Good morning!" or "Good evening!") or give some love to the crowd ("Hello, Chicago!" "Hello, nurses!").

» **Introduce yourself** ("My name is . . .") and emphasize your authority and credibility—why the audience should listen to you ("As a resident of this town for thirty years . . .").

» **Grab 'em** with a killer opening line, a gripping story, a moving piece of Scripture, or a shocking fact.

» **Instead of starting with acknowledgments, weave them into your remarks.** Make them brief and use them to celebrate your hosts, the work they do, and the spirit of the event.

» **Show some love for the audience's Three Fs**—the firsts, foods, and fans that make them who they are and that they're proud of.

» **Instead of trying to tell a joke, just use some humor.** Surprise and delight your audience with unexpected references to the things you have in common.

CHAPTER 6

Be a Uniter

You have to stand for something
bigger than yourself.

—Jose Antonio Vargas

Early in any presentation or speech—ideally right after your opening—it's time to get to your point. Your audience needs to know *why* you're speaking to them: your purpose. And I believe that any good speech—no matter who you are, what you're talking about, or who you're talking to—can have only one purpose.

Here's what I mean.

Around the world, many of our societies are more divided than ever. Leaders unable to deliver real solutions instead demean their opponents and scapegoat vulnerable communities. Ratings-hungry TV pundits stoke our political, economic, and social divisions. The algorithms behind our social media feeds keep us engaged by keeping us outraged, usually at one another.

All of which means that when *we* get up and speak—in our families, our companies, our communities—we have a choice. Do we feed into all this division or try to bring people together? Do we use our words to inflame or to calm, to hurt or to heal?

This is why I believe that a truly good speech can have only one purpose—to *do* good, by uniting people around a *good* cause.

Delivering a toast or a eulogy? Your purpose is to unite your family and friends and reaffirm the values and life's work of the person you're honoring.

Giving a presentation at work? Your purpose is to unite your coworkers around a high-quality product or service that, hopefully, improves the lives of your customers.

Speaking up at a public meeting? Your purpose is to unite your community or elected officials—or at least a voting majority—to support a measure that you believe will make life better for the people in your town, county, or city.

Appealing for support for a cause or charity? Your purpose is to bring your audience together—and bring in new volunteers and donations—so you can alleviate suffering or save lives.

Running for office? Your purpose is to bring together as many voters as possible—not just so you can get elected, but, hopefully, so you can use your power to create a society that's more equal, safe, and prosperous.

So please forget that terrible old advice: "It's not *what* you say, it's *how* you say it." What you say—the substance of your comments, more than the style in which you deliver them—is *the essence* of any great presentation. "You need to deliver a message that is going to resonate and get traction," Obama said to me once.

Here are three big ways to connect with your audience so that your message resonates and motivates your listeners to work together: a shared challenge, a shared identity, and a shared idea.

RALLY YOUR AUDIENCE TO MEET A SHARED CHALLENGE . . .

Think of the times when you felt most united with those around you. Chances are, it's when you faced a common challenge. Your family rallied around a loved one who was stricken with a life-threatening illness. Your community pulled together after a devastating accident or storm. Your company pulled out all the stops when challenged by a competitor. Your country united after being attacked.

"The more a group perceives a threat, the more that group will work together," explains Michele Gelfand, a cultural psychologist at the Stanford Graduate School of Business who studies how communities respond to threats like war, outbreaks of disease, and natural disasters. This holds an important lesson if you're a speaker who is trying to motivate your audience to meet a challenge.

"Make it concrete," Gelfand told me. "If the challenge is too abstract, your audience won't see it." In other words, use vivid language. Gelfand and her colleagues analyzed millions of words that appeared in over a century's worth of publications, in print and online, and developed what they call a Threat Dictionary—240 words that speakers and writers often use when describing a challenge. Their dictionary includes words like "anger," "attack," "chaos," "collapse," "deadly," "devastating," "frightening," "injuries," "murder," "storm," "suffering," "terrorist," and "victims."[1]

Leaders use vivid language like this all the time, especially when trying to summon their people to meet a challenge, whether manmade or natural. Just look at the first two paragraphs of President George W. Bush's speech on the night of 9/11.

> *Good evening. Today, our fellow citizens, our way of life, our very freedom came under **attack** in a series of deliberate and **deadly** **terrorist** acts. The **victims** were in airplanes, or in their offices; secretaries, businessmen and women, military and federal workers; moms and dads, friends and neighbors. Thousands of lives were suddenly ended by **evil**, despicable acts of **terror**.*

*The pictures of airplanes flying into buildings, fires **burning**, huge structures **collapsing**, have filled us with disbelief, terrible sadness, and a quiet, unyielding **anger**. These acts of mass **murder** were intended to **frighten** our nation into **chaos** and retreat. But they have failed; our country is strong.*

Or look at President Obama's remarks after a massive tornado ripped through Joplin, Missouri, killing more than 160 men, women, and children.

*The **devastation** is comparable and may end up exceeding some of the **devastation** that we saw in Tuscaloosa, Alabama, just a few weeks ago. So far we know that **over one hundred people lost their lives**. **Others remain missing**, and hundreds more are **injured**. And obviously, our thoughts and prayers are with the families who are **suffering** at this moment.*

Two presidents speaking in two very different situations but using similar language—the kind of words that Gelfand and her fellow researchers point out "instantly attract our attention" and encourage us to act collectively.*

Trying to rally *your* audience to meet a shared challenge? Don't speak in vague abstractions. Be concrete. Use vivid language so your listeners can see the challenge in their mind's eye.

* For the same reason, leaders in many sectors often invoke the language of "war" to address a range of challenges ("The war on poverty"; "The war on AIDS"; "The war on drugs"; "The war on crime"; "The war on terrorism"). "War" is indeed a powerful metaphor for motivating any audience, and many leaders can't resist portraying themselves as decisive commanders in battle. But there are risks. History shows that a "war" on an issue can easily become a war on people, including dangerous excesses like profiling, discrimination, and violations of civil liberties. My suggestion: Whenever possible, resist declaring "war" on political, economic, or social challenges, especially since they can't be solved by military solutions anyway.

How to Describe a Challenge

Don't be vague	Be concrete and vivid
"Our community is impacted by gun violence."	"Gun violence is killing our children, who don't deserve to be murdered at school."
"Pollution is affecting our town."	"These deadly chemicals are poisoning our drinking water and endangering our lives."
"Our company's market share is being eroded."	"This new competitor is a threat to the survival of our company."
"Climate change touches us all."	"The storms, fires, and droughts fueled by climate change are destroying our homes and devastating our communities."

Of course, when rallying your audience to meet a challenge, be careful. You have to be a leader . . .

. . . BUT DON'T BE A DEMAGOGUE

By overwhelming margins, Americans tell pollsters that they're tired of the vitriol and nastiness in our public discourse and that they want more civility. We've been saying this for years. Yet things only seem to get worse. So here's one way to help us all be a little more civil: when motivating an audience to address a challenge, focus on the *problem*, not *people*—not other human beings.

Of course, there have always been individuals and groups—

bloodthirsty tyrants and terrorist organizations—worthy of our disdain. Their barbarism *is* evil. Even today, there are authoritarians who threaten democracy and human rights and who need to be called out for the danger they pose.

At the same time, good speakers—and by this, I mean speakers who *do* good—don't villainize entire groups of people. Speakers who do this, usually by appealing to the worst passions and prejudices of their audience, are called demagogues. And it's not just leaders. In the heat of the moment, when discussing issues that we're passionate about, it can be all too easy for any of us to succumb to incivility or slip into demagoguery. Here are some ways to avoid it, and more importantly, to know a demagogue when you hear one.

Don't Question Other People's Motives

I once wrote for a Democrat in Congress who proposed a line like this for a speech: "Republicans want to hurt children. Democrats want to help children."

Now, I'm a Democrat. I genuinely believe that, in most cases, Democratic policies are generally better for children than Republican policies. You may or may not see it the same way; reasonable people can disagree. But the idea that Republicans "want" to "hurt" children? Come on. Many Republicans are parents, and they want what's best for their children too.

Yes, there are some bad people out there in the world, including in politics—along all points of the ideological spectrum. Their actions and policies *do* hurt people. And sometimes that really *is* their goal. If you have solid evidence to prove their malevolent intentions, call them out. But here's the challenge: in many cases, it's hard, if not impossible, to really know other people's true motivations.

When we question other people's motives—when we claim that people we disagree with "hate" our way of life or "*want* to tear down our country"—it risks fueling the cycle of distrust and division that's tearing at the fabric of our country. It also makes it harder to persuade other people to embrace our point of view. That's why, even as Obama opposed the U.S. invasion of Iraq, he acknowledged that "there are patriots who opposed the war in Iraq and there are patriots who supported the war in Iraq."

We rarely know what's in someone else's heart, and we should be careful not to talk like we do.

Don't Attack Other People's Character

If others belittle, demean, or degrade us, it's tempting to respond in kind. Your audience may even cheer you on for matching insult for insult. But as the old saying goes, never wrestle with a pig. You both get dirty—and the pig likes it.

By all means, condemn bigotry like racism, sexism, and homophobia as the scourges they are. At the same time, if you're trying to *persuade* someone—a neighbor, a coworker, an employer, an elected official, or your crazy uncle at Thanksgiving—I wouldn't recommend calling them a bigot to their face. "Telling people they're racist, sexist, and xenophobic is going to get you exactly nowhere," explains Alana Conner, of Stanford University's Center for Social Psychological Answers to Real-World Questions. "It's such a threatening message. One of the things we know from social psychology is when people feel threatened, they can't change, they can't listen."[2] I consider that solid empirical evidence for Michelle Obama's good advice for dealing with people who are cruel: "When they go low, we go high."

Leave the pig wrestling to the politicians and the pundits. The rest of us have to live and work together as family, neighbors, and colleagues. If you disagree with someone, don't attack their character; debate their ideas. Take on their arguments—acknowledge them, dissect them, and then rebut them, one by one.

Don't Use Polarizing Language

Every society has its share of criminals and extremists, and they need to be held accountable for their misdeeds. Short of criminal activity, however, differences of opinion between reasonable people are a part of democracy, and I worry that we've sometimes become too quick to brand people that we disagree with as outside the main-stream. I confess that at times I've been guilty of it too.

You see it in the words we use. After analyzing nearly twenty thousand tweets, a group of researchers developed a list of about two hundred words that they found were frequently used by the most partisan social media accounts. They call it a Polarization Dictio-nary.[3] Want to help tone down the divisive rhetoric in our communi-ties and country? The Polarization Dictionary offers examples of the kind of words to avoid. For example, debate vigorously with those with whom you disagree, but resist calling them "idiots," "liars," or "criminals"—especially if you're trying to persuade them. If you're a die-hard liberal, don't refer to all conservatives as "right-wing fas-cists" or disparage entire swaths of America as "flyover country." If you're a proud conservative, resist calling all liberals "leftist radicals" or "coastal elites."

As you've probably noticed, lots of politicians and pundits talk like this all the time. They see debates as zero sum, black and white. It's another reason why so many of us are fed up with politics. In reality, life is full of complexity. So, yes, always stand up for your beliefs. Speak with conviction and passion. But resist the urge to label peo-ple with whom you disagree with language that only deepens our polarization. Every one of us can do our part to cool the incendiary rhetoric that's burning the bridges that connect us to one another.

Don't Otherize, Demonize, or Dehumanize

Beware of the hallmarks of a demagogue.

If someone tends to speak of people who agree with them as "us" and others—especially different racial, religious, ethnic, sexual, or gender groups—as "them," they're a demagogue who *otherizes*. If they describe groups like these as "sinister," "wicked," or "evil," they're a demagogue who *demonizes*. If they refer to other people as less than human—"vermin," "animals," or "hordes"—they're a demagogue who *dehumanizes*. Beware, too, when a speaker characterizes their opponents or their ideas as a "virus" or "poison," which usually is followed by an ominous pledge to "eradicate" them.

But words are just . . . words, right? If only. Language has consequences. The Nazis called Jews "rats" and then murdered more than six million innocent Jewish men, women, and children in the Holocaust. In Rwanda, ethnic Hutus called ethnic Tutsis "cockroaches" and then butchered up to eight hundred thousand people.

In the United States, referring to criminals who were Black as "superpredators" helped pave the way for an era of mass incarceration that fell disproportionately on Black Americans. In recent years, hateful rhetoric—by citizens and politicians alike—against Americans who are Latino, Jewish, Muslim, Asian, and LGBTQ has been linked to a rise in hate crimes against these groups.[4]

Our words matter, especially in an era when social media can instantly carry them far and wide. Every one of us is responsible for the words that come out of our mouth. Good speakers—speakers who *do* good—don't spew hateful rhetoric that can lead to real-world harm.

Don't Threaten Violence

For generations, speakers have urged their audiences to "fight" for their beliefs. It was usually metaphorical. These days, it's all too real. Public officials, judges, election workers, and their families have been physically attacked, shot, and in some cases killed. At his rally on January 6, 2021, as Congress prepared to certify his loss to Joe Biden, Donald Trump said "fight" or "fighting" about twenty times—and then his supporters fought their way into the U.S. Capitol to try to overturn the election. A growing number of Americans—nearly a quarter—believe that it might be necessary to "resort to violence" to "save" the country from political opponents.[5]

When politically motivated violence is a clear and present danger, we'd all be wise to step back from language that could be perceived as threatening or inciting violence. Here are a few places where we might start. We can stop describing people we disagree with as "enemies" who need to be "destroyed" or "crushed." We can stop whipping up audiences to "fight" and "take back our country"—because our diverse society of more than three hundred million people is not something that any one group owns or can "take" from our neighbors. And let's watch our buts—as in, "there's no room for violence, but . . ." Because "but" negates everything that comes before it. In a democracy where we have the power to bring change through peaceful protest and the ballot box, violence is unacceptable. Full stop.

We won't always be able to stop demagogues from spewing fear and hate. Still, the rest of us can make a different choice. Along with rallying our audience to meet a shared challenge without pitting people against one another, we can use the early part of our remarks to appeal to shared identities.

EVOKE A SHARED IDENTITY

In one sense, you have to give the demagogues credit. They know exactly what they're doing. They understand that, as social animals, we humans gravitate toward groups—usually people who look, act, or think like we do—especially when we feel vulnerable or afraid.[6] Demagogues exploit our racial, religious, ethnic, gender, and sexual identities to try to divide us and do harm. Here's the good news: we can evoke our identities too—to bring people together and do good.

"One of the biggest myths about groups is that they inevitably lead to discrimination toward outgroup members," explains Jay Van Bavel, a professor of psychology and neural science at New York University. "However, this is not always the case. When people join a group that cares deeply about diversity and inclusion it can lead them to embrace" people from outside the group.[7]

In fact, evoking a shared identity can be one of the most powerful ways to inspire your audiences to do good—and it starts with how you identify yourself.

The Power of You

Let me introduce you to two guys.

The first guy lives in Virginia. He's white. His father was in the military, many of his friends and colleagues are veterans, he's a husband and father who wants to keep his family safe, and he's a proud American.

The second guy considers himself liberal and progressive, he joined a rally for justice after the murder of George Floyd, and he believes America still has a long way to go to achieve true equality for all people.

As you read those two descriptions, I suspect you started to make some instant judgments about each person. Maybe you identified with, and were drawn to, one more than the other. Which, in turn, might make you more inclined to listen to what he had to say.

Here's the thing: both guys are the same person. Both guys are me.

None of us are one-dimensional. Every one of us, as Walt Whitman wrote, "contain multitudes." So, too, when we're speaking. How we identify ourselves to our audience can have a profound effect on how they perceive us—whether they see us as part of their group and therefore whether they're open to what we're saying. It's the essence of group loyalty—we're more likely to align with and believe people who we perceive as similar to ourselves or as part of our own group.[8]

Which means persuasion starts with you. Whenever you speak, think about which of your many identities—all of which are true and authentic—might allow you to best connect with your audience. "I'm speaking to you today as . . ." "a mother," "a father," "a daughter," "a member of this community," "a person of faith," "a veteran," "a child of immigrants," "the first person in my family to go to college."

We have so many identities to choose from. And it doesn't have to be the same one every time you talk. Whenever you speak, ask yourself: How best can I present myself to—and connect with—*this* audience?

The Power of "We"

Here's another powerful word in our rhetorical arsenal: "we." Unfortunately, we don't hear it enough. In contrast to demagogues who speak in terms of "us" versus "them," "we" can rally our audience by reminding them of what we have in common. "We" can be members of our family, our neighbors, our colleagues, or our fellow citizens. "The single most powerful word in our democracy is 'We,'" Obama declared when marking the fiftieth anniversary of the civil rights marches in Selma, Alabama. "'We the People.' 'We Shall Overcome.' 'Yes We Can.' That word is owned by no one. It belongs to everyone."

When you appeal to everyone—"we," "our," "all of us"—you can bring more people to your cause, as Jay Van Bavel and Dominic Packer, a professor of psychology at Lehigh University, show in their book *The Power of Us*. One study found that reminding people of the identities they share—which any of us can do, for example, by appealing to our "fellow Americans"—can decrease negative attitudes toward people from another political party.[9] Another study showed that candidates who use words like "we" and "us" more often in their speeches are more successful at the ballot box.[10] It's a winning recipe for any organization, including businesses. In the face of those who *exclude*, we have to *include* so that our families, communities, companies, and countries benefit from the talents and skills of every person.

When trying to win people over to your cause, try putting aside the usual labels that could turn off parts of your audience ("Democrat," "Republican," "liberal," "conservative") and appeal to the more inclusive identities that they cherish—"fellow Pennsylvanians," "fellow Georgians," "fellow Americans."

And what if you're appealing to your audience to help people on the other side of the world with whom they may feel they have little or nothing in common? Remind them of the most fundamental identity that we share with every other person on the planet—"our fellow human beings."

The Power of What We Do

Tapping into the shared identities of our audience doesn't just feel good, it can help get things done. How? Jonah Berger, a marketing professor at the Wharton School of the University of Pennsylvania, urges us to use fewer verbs and more nouns. He points to one study where encouraging people to think of themselves as "a voter" made them more likely to vote than people who said they simply planned "to vote."[11] Berger calls this "turning actions into identities."[12]

We can do it too. When addressing our communities, we can appeal to our school board members' identities as "educators" and to police officers' identities as "protectors." When addressing our co-workers, we can lean into their pride as "problem solvers," "creators," and "innovators."

Imagine your audience. How do they see *themselves*? What do they take pride in? Speak to those identities and they'll be more likely to take the action—and deliver the results—you want.

APPEAL TO A SHARED IDEA

Alongside our shared identities, we can also motivate our audiences by appealing to the beliefs we hold in common. Over the years, I've found that many speakers don't fully appreciate the opportunity they have to wrap their remarks in a larger idea. I see it most often with business leaders. "My CEO," I've heard many corporate speechwriters say, "just wants to talk about our services and products. She doesn't want to talk about anything bigger." Which is too bad, because, let's be honest, a lot of services and products are . . . not that exciting. And if that's all you're talking about, then, yeah, your presentation probably won't be that exciting, either.

Whenever we speak, we have an extraordinary opportunity—not simply to talk, but to impart an idea that can inspire our audience. And the bigger the idea, the better. Most of the speeches Obama gave as a candidate and president were, in one way or another, about one simple yet profound idea—our founding belief, as Americans, that "all men are created equal, that they are endowed by their Creator with certain unalienable Rights, that among these are Life, Liberty and the pursuit of Happiness." That's a pretty powerful idea—one that Americans have been striving to uphold, and that has inspired people around the world, for more than two centuries.

Maybe you're speaking at a public meeting. When discussing the danger of racial profiling or hate crimes, try uniting your neighbors around an even bigger idea: "We believe in a community that is safe, where every person can walk down the street and not be targeted because of who they are or what they look like."

Maybe your company is launching a new product. Of course, give a presentation that showcases all its cutting-edge features and benefits. But don't forget to wrap your product, and rally your employees, around a bigger idea—if you're a tech company, perhaps something like "We believe that every person has a right to privacy and to control their own data."

Or maybe you're an ecopreneur—an entrepreneur developing mind-blowing products to help the environment. Yes, make the financial case for why venture capital firms will make money by investing in your innovation to capture carbon dioxide emissions before they pollute the atmosphere. But don't miss the chance to inspire them with a broader mission, perhaps: "We believe that we have an obligation to leave our planet safer and healthier for future generations."

With every presentation, you have the opportunity to unite and inspire your audience around a big, bold idea. What's *yours*?

Challenge an Idea

Then again, maybe you want to use your remarks to *change* the way your audience thinks—by reframing an old idea or by challenging them to embrace a new one.

Dr. King's "I Have a Dream" speech was a stirring challenge to America to "rise up and live out the true meaning of its creed" that we're all created equal.

When David McCullough, Jr., a Massachusetts teacher, spoke at his high school's commencement, he surprised the graduates by telling them they'd been "pampered" and "you are not special," sparking a national discussion about parenting and education.

Reshma Saujani, the founder of Girls Who Code, used her commencement address at Smith College to push back on the idea that "imposter syndrome" is something that women need to fix in their own minds. The real problem, she argued, is systemic inequalities—

like women getting paid less than men for the same work—and that it's everyone's job, including men's, to "fix the system."

Defend an Idea

Or maybe you want to use your time at the podium to *defend* an idea that's under threat. That's what Amanda Jones, a librarian in Louisiana, did at a meeting of her local library board a few years ago.

A proud native of Watson, Louisiana—a small town in Livingston Parish outside of Baton Rouge—Amanda says she "loves everything about Louisiana." Along with her husband and teenage daughter, she cheers for the LSU Tigers, dances to Zydeco, and savors Cajun cuisine—"Beignets, boudin, and King Cake during Mardi Gras."

Raised a Southern Baptist, "I'm a Christian, and I'm vocal about my faith," she told me. "God's purpose for me is to educate children," which led her to become a middle school librarian, a role she balances with her responsibilities as a parent. "As a mother, I get to decide what my child sees." A lifelong Republican, she voted for Donald Trump in 2016.

At the same time, Amanda is an educator. "I make sure that our students have the books they need," she says. It's why she works to make her school library's collection "as diverse as possible, so that all our students see themselves in our books."

So when Amanda noticed an unusual item—"Book Content"—on the agenda for an upcoming meeting of her local library board, she knew instantly what it was about. A group had been working to remove books from libraries across the state. It was part of an aggressive national effort targeting certain books, most of them by or about people of color and the LGBTQ community. Now they had their sights set on Amanda's school.

"I had to speak up," she said.

The night before the meeting, Amanda sat on her couch, flipped open her laptop, and quickly typed out everything she wanted to say. Her fury came through in her first draft. "I was going to go in guns blazing," she told me. When she shared her draft with a few fellow librarians, they suggested a less confrontational approach. "I was a little inflammatory," Amanda concedes. "So I toned it down to make it more conciliatory."

The night of the meeting, nearly sixty people gathered at the local library. Amanda walked up to the microphone and began to speak. "I started feeling very angry," she told me later, "but I worked really hard to control my voice and be even-tempered." In fact, the remarks she went on to deliver show how anyone can speak with the civility and grace that can bring people to a cause.

Despite her anger, Amanda didn't attack those who disagreed with her. She didn't question their motives. Instead, she invited the board member who had put "Book Content" on the agenda to work with her to learn about the harmful effects of censorship on young people.

Amanda tapped into her shared identity with her audience. "I am here," she said, "as a lifelong resident of Livingston Parish, parent of a child in this district, and taxpayer." She grew up, she explained, "being taught that God is love."

She spoke in concrete terms about the challenge as she saw it—her "fear that a member of the board is trying to censor books." She called for an end to "the false narrative," because "nobody is putting pornography in children's sections of the library." Finally, Amanda spoke up forcefully for an idea—the freedom to read—and explained why it was important to her audience.

> *The citizens of our parish consist of taxpayers who are white, Black, brown, gay, straight, Christian, non-Christian—people from all backgrounds and walks of life, and no one portion of the community should dictate what the rest of the citizens have access to. Just because you don't want to read it or*

see it, it doesn't give you the right to deny others or demand its relocation.

When Amanda finished speaking, her supporters in the room broke into applause. Her impassioned plea, and that of other speakers that night, worked. The library board moved on to the next item on the agenda without removing any books.[*]

Within days, however, Amanda was subjected to what she calls "a coordinated attack." In Facebook posts that were shared hundreds of times, one person asked why she wanted to "keep sexually erotic and pornographic material in the kid's section." She was called a "pervert" and a "sick pig." One man sent an email threatening to kill her.

"I was terrified," she told me a year later. "I bought security cameras, a taser, and started keeping a shotgun under my bed." The threats took a heavy emotional toll. "I broke out in hives, started having panic attacks, and slipped into depression. I took medical leave from work and didn't leave the house for months." She feared most, though, for the students at her school. "If a child was ever hurt . . ." she said, her voice trailing off as she started to cry.

Still, Amanda refused to back down. "If they wanted me to be quiet, they picked the wrong person. I'm going to roar." She kept speaking up at local meetings. She received hundreds of letters of support and inspired people across the country, including my sister Katherine, a dedicated librarian in Massachusetts, who told me that "seeing Amanda stand up for free speech makes me proud to be in a profession that defends the very foundation of our country."

For Amanda, this is the greatest reward—helping to unite people in support of the freedom to read, especially the freedom of children to read books about the beauty of their own lives. "I'm here to

---

[*] There is no video of Amanda's speech to the library board; there were no video cameras at the meeting. A full transcript of her remarks can be found on her website, Amanda Jones, Defender of Wonder.

support these kids. They need to feel accepted and loved," she said. "And it can't just be up to the people being targeted to defend themselves alone. Everybody has to speak up."

The Download

Early in your presentation or speech, you have to get to your point. You have to tell your audience *why* you're speaking: your purpose, your goal. I believe that a good speech—a speech that *does* good—can have only one purpose: to bring your audience together and motivate them to work for a good cause. For example, you might . . .

» **Rally your audience to meet a shared challenge** by describing the problem in concrete terms with vivid language. But always be careful to avoid any demagoguery that otherizes, demonizes, or dehumanizes our fellow human beings.

» **Evoke a shared identity with your audience** by leading with your own identity (the Power of You), appealing to common bonds (the Power of "We"), or showing the actions you want your audience to embrace (the Power of What We Do).

» **Appeal to a shared idea** that inspires your audience, challenge your listeners to embrace a new idea, or defend an idea that's being threatened. Don't just tell your audience what you think, tell them what you *believe* ("I believe our community/company/country is stronger when . . .").

CHAPTER 7

Appeal to Values

Though we see the same world, we
see it through different eyes.

—Virginia Woolf

You've greeted your audience and grabbed their attention. You've started to bring them together around a shared cause, identity, or idea. Now what?

The next thing I try to do in any speech is frame the main idea or argument around the values that the audience cherishes most. It's one of the most powerful ways to connect with and persuade your listeners.

Unfortunately, many of us miss the chance to do it.

In a fascinating experiment, researchers from Stanford and the University of Toronto examined how we try to persuade other people to change their mind. It involved roughly two hundred people—half of whom identified themselves as politically liberal and half as conservative.[1] The liberals were asked to write a few sentences to convince conservatives to support same-sex marriage. The conservatives were asked to write a few sentences to convince liberals to support English as the official language of the United States. What happened?

Almost everyone failed.

Among the liberals, the vast majority (74 percent) made their argument for same-sex marriage using arguments and values often favored by *liberals*, like fairness and equality. (For example, "They deserve the same equal rights as other Americans.") Only 9 percent of liberals appealed to conservatives with values often favored by conservatives, like loyalty and unity. ("Our fellow citizens of the United States of America deserve to stand alongside us.") Worse, a third of liberals (34 percent) used arguments that *contradicted* values favored by conservatives, like the importance of faith. ("Although you may personally believe your faith should be against such a thing . . . your religion should play no part in the laws of the United States.") Talk about not reading the room!

The conservatives fared no better. The vast majority (70 percent) argued for English as the official language of the United States using values often favored by *conservatives*, like loyalty and unity. (For example, "Making English the official language will help unify the country as we all can communicate with one another and speak the same national language.") Only 8 percent of conservatives appealed to liberals with values favored by liberals, like fairness. ("By making English our official language, there will be less racism and discrimination.") And 14 percent of conservatives used arguments that *contradicted* values favored by liberals. ("So those of you preaching diversity and equality, who think everyone should take advantage of us, should think real hard.") Attacking your audience is . . . not persuasive.

At one time or another, we've all done it, whether at Thanksgiving dinner with our family or a community meeting with our neighbors. We often try to convince someone of something by using the arguments and values that make sense *to us*. And other people do it right back to us. We talk past each other. "Most

people are not very good at appealing to other people's values,"
said Matthew Feinberg, a coauthor of the study and a professor of
organizational behavior at the University of Toronto.[2]

Which may also explain why sometimes the more we talk, the
less likely we are to change the minds of people who see the world
differently than we do. In another study, researchers asked hundreds of liberals to follow prominent conservatives on what was then
Twitter and hundreds of conservatives to follow prominent liberals.
Think anyone was persuaded? Of course not. In fact, after about a
month, the conservatives were even *more* conservative in their beliefs and the liberals were even *more* liberal.[3]

Why are we *so bad* at persuading people who see the world
through different eyes?

Researchers at the University of California Irvine have one possible answer. They argue that many of us have a "moral empathy
gap"—we often fail to appreciate that other people have a different
moral worldview than our own. "Our inability to feel what others
feel," the researchers explained, "makes it difficult to understand
how they think"—which, in turn, makes it difficult to connect,
communicate, and persuade.[4]

But there's hope.

Some social psychologists argue that we humans tend to see the
world through several major prisms, or "moral foundations."[5] These
foundations go something like this:

- Care/Harm—a focus on caring for and protecting others
  from harm.

- Fairness/Cheating—an emphasis on equal treatment and an
  opposition to cheating.

- Authority/Subversion—a deep respect for hierarchy and
  authority and a disapproval of subversion.

- Loyalty/Betrayal—devotion to family, community, and country and a disdain for betrayal.

- Sanctity/Degradation—a belief in upholding the sanctity of our bodies, institutions, and lives.

- Liberty/Oppression—an emphasis on independence and a rejection of oppression.

Of course, these six moral foundations alone can't explain everyone's beliefs about every issue, and few of us identify with just one. Still, as you read through them, you may find yourself drawn more to certain ones. Consider yourself more progressive or liberal? You might gravitate toward care and fairness. More traditional or conservative in your views? You might see a lot to like with authority, loyalty, and sanctity.[6] And whatever our ideological orientation, what's not to like about liberty?

When I first learned about moral foundations after leaving the White House, it felt like an epiphany. I felt like I'd finally found the theory behind what I'd been practicing for decades as a speechwriter. Because, to me, "moral foundations" is another way of saying "values," and values can help you build bridges with any audience, even in these polarized times.

THE VALUES WE SHARE

One Saturday a few years ago, I spent the day in a church basement in Virginia listening to about a dozen Americans talk about their lives, their beliefs, and their country. Half identified themselves as conservative and half as liberal. As you'd expect, things got heated. Fast. Some people struggled to express themselves without disparaging the other side. A few folks fell back on familiar talking points they'd heard from politicians and TV pundits.

But there were also some surprises, which was the point. The meeting was convened by Braver Angels, a group devoted to helping Americans bridge partisan divides. Over seven hours of intense and emotionally exhausting conversations, some of these conservatives and liberals started to sound like . . . one another. Liberals proudly described their deep religious faith, their service in the military, and how they value family above all else. Conservatives said it was important for communities to welcome immigrants of all backgrounds and that America needs to be a place where people of all races and religions can thrive.

At times, these conservatives and liberals even used the exact same words to describe their beliefs and goals—"the dignity of the individual . . . respect for all people . . . creating opportunity for more Americans to succeed."

"The other side," joked one person, "was not as unreasonable as I expected."

It's true. Many of us fail to realize that—even as we disagree with one another on specific issues, sometimes vehemently—most people share our basic values. In one survey, Republicans and Democrats were asked about their own views and those of one another.[7] Less than a third of Democrats believed that Republicans think it's "extremely or very important" for Americans to learn from the past so the country can make progress. In fact, 91 percent of Republicans said they believe that. Likewise, only about a third of Republicans believed that Democrats think it's "extremely or very important" that government is accountable to the people. In fact, 90 percent of Democrats said they believe that.

It's true across other values as well. Roughly 90 percent of the people in the survey, Republicans and Democrats alike, said that personal responsibility, fair enforcement of the law, compassion, and respect across differences were important to them. What one person in that church basement in Virginia said seems to be true: "We have sincere differences, but I think we're motivated by deeply shared principles."

This is why, as a speaker, appealing to values can be so effective. Values (moral foundations) like care, fairness, authority, loyalty, sanctity, liberty, and so many others, are not exclusive to any one group or community—which means they can help us transcend the usual fault lines in our families, companies, communities, and countries.

Of course, cherishing the same values can sometimes lead people to hold profoundly different opinions on specific issues. To many conservatives, "freedom" means freedom from excessive government regulation; to many liberals, it means a larger role for government in areas like education and health care to help people live their lives in freedom and security. To many conservatives, "caring for others" and "protecting life" means protecting the unborn from abortion; to many liberals, it means protecting the life and choices of the mother.

But that's the beauty and the power of values. Your audience may or may not agree with you on every issue. But, in many cases, you *can* find some common ground—and build support for your position— by speaking to the broader, deeper values that you share. In this way, speaking to values—Values-Based Public Speaking—can lead to greater understanding, empathy, and cooperation, even across communities and cultures.

VALUES ARE UNIVERSAL

One of the things that Obama had to learn as a speaker, he told me once, was "to speak to values."

Look at some of the words he used in his first big national speech at the convention in Boston in 2004: "hard work . . . freedom and opportunity . . . love . . . diversity . . . equal . . . rights . . . liberty . . . change . . . choice . . . faith . . . service . . . individualism."

Flash forward thirteen years later to his farewell address in Chicago as he prepared to leave the White House: "faith . . . change . . . rights . . . liberty . . . freedom . . . individual . . . equality . . . change . . . diversity . . . opportunity . . . hard work . . . love . . . service . . . choices."

Two speeches, more than a decade apart, but rooted in the same fundamental values that most Americans share—values that Obama believed, if we could remember and reaffirm them, might bring us closer as a people.

Obama wasn't perfect. At a fundraiser, he committed a gaffe that he later called the "biggest mistake" of his first presidential campaign.[8] He said that in "a lot of small towns" hammered by decades of job losses, "they get bitter, and they cling to guns or religion or antipathy toward people who aren't like them, or anti-immigrant sentiment . . . as a way to explain their frustrations."

He was trying, he subsequently said, to explain why many people find comfort and strength in the constants of their traditions, including their faith. But his comments—what he admitted was a "string of poorly chosen words"—sent a very different message. It seemed like he was disparaging some peoples' most deeply held values. "Even today," he reflected years later, "I want to take that sentence back."[9]

An appeal to common values was also one of the hallmarks of Obama's speeches to audiences around the world, especially among friends and allies. His entire speech to the Canadian Parliament was organized around "a common set of values"—Canadians' and Americans' belief in "freedom;" military cooperation made possible by the "service" and "sacrifice" of those in uniform; international alliances designed to promote "peace"; economic cooperation that fosters "openness," "innovation," and "opportunity"; investments in democracy and human rights to uphold "pluralism and tolerance and equality."

"His speech was a full-throated defense of democratic values," said Zev Karlin-Neumann, a speechwriter on the National Security Council staff who was in the House of Commons when Obama spoke. "He was reminding people in both countries about who we are at our best." The Canadian legislators in the audience seemed to agree. By the end of his remarks, they broke into chants of "Four more years!"

Evoking shared values can help you connect with audiences across cultures. Here are some lines from three different Obama speeches.

Speech 1: "We all seek to be free. We all seek to be heard. We all yearn to live without fear or discrimination."

Speech 2: "We all share common aspirations—to live in peace and security; to access education and opportunity; to love our families and our communities and our faith."

Speech 3: "We believe in . . . free expression . . . the freedom to worship as you please . . . your right to basic human dignity . . . the right of all people to live free from fear."

Obama delivered those remarks in Brazil, Ghana, and Myanmar, respectively—three very different countries, each with their own unique histories, cultures, and demographics. But the language is remarkably similar. And in all three cases, the audiences greeted them with enthusiastic applause. That's because some values are truly universal and, when you appeal to them, you can forge a connection with just about any audience anywhere—even in the cutthroat world of business.

VALUES ARE GOOD FOR BUSINESS (USUALLY)

Marc Benioff, the founder and CEO of Salesforce—the cloud-based software company that helps businesses digitally connect with their customers—gives dozens of speeches every year to his employees, customers, investors, and at international conferences. Most of the time, he focuses on his company's products. But in just about every speech, he also talks about something bigger—his company's values.

"The days when a CEO could focus on profit alone are over," he told me. "I'm responsible to all our stakeholders. That includes shareholders. It also includes our employees, the communities where we work, and the planet we all depend upon. That means, even as we make a profit, we have to stand up for a set of core values, including our commitment to trust, innovation, customer success, equality, and sustainability." I've worked with Benioff and Salesforce for several years, but he's been talking like this since he started the company more than two decades ago.

If you're an executive, framing your work around larger values can be good for business. "It's what employees expect," Benioff says. In fact, nearly two-thirds of employees say they'll only work for a company with values that are similar to their own.[10] Today, the vast majority of younger employees say they'd leave their company if it doesn't stand up for diversity, equity, and inclusion.[11] "Our values are a major reason we're able to recruit and retain the talented people that we do," explains Benioff.

Appealing to the values that customers cherish can also be good for the bottom line. More than 80 percent of consumers, according to one survey, prefer brands whose values align with their own.[12] Studies have found that companies with a purpose beyond profit alone tend to grow faster and deliver higher revenues.[13] "Values create value," says Benioff, whose company generates quite a bit of value—annual revenues of nearly $40 billion.

Of course, different executives will inevitably wrap their company's work in different values. Hobby Lobby, the arts and crafts retail chain, has attracted employees and customers by espousing values that include "honoring the Lord in all we do by operating in a manner consistent with Biblical principles." Some customers love Chick-fil-A not only for its delicious chicken sandwiches but because of its corporate purpose: "To glorify God by being a faithful steward of all that is entrusted to us." Some investors practice what they call BRI—Biblical Responsible Investing—choosing to invest in companies they view as upholding Christian values. Tens of thousands of businesses use the online marketplace PublicSquare, which calls itself "pro-life, pro-family, pro-freedom."

Julie Sweet, the CEO of the professional services company Accenture and a leading voice in the corporate world for equity and diversity, has told executives that "if you serve your communities, then you have to think . . . beyond your four walls." For Hamdi Ulukaya, the CEO of Chobani yogurt, that has meant speaking eloquently about upholding a sense of "community," which he does by hiring refugees from war-torn regions.

Yvon Chouinard, the founder of Patagonia, says his company works to "maintain our values," including meeting its "responsibility" to earth. He even gave away ownership of the company to a nonprofit and trust so that future profits can be used to fight climate change. "We're in business," Chouinard has said, "to save our home planet"—a values-based message that helps explain why Patagonia ranks as the most respected brand among American consumers.[14]

Conversely, failing to uphold values that are important to customers can damage a brand. Consider Meta (the owner of Facebook) and X, formerly Twitter. Both companies argue that they uphold the value of free speech. At the same time, by not doing more to stop conspiracies, hate speech, and the exploitation of children on their platforms, both companies have often failed to uphold other values, including the trust and privacy of users and the safety of vulnerable communities. Not surprisingly, in surveys of consumers, the reputations of both Meta and X have tanked in recent years.[15]

Some critics are skeptical when executives lace their presentations with talk of values. CEOs who warn against inequality, they point out, often receive salaries that are hundreds of times higher than most of their employees, and some of their companies pay little or nothing in federal taxes, thereby reinforcing broader economic inequalities. In some cases, soothing rhetoric about sustainability is a cover for "greenwashing"—harmful practices that degrade the environment. All of which is to say, if you're an executive who's going to speak about values, make sure you back up your words with deeds (more on that in chapter 12).

There is, of course, another challenge for business leaders who frame their work around larger values: what to do when those values are at risk. In recent years, a new generation of business leaders has been willing to raise their voices in the defense of the values they see as fundamental to their business and to society at large.

Countless executives and their companies affirmed their commitment to equality after the gut-wrenching murder of George Floyd and pledged to take action to address systemic racism (and many still need to make good on their pledges). Kenneth Chenault, the former head of American Express, and Ken Frazier, then the CEO of Merck, two of the country's most prominent Black CEOs, rallied dozens of executives to speak out against state laws they believed would undermine voting rights—laws they called a threat to "fairness and equity for all."

Guided by his company's commitment to equality, Marc Benioff speaks regularly about the importance of equal pay for women. He vocally championed an initiative in San Francisco, where Salesforce is based, to raise taxes on companies like his to help address the city's homelessness crisis, and has said that billionaires like himself should pay higher taxes as well. He's publicly opposed state laws that his LGBTQ employees feared would discriminate against them and their families. To address the threat of climate change, he's called on companies to make sustainability "a core value."

To be sure, a company framing its work around values—and then publicly defending those values—can sometimes come at a cost. Some politicians are quick to target business leaders who object to their policies. Giving voice to values cherished by one group of employees and consumers can also sometimes trigger a backlash from others. Hobby Lobby and Chick-fil-A's longtime support for groups they've seen as "pro-family" has been deemed by critics as "anti-LGBTQ."

After Disney publicly opposed Florida's so-called "Don't Say Gay" law, its reputation rose among liberals and dropped among conservatives. After some customers took issue with Target for selling LGBTQ-themed clothes, the company relocated the displays—a move that was, in turn, condemned by other customers and human rights organizations. After a transgender social media influencer publicly thanked Bud Light for sending her a commemorative can of beer with her face on it, a boycott by conservatives caused sales to plummet. All of which helps explain why about 40 percent of Americans say that companies are "speaking out too much these days."[16]

If you're a business leader, what are you to do? How do you know whether and when to frame your work around a larger set of values? Or whether to speak about the values you support when you feel they're threatened?

Of course, just because you care about a certain set of values doesn't mean you have to speak about them in every presentation or every single time they're in the news. My suggestion: ask yourself a version of those questions from chapter 1, where all effective speaking begins.

Who am I?

What do I believe?

What are my values and the values of my company?

What values do our employees and customers expect us to represent?

*If we stand up for a value that we believe in and there's a backlash,
   what price are we willing to pay?*

*And what price are we willing to pay if we don't speak up for our
   values?*

Not every executive and company will answer these questions the same way. Despite criticism from some consumers and politicians, Disney, Anheuser-Busch, the maker of Bud Light, and Target—despite scaling back its LGBTQ merchandise during Pride Month in 2024—reaffirmed their commitment to the LGBTQ community, even as some advocates felt it was too little too late.[17] Some executives who have spoken out against systemic racism in the name of equality have chosen not to weigh in on other issues, such as the debate over abortion.

In the end, your best guide may be your own colleagues and employees. Benioff points out that it was his LGBTQ employees at Salesforce who first urged him to speak out on behalf of equality in states considering laws that could discriminate against them. "I'll always have my employees' backs," he said. "Today, being an executive means looking out for everyone and the core values that we share. It's a business imperative."

VALUES CAN CHANGE MINDS

Tapping into values is not only a great way to connect with your audience; it's a powerful way to persuade them. Researchers call it "moral framing"—precisely what so many people failed to do in the experiment at the beginning of this chapter. How to do it right? In another study, participants, including conservatives, were more likely to support legal immigration when the argument was framed in terms of loyalty and patriotism—that hardworking immigrants help fuel America's economic strength and leadership position in the world.[18] Another study found that liberals were more likely to support higher levels of military spending when it was framed in terms of fairness—that, as a diverse institution, the military helps service members overcome poverty and inequality.[19]

It works in the real world too. Conservatives have long couched many of their policies in broader values, such as upholding "law and order" and defense of "the family." Public funding for charter and religious schools is framed as giving families "choice." Removing certain books from libraries is billed as "protecting children." In his first year in office, President Obama was able to boost public support for his plan to reform health care with appeals that his proposal would reward "hard work" and "fair play" and create more "opportunity," "security," and "stability" for American families.[20]

~

A deliberate appeal to values also fueled one of the most rapid shifts in public opinion on an issue in American history.

By 2010, according to some polls, a slight majority of Americans supported giving legal recognition to marriages between same-sex couples. But for advocates like Evan Wolfson, of the group Freedom to Marry, that level of public support was not nearly enough. "We wanted to build a critical mass of support and win over at least another five to ten percent of the country," Wolfson told me.

But how?

For starters, it meant not demonizing people who held a different opinion or who were conflicted about the issue. "We were trying to persuade people," Wolfson said, "and slamming the door on them and denouncing them would only turn people off."

Wolfson and his colleagues at Freedom to Marry looked hard at the language they used. For years, they'd made their case by citing a litany of reasons for supporting same-sex marriage—upholding equal rights and freedom; opposing discrimination; ensuring legal, health, and tax benefits; and allowing same-sex couples to share in the love, commitment, and family that comes with marriage. Yet when it came to persuading more Americans, "some of our messaging," explained Wolfson—such as legal and tax benefits—"was getting in the way." The most persuasive message, their research found, was that same-sex couples simply wanted to share in the values of marriage.

In the years that followed, advocates "doubled down on 'love,' 'commitment,' and 'family,'" Wolfson said. Social media was flooded with hashtags like #LoveIsLove. In speeches and interviews, same-sex couples shared stories of their commitment to each other. In moving testimonials, their fathers, mothers, sisters, and brothers spoke about the bonds of family that united them.

The results were remarkable. Whereas voters had previously rejected marriage equality in some thirty states, by late 2012 voters approved it in all four states where it was on the ballot. By 2015, more than 60 percent of Americans supported marriage equality, and the U.S. Supreme Court affirmed same-sex couples' freedom to marry. By 2022, more than 70 percent of Americans supported it, and Congress passed, and the president signed into law, federal protections for same-sex marriage.

Of course, this shift in public opinion wasn't only because of the language used by advocates. People's views changed for many reasons—protests, legislation, lawsuits, and because so many brave Americans had the courage to come out to their families and friends.

But the words mattered too. "We showed people that marriage

equality *did* match up with their values of love, commitment, and family," Wolfson explained. "We got them to think of their own values, which is how you move people and create a better country true to American values."

~

Ashley All—a Kansas mother of five, including three young girls—knows the power of values too.

Ashley was driving her kids to camp one morning when she heard the news on the radio that the Supreme Court had struck down *Roe v. Wade*, ending the constitutional right to abortion in the United States. "I was enraged that my daughters would have fewer constitutional rights over their bodies and health than I did," she told me. "And that was unacceptable."

As a two-time-Obama-voting, National Public Radio–listening, Volvo-driving Democrat, Ashley admits she's "pretty darn progressive." But as an advocate working to protect the right to abortion in Kansas, she also understood "the importance of communicating with people with different opinions." And she didn't have any time to lose. After the Supreme Court ruling, Kansas was the first state to put the issue to a popular vote.

At first glance, it didn't look good. Kansas is one of the most conservative states in the country. The state hasn't voted for a Democrat for president in about sixty years.

What were advocates like Ashley to do?

Here's what they *didn't* do. They didn't demonize people they disagreed with. And in their speeches, conversations with voters, and commercials, they didn't emphasize values that tend to resonate more with liberals, like "equality" or a woman's "right to choose." Often, they didn't even mention the word "abortion" at all.

Instead, Ashley and her fellow advocates spoke to the values shared by the broadest possible number of Kansans, including many conservatives. Ashley's group—Kansans for Constitutional Freedom—said people deserve the "freedom to make their own private medical decisions." Restricting a woman's right to abortion would be "government interference" and "a strict government mandate" that would threaten "core freedoms" and put "your personal and individual rights at risk."

"Don't let politicians take away your freedom," they declared, urging Kansans to "say no to more government control" and "stand for liberty."

It worked. Turnout was huge, and by a whopping 59–41 percent, Kansans—even some conservative voters in rural counties—stunned the nation by voting to protect a woman's right to choose. Since then, similar messaging has also helped win reproductive rights victories in every state where it's been on the ballot, including conservative Kentucky and Montana.

"We can't just yell at people and demand that they agree with us," Ashley told me. "It doesn't work. It turns people off. Whatever the issue, we have to use language that brings people together around common values and ideals. It's the only way we'll make progress."

The Download

If you're trying to persuade an audience to embrace your point of view, don't just argue the points that make sense *to you*. Practice Values-Based Public Speaking by wrapping your argument in the values that matter to your listeners. The six moral foundations mentioned earlier can be a useful guide. Next to each one, I've offered some themes that you might emphasize in your presentation.

If your audience values . . .	Consider framing your ideas and arguments around . . .
Care	charity, community, compassion, dignity, empathy, peace, protection of the vulnerable, responsibility, sacrifice, safety, security, selflessness, service, sustainability, tolerance, understanding
Fairness	acceptance, access, altruism, community, compassion, dignity, empathy, equality, equity, fair play, inclusion, individuality, openness, opportunity, protection of the vulnerable, reciprocity, respect, rights, social justice, trust
Authority	continuity, discipline, hierarchy, lawfulness, leadership, obedience, order, respect, sacrifice, security, stability, strength, toughness, tradition, trust
Loyalty	bravery, courage, citizenship, community, country, discipline, family, honor, obligation, patriotism, reliability, responsibility, sacrifice, selflessness, service, solidarity, unity
Sanctity	devotion, dignity, discipline, faith, God, humility, innocence, integrity, obedience, prudence, modesty, morality, respect, restraint, sacrifice, self-control, tradition
Liberty	choice, creativity, curiosity, entrepreneurship, flexibility, freedom, independence, individualism, innovation, justice, opportunity, rights, self-reliance, self-sufficiency

Of course, different members of your audience may prioritize different values. As a speaker, focus on the values that will allow you to connect with the most people—and then weave those values throughout your presentation, including as you move from the beginning to the middle . . .

The Middle

Hold 'em

CHAPTER 8

Speak from Your Heart . . . and to Theirs

There are those who have the truth within
them, but they tell it not in words.

—Kahlil Gibran

On a December day in 2019, several thousand political leaders, business executives, and activists gathered in Madrid for a global conference on climate change. One of the speakers was Greta Thunberg, the Swedish teenager who—at just sixteen years old—had emerged as one of the world's leading climate activists. She took the podium and in a soft yet firm voice began to speak. Here's some of what she said, referring to a report by the United Nation's Intergovernmental Panel on Climate Change.

In chapter two, on page 108 in the SR 1.5 IPCC report that came out last year, it says that if we are to have a 67 percent chance of limiting the global temperature rise to below 1.5 degrees Celsius, we had, on January 1st, 2018, 420 gigatons of CO_2 left *to emit in that budget. And, of course, that number is much lower today as we emit about 42 gigatons of CO_2 every year, including land use.*

Got it?

Don't worry if you didn't. Thunberg later acknowledged that rattling off so many statistics probably wasn't the best way to make her point. "I basically only spoke about facts and numbers," she told a reporter. "And then people watched it, and it felt like no one understood a word I said."

Thunberg has inspired millions of people around the world, especially young people, to demand that governments take faster action to address climate change. But in that moment in Madrid, she made one of the most common mistakes in public speaking—trying to persuade an audience with a blizzard of facts, figures, and statistics.

Why do so many speakers overload their presentations with a deluge of data?

Ever since Aristotle, we've been told, correctly, that *logos*—logic—is one of the three pillars of effective rhetoric. In school, we're rightly taught to back up our assertions with evidence. Some speechwriters have even argued that the most moving thing about a speech is not its language, but its logic—not the emotion, but the argument. All of which leads many speakers to pack their speeches with statistics.

THE DANGER OF DATA

In any presentation—especially in the middle as you make your case—there are all sorts of reasons to be cautious about relying too much on facts and figures.

For one, a lot of folks in your audience may be inherently skeptical of any numbers you throw at them, especially in this age of misinformation. They know that statistics, graphs, and charts can be misleading or manipulated to serve the agenda of the speaker. There was even a famous book about it, *How to Lie with Statistics*.

Remember, too, that your audience may not *want* to accept the evidence you're offering. As we all know, being confronted with information that challenges our views can be unsettling—creating what psychologists call cognitive dissonance. And one of our defenses against this discomfort, often without even realizing it, is confirmation bias—best defined, I think, by the old Simon & Garfunkel lyric: "a man hears what he wants to hear / and disregards the rest." If your audience isn't open to your argument because it's at odds with their beliefs, no statistic is likely to change their mind.

Facts are also no match for fear. When I was at the White House, an outbreak of the Ebola virus in West Africa and the first cases of the disease on American soil triggered panic across the country. Still, the number of Americans who contracted the disease on U.S. soil? A grand total of . . . two (both nurses in a hospital). Our speechwriting team cranked out speech after speech in which Obama tried to calm people's anxieties with evidence. "We have to remember the basic facts," he cautioned, noting, for example, how difficult it would be to catch Ebola in America. Stressing the science-based facts was the right thing to do. But it didn't do much to calm the panic. "You can't use reason," the fact-based astrophysicist Neil deGrasse Tyson has observed, "to convince anyone out of an argument that they didn't use reason to get into."

Sometimes, data can even backfire and make your audience *less* likely to support your position. One study found that presenting parents who were skeptical of vaccines with more information about vaccines actually made some parents *more* skeptical of vaccinating their children.[1] "Numbers and statistics are necessary and wonderful for uncovering the truth," explains Tali Sharot, a neuroscientist and professor of cognitive neuroscience from University College London and the Massachusetts Institute of Technology, "but they're not enough to change beliefs, and they are practically useless for motivating action."[2]

Statistics can also sometimes make people *less* likely to support a worthy cause. Suppose you're making an appeal for donations. The bigger you make the problem, the more money people will give, right? Wrong. In multiple studies, participants were asked to donate money to help children in need. But as the number of children needing help went up, the donations went *down*.[3]

In another study, one group of participants donated generously to address a food crisis in Africa when the appeal was framed as helping a single child, a little girl named Rokia. But when another group of participants heard the same appeal to help Rokia—along with a few statistics to show the larger humanitarian crisis—they donated *less*.[4] It was as if the statistics about the larger problem undermined the listeners' sympathy for Rokia's plight. Psychologists call this "psychic numbing"—the larger the scale of the suffering, the more overwhelmed people tend to get and the less likely they are to help. As Deborah Small, the lead researcher on the Rokia study, explained: "It's hard for humans to generate feelings toward statistics."[5]

If You Must Use Statistics . . .

I'm not saying you should *never* use statistics when you give a talk. If you're at work—pitching investors or courting a customer—or if you're speaking up at a local meeting in support of a new project in your community, you better have *some* numbers to back up your claims. And if you're speaking at the American Statistical Association, a stream of statistics may send your audience into a frenzy.

In most cases, though, I suggest using facts and figures sparingly—and strategically. Use them to do what all good presentations must do—tell a story, with a beginning, a middle, and an end. That's what Obama did in the final year of his presidency after a series of tragedies in which unarmed Black Americans were shot by police. Multiple studies, he said, showed that:

African Americans are thirty percent more likely than whites to be pulled over. After being pulled over, African Americans and Hispanics are three times more likely to be searched. Last year, African Americans were shot by police at more than twice the rate of whites. African Americans are arrested at twice the rate of whites. African American defendants are seventy-five percent more likely to be charged with offenses carrying mandatory minimums. They receive sentences that are almost ten percent longer than comparable whites arrested for the same crime.

That's a lot of statistics. But, together, they told a story, including this ending: "If you add it all up, the African American and Hispanic population, who make up only thirty percent of the general population, make up more than half of the incarcerated population." That was the story Obama wanted the American people to know—and to deal with—and, in that case, statistics were a powerful way to tell it.

Thinking of using statistics in your presentation? Ask yourself:

- Will this number clarify the issue for my audience?

- Will this piece of data increase the chance that my audience will act?

- Does this statistic tell a story?

If the answer is no, then the number isn't necessary.

FEEL WHAT YOU'RE SAYING

If a lot of data is the *wrong* way to connect with your audience, what's the *right* way?

Let's go back to Greta Thunberg.

A few months before she spoke in Madrid, she gave another speech, at the United Nations in New York City. Her remarks were deeply emotional, laced with fiery indignation. "My message," she began, aiming her comments directly at the world leaders gathered at the UN, "is that we'll be watching you." Later in the speech, she declared:

> *You have stolen my dreams and my childhood with your empty words. And yet I'm one of the lucky ones. People are suffering. People are dying. Entire ecosystems are collapsing. We are in the beginning of a mass extinction, and all you can talk about is money and fairy tales of eternal economic growth. How dare you!*

With each sentence, Thunberg jabbed her hand for emphasis, her voice practically breaking, tears welling up in her eyes. There were countless speakers that week at the United Nations. But it was the words of a sixteen-year-old girl that broke through—a speech seen and heard around the world—because she did what great speakers do. She spoke from her heart, with passion and the power of her convictions. More than that, she didn't just speak her words, she *felt* them.

Michelle Obama excels at this. Tyler Lechtenberg, who wrote speeches for both the First Lady and President Obama, remembers a prep session when she was not happy with the draft she'd been given.

"'What are we doing here?'" Tyler remembers her asking. "It was her way of saying, 'There's no emotional core in this speech.'"

"One of her powers as a speaker is the emotional force she brings to her remarks," he said. "She won't give a speech unless she *feels* something. And then, in turn, the audience feels it too."

It's true for the rest of us too. We can't tap into the emotions of our audience—the third pillar of rhetoric that Aristotle called *pathos*—unless we first feel it ourselves. So, no, the most moving thing in a speech, in my view, is not its logic. It's the emotion—the feelings, sincerity, and authenticity—that we, the speaker, bring to our remarks. If we really want to connect with, persuade, and motivate our audience, pathos beats logos.

This is another reason why I beg you *not* to use a chatbot to write your presentation, especially one that's meant to be personal. As we've discussed, giving a speech is a fundamentally *human experience* between the human who is speaking (you) and humans who are listening (your audience). And no machine, no matter how sophisticated it is, will ever truly know what's in your heart. Your audience wants more humanity, not less.

USE EMOTIONAL WORDS

A growing body of research shows why speaking from the heart is so powerful.

Jonah Berger—the Wharton School professor you met in chapter 6—along with his colleague Katherine Milkman, wanted to find out why readers share some online news stories more than others. Berger and Milkman examined around seven thousand news articles and found that readers were more likely to share articles that trigger strong emotions, like awe, anger, or anxiety.[6] Emotions like these create a physical reaction—"physiological arousal," Berger and Milkman wrote—which makes us want to share that experience with others. We're seeking an emotional connection with family and friends, Berger explains. "If you read the article and feel the same emotion, it will bring us closer together."[7]

A different group of researchers found something similar on what was then Twitter. Psychology professors from New York University studied more than 560,000 tweets about issues like gun safety, same-sex marriage, and climate change. They compared tweets with moral and emotional words—like "crime," "mercy," "right," "afraid," "love," "weep," "abuse," "honor," "spite," "faith," and "sin"—with tweets that contained more neutral language. What did they find? Every time a moral-emotional word was used, the tweet was 20 percent more likely to be shared.[8]

What's true online is often true in life. We're drawn to language that makes us *feel* something—that stirs our hearts. And it starts with the words we use. As you prepare your presentation, go online and search for "Feelings Wheel" or "Emotions Wheel." Suddenly, your screen will be filled with rainbow-colored circles full of words. These wheels are a favorite of copywriters and communications professionals and are shared often on social media. But these word wheels weren't created by writers at all. They were originally designed by psychologists to help their clients better identify and express their feelings.[9] Which is exactly why they're such an effective tool when you want to bring more emotion to your presentations.

Don't just say you're "happy." Say you're "proud," "optimistic," "joyful," or "hopeful." Don't just say you're "angry." Say you're "frustrated," "furious," or "indignant." Instead of "surprised," say you're "amazed," "excited," or in "awe." When you give a speech, don't just use words. Whenever possible, use *emotional* words that truly convey what's in your heart and allow you to create a deeper connection with your audience.

GET EMOTIONAL

If I were writing this book decades ago, I might have suggested that you keep your emotions in check when you give a speech. For too long, leaders, especially women, were unfairly ridiculed as "weak" or "unstable" for showing too much emotion, even if it was just shedding a tear. And yes, some stereotypes linger. Women leaders are still sometimes unjustly perceived as "too emotional" or "less effective" for expressing emotions like anger, fear, and remorse.[10] One study found that people of color who express anger at work are more likely to be dismissed as "radical" or "not viewed as team players," while white employees who show anger are seen as having "passion for their work"—another reminder of the persistent biases that we have to address in our workplaces, our communities, and in our own hearts and minds.[11]

"Showing emotion is always going to be hard, especially for women and people of color," said my fellow White House speechwriter Sarada Peri. "But sharing our emotions is one of the best ways to build trust with your audience." Conversely, as Sarada points out, "an empty, cold speech with no emotion is always a risk—for anyone." I've seen it myself. I've worked with speakers of many different backgrounds over the years, and I've never heard an audience clamor for less emotion; if anything, they always want more.

Today, sharing what's in our heart is widely admired as a sign of a speaker's authenticity. When Hillary Clinton grew emotional during a campaign stop in 2008 while speaking about her commitment to public service—something that would have once been seen by many people as disqualifying—it was widely seen as humanizing.

And it's not just women. In an emotional postgame interview, Detroit Lions running back Jamaal Williams tearfully dedicated his team's win—and personally breaking a team record—to his late great-grandfather, and then he defiantly shot back at critics who had doubted his team. Now that's what you call a person's "passion for their work." And his remarks resonated with millions of people; the video of his comments went viral. Likewise, when Jason Kelce of the Philadelphia Eagles repeatedly cried as he announced his retirement from the NFL, he was widely praised for his emotional authenticity, which one sportscaster called "beautiful, just beautiful."

I saw the power of speaking from the heart at the White House too. In Obama's eight years in office, our speechwriting team worked on 3,477 speeches and statements for the president. Of those, how many can you recall? (It's okay. I can't even remember all his remarks either, even some of the ones I worked on.) But here's one speech I bet you *do* remember.

After a gunman in Newtown, Connecticut, murdered twenty little children and six educators at their elementary school, Obama entered the White House briefing room. He couldn't get through the first minute of his remarks without choking up.

"The majority of those who died today were children—beautiful little kids between the ages of five and ten years old." He paused, unable to go on, and dabbed a tear in his eye. He sighed and fidgeted with his speech. He tried to start speaking again, but paused again. For about ten seconds, he stood there in silence, struggling to keep his composure. Finally, he looked up and continued his remarks, wiping away the tears as he spoke.

"They had their entire lives ahead of them. Birthdays. Graduations. Weddings. Kids of their own."

Those remarks were among the most watched videos from Obama's entire presidency, viewed millions of times. Why? It wasn't the elegance of his words. He was speaking in simple and plain language. And it wasn't *logos*—the logic of his argument. His remarks resonated with so many people because of the raw human emotion that Obama displayed in the moment, unplanned and unscripted. He was speaking not only as a president, but as a parent. He was speaking as we all should—from the heart, unafraid to share our most intimate feelings.

BE VULNERABLE

Sometimes, sharing what's in our heart means sharing the parts of ourselves that we usually keep private—our setbacks, pain, and trauma. For many of us, this can be terrifying, especially with an audience of strangers. I've even heard some speech coaches say, "Don't get too personal."

I couldn't disagree more.

Getting personal and being vulnerable is one of the most effective ways to emotionally connect with your audience and maybe even bring them around to your point of view. That's what Olivia Vella, a thirteen-year-old girl in Queen Creek, Arizona, discovered when she wrote and delivered a slam poem to her seventh-grade English class.

In many ways, Olivia seemed to be thriving. She excelled academically, enjoyed playing volleyball, and spent evenings and weekends at community theater, where she loved ballet. Privately though, she was struggling. Like so many young people, especially girls, she felt unrelenting pressure from her classmates and a society obsessed with physical appearance. On top of that, "I was very self-conscious about my body. I thought I was hideous," she said. Diagnosed with body dysmorphia, anxiety, and depression, "I had a really hard time making friends and was excluded at the cafeteria." And so, when her English teacher told her class they'd have to read a personal essay out loud, Olivia knew immediately that she'd share what was in her heart. "It was my way of telling my classmates how I felt."

A cellphone video, taken by a classmate, captured the six minutes when Olivia stood in front of her class and recounted the pain and pressures that girls like her endure every day.

> *Pick out an outfit that will fit in with the latest trends . . .*
> *Put on some makeup so you can actually show your face in*
> *public and be a little bit pretty . . .*
> *Don't forget to style your hair in elegant curls . . .*
> *Shove your fat feet into those toe-pinching blood-blistering*
> *Converse that everyone at school is wearing and you*
> *cannot be the odd one out . . .*
> *Every part of your outfit is uncomfortable.*
> *But even though you spend hours trying to look pretty, you*
> *will never be as good as those other girls at school.*
> *You are actually holding back a few tears, but you feel like you*
> *are holding back a tsunami of emotion . . .*
> *Why am I not good enough? . . .*

Toward the end of her poem, Olivia's voice rose as she built to her impassioned conclusion.

> *You tell yourself, "I just want people to like me, I just want to*
> *be accepted."*
> *But skipping meals and marking up your wrist isn't going to*
> *fix that.*
> *You look at other girls wishing you were them, but other girls*
> *are looking at you wishing they were you . . .*
> *But society is wrong.*
> *You are loved.*
> *You are precious.*
> *You are beautiful.*
> *You are talented.*
> *You are capable.*

You are deserving of respect.
You can eat that meal.
You are one in seven billion.
And, most of all, you are good enough.

When Olivia finished, her teacher and some of her classmates were in tears. Others clapped and cheered. Pouring her heart out, she told me several years later, was "life-changing" in several ways. "I was nervous," she recalled, "because I thought people would laugh at me. But this was my moment to express how I was feeling. I still deal with anxiety and depression, but sharing these difficult emotions was my way of giving power back to myself."

She noticed a change in her classmates as well, including some who had treated her poorly in the past. "As I was speaking, I could see how my words were affecting them. Almost every person who came up to me after said, 'I'm so glad you said that, because I feel the exact same way.' It taught me that I wasn't alone, and I think we all saw each other as more human."

To her amazement, Olivia's words reverberated around the world. The video of her reciting her poem went viral, sparking a larger conversation about the social pressures facing teenage girls, especially around body image. "Your poem saved me," a girl in Wyoming wrote her in a letter. "It allowed me to be happy." A sixty-year-old woman who said she struggles every day with "never feeling good enough" wrote that Olivia "was talking directly to me."

"I feel like we try to lock up our feelings and put up a façade that we're all really doing well," Olivia told me. "But when we're vulnerable, we allow people to see us as we really are. We're not perfect. We're flawed. Honoring our emotions is being who we really are and lets us create a connection with other people, who know they can be themselves too."

Even as you speak from *your* heart, there's an equally powerful way to emotionally connect with your audience—speak to *theirs*. There are several ways to do it.

SPEAK TO ONE PERSON

On April 15, 2013, two explosions ripped through the final blocks of the Boston Marathon, shocking the city and the country. Amid the carnage, three people were killed and nearly three hundred were injured. A day after the bombings, we got word that Obama might travel to Boston and speak at a memorial service later in the week. Which meant we had only about forty-eight hours to prepare his remarks.

The tragedy struck close to home for Obama. He knew the city, as did the First Lady, from their days as law students at Harvard. He'd given his 2004 convention speech in Boston. The bombing hit close to home for me as well. I was born in Boston, and even after our family moved down to Cape Cod, we returned to the city often to be with relatives for holidays, baptisms, and weddings.

Whenever I work on a speech, I try to think of someone specific— a real, living person the speech should connect with, deeply, emotionally—and I try to write for them. In those days after the bombing, I kept thinking of my family and friends across Massachusetts, especially my Uncle Dan. He was Boston to his core—an altar boy at church, Catholic school graduate, season-ticket holder to Boston College football and hockey games, and a fixture at more than a few Boston bars. A staunch conservative, though, he was no fan of Obama (and let me know it every Thanksgiving!). Still, as I worked on the president's remarks, I imagined Uncle Dan watching the speech at a pub with his friends, and I asked myself, *What would he want to hear?*

The evening before the service, I sent a draft to Obama. The next morning, his edits were waiting on a desk just outside the Oval Office. Much of what I'd written was intact, but he'd made changes to just about every paragraph. On the flight to Boston, he made more edits. Even as Air Force One started the descent into Boston, he casually walked back to my seat and handed me yet another round of changes. He was making the speech his own.

Just after noon, from the pulpit overlooking a cathedral filled with mourners, Obama began to speak. He painted a picture of "a beautiful day to be in Boston"—the sun rising over the city, spring in bloom, runners lacing up their shoes—and how "in an instant, the day's beauty was shattered." He paid tribute to the three innocent people who lost their lives in the blasts. He spoke to the injured, watching from their hospital beds across the city, telling them, "You will run again."

Then, about halfway through his speech, Obama's tone shifted. He spoke directly to the people of Boston and channeled the "Boston Strong" spirit of defiance and resilience that had taken hold that week.

> Your resolve is the greatest rebuke to whoever committed this heinous act. If they sought to intimidate us, to terrorize us, to shake us from those values . . . that make us who we are, as Americans—well, it should be pretty clear by now that they picked the wrong city to do it.

The church erupted into applause, and the audience was on its feet. Obama leaned in to the microphone and continued over the cheers.

"Not here in Boston! Not here in Boston!"

A few moments later, he described a runner being knocked down by the blast but getting back on his feet. "We'll pick ourselves up. We'll keep going. We will finish the race!"

Obama was turning a sermon into a rally—a summons not only for how to deal with death, but how to live our lives. As his remarks built to a crescendo, he rode the emotion in the church, practically yelling over the applause.

> *And this time next year, on the third Monday in April, the world will return to this great American city to run harder than ever, and to cheer even louder, for the one hundred and eighteenth Boston Marathon. Bet on it!*

The Bostonians in the pews were on their feet again, clapping, cheering, and hollering. Some pumped their fists in the air—a city and a country that was strong, resilient, refusing to be terrorized.

Later that day, a White House staffer told me the speech was "a love letter to Boston." I felt that way too. So, it seemed, did the people of Boston. News coverage showed people gathered outside the cathedral and crowded into restaurants and bars, taking in Obama's words the way a speech is meant to be received—together, a communal experience.

Sometime that afternoon, I noticed a new voicemail on my phone.

"Terry, this is your Uncle Dan," he said, in his thick Boston accent.

I was surprised. He rarely called, and he couldn't have known that as I had worked on the speech, I was doing it for him. From the noise in the background, I could tell he was at one of his favorite pubs.

"I just watched the president's speech. We all did. He did a good job. It was a very fine speech, and I just wanted you to know that."

It wasn't much. But coming from my uncle, it was high praise. For a moment, however brief, Obama had connected with someone with whom, on the surface, he had little in common. And he did it by speaking to my Uncle Dan's heart—the city that he loved and the spirit that defined him.

When you give a speech, find your Uncle Dan.

SPEAK TO THEIR EXPERIENCE

In his final year in office, Obama made three historic trips.

That spring, he became the first U.S. president to visit Cuba in nearly ninety years. In his speeches in Havana, he paid tribute to the Cuban people's achievements in medicine, education, and entrepreneurship. He celebrated Cuban culture, including how both Cubans and Americans "dance the cha-cha-cha or the salsa, and eat *ropa vieja*." Most importantly, he bluntly acknowledged what no U.S. president had ever said—that the U.S. trade embargo on the country was an "outdated burden" that was "only hurting the Cuban people instead of helping them."

A few months later, he became the first sitting American president to visit Hiroshima, where the United States dropped the first atomic bomb to end World War II. Obama met with elderly survivors of the bombing and acknowledged the victims who perished when "death fell from the sky." Standing at the memorial park dedicated to their memory, he asked the world to consider the horror that they had endured.

> *Why do we come to this place, to Hiroshima? We come to ponder a terrible force unleashed in a not so distant past. We come to mourn the dead, including over a hundred thousand Japanese men, women, and children; thousands of Koreans; a dozen Americans held prisoner. Their souls speak to us.*

Later that year, Obama became the first U.S. president to visit Laos, the small country in Southeast Asia that endured a massive American bombing campaign during the Vietnam War. As I worked on his remarks, I was stunned to learn that no American president had ever fully acknowledged the devastation caused by the so-called Secret War. Over nine years, U.S. aircraft dropped more than two million tons of bombs on the country, making Laos, per person, the most heavily bombed nation in history. Sitting in the audience with a thousand Laotians in the capital, Vientiane, I watched as Obama spoke words that none of his predecessors had uttered.

> As one Laotian said, the "bombs fell like rain." Villages and entire valleys were obliterated. . . . Countless civilians were killed. And that conflict was another reminder that, whatever the cause, whatever our intentions, war inflicts a terrible toll, especially on innocent men, women, and children. Today, I stand with you in acknowledging the suffering and sacrifices on all sides of that conflict.

Obama's political critics liked to claim that remarks like these were part of an eight-year "apology tour" for past American misdeeds around the world. Nothing could have been further from the truth. Obama was doing what any good speaker does. He was showing empathy for his audience and acknowledging the histories that shaped who they are. As speakers, we should never underestimate just how powerful this kind of empathy can be—including in the workplace, where research shows that empathy is a critical skill for effective leaders.[12]

I saw it myself. Sometimes after a speech, especially overseas, I'd find someone from the audience and ask them what they thought of Obama's remarks. They probably thought I was a reporter. Our conversation usually went something like this:

Audience member: "Oh, I loved the speech!"

Me: "Was there a particular line you liked?"

At this point, they'd usually pause and think.

"Not really."

"Or a certain part of the speech?"

Another pause.

"It wasn't really any one part," they'd say. "It was more how it made me feel. He saw us. He understands us." I heard a version of this over and over, all around the world.

Think of the speeches that mean the most to you, whether it was president at their inaugural or a sibling delivering a eulogy for your grandparent. Yes, you might recall a great line or two. But I bet what you remember most is how the speaker made you *feel*—how you felt seen, heard, and understood. You know what this feels like when you're in the audience. That's the feeling *we* should try to create when *we're* the speaker.

Even as you show empathy for your audience, there's another powerful way to speak to their hearts, especially if you want to rally them to a cause: tap into their empathy for the people you're trying to help.

SHOW A HUMAN FACE

By the summer of 2016, the brutal civil war in Syria had been raging for more than five years. Hundreds of thousands of men, women, and children had been killed. More than eleven million people had been driven from their homes, part of the estimated sixty-five million people displaced by conflicts and famine globally, at the time the largest refugee crisis since World War II. And yet, for so many people around the world, those numbers were too often . . . numbers.

And then they saw Omran.

After airstrikes in the Syrian city of Aleppo, video emerged of a little boy in an ambulance. Omran Daqneesh was just five years old, in shorts and a T-shirt, covered in dust, the left side of his face smeared with blood. He sat in the ambulance, silent, in shock, at one point trying to wipe the blood from his little hand. Soon, Omran's image was seen all over the world. A crisis of epic proportions suddenly seemed relatable. Parents could see their own children.

Psychologists call this the identifiable victim effect. We're often more likely to have empathy for a specific, identifiable person than for a larger group of people. Remember the study about the food crisis in Africa. Participants were more likely to donate to help little Rokia—a specific, identifiable person—than when they were told that "more than three million children" were suffering.

What's going on?

Dr. Paul Zak, a neuroeconomist at the Claremont Graduate School, discovered that when we listen to human-centered stories, our brains release oxytocin, the hormone that he found is associated with increased levels of compassion, generosity, and charity.[13] Which is why Zak calls oxytocin "the moral molecule."

His research bears it out. In an experiment, Zak and his colleagues showed study participants more than a dozen public service announcements on issues like smoking, drinking, and speeding and then asked whether they wanted to donate to a charity that addressed the problem. Some of the participants were given a placebo; others were given an injection of synthetic oxytocin through the nose. What happened? You guessed it. Compared to the people in the study who were given the placebo, those who received the oxytocin reported more concern for the people in the PSAs and even donated more money—56 percent more.[14]

Research like this confirms what we've always known. "If I look at the mass, I will never act," goes the saying (attributed, perhaps apocryphally, to Mother Teresa). "If I look at the one, I will."

I don't recommend trying to inject synthetic oxytocin into the noses of your audience. But if you want to motivate them, do the next best thing: tell the stories of the people you're trying to help. Better yet, tell the story of a single person. Force them to "look at the one." Obama had to learn this too. One of the things that he came to appreciate as a speaker, he told me, was "to tell stories rather than facts and appeal to people's hearts, not just their heads."

Appealing to people's hearts is something anyone can do.

~

At his home in Scarsdale, New York, six-year-old Alex Myteberi caught a glimpse of Omran Daqneesh on his mother's cell phone as she scrolled through the news. Suddenly, Alex was obsessed with the little boy from Syria. "It was all Alex was talking about," his mother, Val, remembers. "He was upset. He had tears in his eyes. He wanted to do something to help." So Alex sat down at his dining room table, pulled out a blue pen and his parents' yellow legal pad, and wrote a letter—to President Obama. Alex said he wanted Omran to come live with him and his family in New York.

When the folks at the White House correspondence office read Alex's letter, they immediately flagged it for our speechwriting team. Obama was getting ready to give a speech to a summit on refugees at the United Nations, and we knew instantly that Alex's words could focus the world's attention on the crisis.

In his remarks, Obama made the case for more international support for migrants and refugees. Nearing the end of his speech, he read parts of Alex's letter, clearly moved by a young boy's generous spirit. A room of presidents and prime ministers at the United Nations is usually a somber audience. After hearing Alex's words, they broke out into a rare burst of applause, and the story of Alex's letter made headlines around the world. But even that paled beside what happened next.

Days earlier, a White House film crew had visited Alex at his home. Sitting at the same dining room table where he had written his letter, he read it out loud. His letter, in a sense, became a speech.

Omran "will be our brother," Alex said. "Catherine, my little sister, will be collecting butterflies and fireflies for him . . . We can all play together." Since Omran "won't bring toys," he said, "I will share my bike and I will teach him how to ride it . . . I will teach him additions and subtractions in math."

Did the world do enough to help the Syrian people during those awful years? I believe we could and should have done more. I also believe that the refugee summit—and Alex's heartfelt words—made a difference. Video of him reading his letter went viral, helping more people see the plight of children like Omran and raising more money for humanitarian relief.

"So what if we have different color skin or a different religion?" Alex told me when I spoke with him several years later. "I wish compassion was as common as breathing. We're all humans just trying to be cared for and have a good life. And we can, if we just help each other."

As Obama said in his speech, "We can all learn from Alex." When we speak, we can remember how the story of a single person, like Omran, can break through all the numbers and humanize a cause that might seem overwhelming. We can remember that sometimes—no matter how good a speaker we may be—the most powerful words we utter may come from someone else, like a boy in

New York who saw a boy in Syria and knew that we're all humans who have to help each other.

The Download

Want to connect with your audience and inspire them to action? Don't overwhelm them with data. Just speak from your heart. Remember that the most beautiful and moving part of your presentation is the emotion—the authenticity, sincerity, and feelings—that you bring to your remarks.

» **Feel what you're saying.** You'll be at your best—your most authentic and your most passionate—when you speak about the people, causes, and communities that you care about most. What do you love? Who do you love? If you're honoring someone with a toast or eulogy, what are the three or four emotions they make you feel? Speak about that.

» **Use emotional words.** Connect with your audience by using words that convey the depth of your own feelings. An "Emotions Wheel" online can help you find the words that capture the intensity of your indignation or your pride, your frustrations or your excitement.

» **Get emotional.** Don't just tell your audience what you think; show them how you feel. Avoid cold, heartless presentations. Share your innermost emotions; it's not a sign of weakness, it's a sign of strength.

» **Be vulnerable.** What has caused you pain? How have you struggled? When you let your guard down and share your own doubts, insecurities, or failures, you give your audience the space to reflect on their own, creating an opportunity for greater empathy and understanding.

Even as you speak from your own heart, speak to the hearts of your audience.

» **Speak to one person.** As you develop your presentation, think of someone specific: a real, living person your remarks should connect with emotionally. Write and speak to them. When addressing your audience, speak *to* them ("you") not *about* them ("they").

» **Speak to their experience.** Try to put yourself in the shoes of your listeners and speak to their reality. What experiences have shaped their lives? Are there achievements that they're proud of that I can celebrate? Do they carry any pain, trauma, or sense of injustice that I can acknowledge and perhaps address?

» **Show a human face.** Don't describe an issue or problem in vague terms and statistics. Humanize it. Bring the problem alive by telling the stories of real people—or a single person—who embody the challenge that you want your audience to care about.

Here's another great way to connect with the humans in your audience . . .

CHAPTER 9

Talk Like a Human

If I had a world of my own, everything would be nonsense.
Nothing would be what it is because
everything would be what it isn't.
And, contrariwise, what it is, it wouldn't be.
And what it wouldn't be, it would. You see?

—Alice, *Alice in Wonderland*, adapted from Lewis Carroll's
Alice's Adventures in Wonderland

With another speech on the horizon, I popped into the office of the
White House official who was busy developing the proposals that
President Obama would unveil in his address. I'll call him Greg.
Several minutes in, he tried to boil it down for me. His explanation
went something like this.

"The old economic models haven't worked. The U.S. government
needs to put more skin in the game."

Intrigued, I asked for details.

"We're proposing a new model—public-private partnerships that
leverage innovation."

Perhaps sensing I was confused, he tried again.

"There's no one silver bullet. This is about harnessing multisector
collaboration."

He must have seen my eyes starting to glaze over. So he clarified. Or tried.

"It's about creating synergy, so we can catalyze solutions at scale."

I was writing it all down, but my head was starting to hurt.

"At the end of the day," he said, "the president has an opportunity to really move the needle."

By now, my skepticism must have been showing. He tried one more time.

"Terry, this is a real paradigm shift. It has the potential to unleash transformational change."

I must have listened to Greg speak for half an hour. I left more confused than when I had arrived—and I needed an aspirin.

Why do so many people talk like this?!

Call it whatever you want. Jargon. Buzzwords. Bureaucratese. Gibberish. Gobbledygook. Pablum. Bafflegab (yes, that's a real word). Word salad. The one thing you *can't* call it is English. And yet, this sort of rhetorical nonsense infects so many of the conversations and presentations that we hear every day.

Many business executives refer to their employees as "human capital," urge them to "align around core competencies," focus on what's "mission-critical," but also "think outside the box." When times get tough, instead of being laid off, employees are "impacted" or "affected."

I've heard nonprofit leaders urge their teams to "push the envelope," engage in "blue-sky thinking," and "incentivize best practices" in order to pursue "holistic approaches" that "deliver positive outcomes." So many words. So little clarity.

Financial experts often speak a language all their own. "It's a tricky problem," Alan Greenspan reportedly said when he was chair of the President's Council of Economic Advisors, "to find the particular calibration in timing that would be appropriate to stem the acceleration in risk premiums created by falling incomes without prematurely aborting the decline in the inflation-generated risk premiums."[1]

Say what?

Speakers like these have an affliction. It's called the Curse of Knowledge—assuming that their audience possesses the same knowledge and vocabulary as themselves.[2] It happens everywhere, including in medicine. If you're like me, you've sometimes struggled to understand your doctor as they overwhelm you with medical terminology—until they finally say something like "That's a fancy word for bruising."

So why not just say "bruising"?!

There's "too much mumbo jumbo" when doctors speak to patients and the public, says Laura Dean, an emergency physician at Massachusetts General Hospital in Boston. She should know. Before going to medical school, she was a member of our speechwriting team at the White House. She's probably one of the few speechwriter-doctors in the world. "Technical jargon," she points out, "can be a barrier to understanding."

We saw this during Covid. In their defense, public health officials had the near-impossible task of communicating with a frightened public even as our knowledge of the virus evolved. Still, watching the news I often shook my head in disbelief as officials spoke about how some variants of Covid were "more pathogenic" than others, that we should avoid "congregate settings" (was this different than "crowded settings"?), and how some "medical countermeasures" were more "efficacious" than others. We shouldn't need a medical degree to understand what officials are telling us, especially in a crisis when our very lives depend on it.

Even presidents can fall victim to verbosity. "There are times when I am saying things in complicated ways where they could be simpler and punchier," Obama admitted to me once. "There's no doubt that when I'm not good," he remarked with a smile, "I'm not good in a certain kind of way."

One habit, he said, was "to talk a lot about policy and the details of it. Some of this is the training you get from being a lawyer and making sure you've covered every base. It's a certain kind of academic training that probably I embodied. Some of it is temperamental. Some of your strengths are going to be weaknesses and vice versa."

The former college lecturer, Obama could sometimes get downright professorial. For instance, he spoke often (and rightly so) about the importance of upholding "international rules and norms." Watching offstage, though, I often wondered, *Does anyone in the audience actually know what a "norm" is?* Every time we heard him say this, Cody Keenan would yell out, like the gang on *Cheers* welcoming their buddy to the bar: "Norm!"

One of my all-time favorites, though, was when Obama was at an international conference in South Korea. At a press conference, he grew frustrated that journalists seemed dismissive of the role that U.S. negotiators had played in forging the summit's final communiqué.

> *Let's just reflect on this summit. The Framework for Balanced and Sustainable Growth is one that we helped to originate. The financial reforms and Basel III are based on ideas that came out of our work. . . . The development document that was set forward in this communiqué tracks the development ideas that I put forward. . . . The corruption initiative that's reflected in the communiqué was prompted by recommendations and suggestions that we made.*

To this day, I'm still not sure what Basel III is (although I assume it's better than Basel II). And, in Obama's defense, maybe his audience of international economic experts *did* need to hear a forceful defense of the Framework for Balanced and Sustainable Growth. Maybe. It obviously wasn't intended for Americans back home, who I'm pretty sure weren't glued to their TVs chanting "Basel III! Basel III!"

As with statistics, I'm not saying you should *never* use technical language. If everyone in your audience is a subject matter expert, speak the language they know. If you're giving a lecture at the International Geological Congress, drill down. Dig deep. Get as technical as you want. Your audience may love it. Rock their world.

In most cases, though, be careful not to use words that some people in your audience may not understand. Don't serve word salad, which leaves a bad taste in the mouth. Avoid jargon that forces your listeners to try to decipher what you're saying. It creates divisions between insiders who understand the code and outsiders who don't. Jargon is hackneyed when we should be original; vague when we should be precise; confusing when we should be clear; evasive when we should be direct.

All of which is why jargon can undermine our credibility as a speaker. It breeds mistrust among our listeners who sense we're either not being candid or don't know what we're talking about. Jargon and bureaucratese push our audience away with unfamiliar terms—especially if it's a diverse audience that includes non-native speakers—when we should be welcoming them with words they understand. If it's a mouthful, it shouldn't come out of our mouth.

Fortunately, there's an alternative.

HOW TO SPEAK HUMAN

For years, if a speaker I was working with wanted to inject any sort of jargon or pablum into a speech, my suggestion to them was simple:

Don't Speak Like a Robot. When I got to the White House, Jon Favreau, the chief speechwriter, had a nicer way to put it: Talk Like a Human.

It makes sense. We're humans talking to other humans. It turns out, speaking Human is easier than you think.

Speak Like a Normal Person

Remember, the best speakers are having a conversation with their audience. Obama once described it to me like talking with a loved one, a best friend, or a coworker. "It's like, 'Man, this is great. We're having so much fun. Ideas are bouncing around. You're syncing."

As First Lady, Michelle Obama "had no patience for jargon" either, remembers Dave Cavell, one of her speechwriters. "She was determined to speak like a normal person. It's why, for example, she didn't call her initiative for kids 'The First Lady's Program to Encourage Exercise and Healthy Dietary Practices Among Youth.' She called it 'Let's Move!' She spoke to young people the same way she spoke to her daughters' friends."

That's why I urge speakers to follow the BBQ Rule: if you wouldn't say it at a BBQ with your family and friends, don't say it in a speech. Why a BBQ? Because at a BBQ, you might be having a conversation with your grandma, your crazy uncle, or your thirteen-year-old niece in the eighth grade—or all of them at the same time. Suppose they ask what you're doing at work. Hopefully, you wouldn't say, "I utilize next-generation innovations to create synergies that optimize technology for positive health outcomes." Say that, and your niece is already wandering off.

Instead, I hope you'd say something like "We make watches that monitor your heart rate and then share that information with your doctor so you can stay healthy."

No gibberish. No jargon. Everyone at the BBQ understands

what you're saying, even your eighth-grade niece. Because you followed one of the most fundamental rules in communication—Keep It Simple.

It's no coincidence that many speeches, even some State of the Union addresses, are written at about the eighth-grade level.[3] It's the reading level of the average American. And the more people who understand your presentation, the more effective it will be.

I'm not saying you have to deliver every presentation like you're speaking to an eighth grader. Still, as you prepare your remarks, beware the Curse of Knowledge. Look closely at every word. If you find yourself using jargon or language that's perhaps over the heads of some of the people in your audience, look for a more human way to say it. Use everyday words.

Can't come up with a normal word for your jargon? This is another place where a chatbot can help. Type in: "Give me ten simpler words for _____." Yes, sometimes a robot can help you speak more like a human.

Talk About People (Not Programs)
Here are two actual quotes from two different speakers.

"In the future, we will redefine personal mobility."

"The world needs to aim for a new global compact on human mobility."

Any idea what they're talking about? I don't blame you.

Sure, both are out of context. But even *in* context, they're still not entirely clear. Both use similar words and yet they're talking about wildly different things. The first quote is from an automobile executive's remarks about how we get around in our cars. The second

The BBQ Rule: Use Everyday Words

Instead of . . .	Just say . . .
Align	Coordinate
Architect (the verb: "To architect . . .")	Create/come up with
Bandwidth	Availability
Cogitate	Think
Core competencies	Unique strengths
Dialogue it	Talk it through
Incentivize	Motivate
Interdependent	Connected
Leverage	Harness
Noncitizens	People
A paradigm shift	A change
Synergize	Collaborate
Utilize	Use

quote is from a United Nations official about the rising number of migrants around the world. Similar words. Totally different meanings. And largely devoid of the humanity—the living, breathing human beings—at the core of each issue.

Many of us speak this way. We talk about concepts that can seem abstract ("pay equity") rather than tangible goals (making sure people are paid the same for the same work); inputs (dollars invested) instead of outcomes (the real-world impact of those investments). Politicians refer to their "infrastructure plan" (mistakenly assuming that we know or remember what's in the plan) instead of the difference that their plan will make in our daily lives—more jobs, better roads, less time in traffic, more time with family.

Several years ago, the cofounder of a new nonprofit where I live in Virginia was struggling with how to talk about her work. From a small basement space called The Clothesline for Arlington Kids, Ellen Moy gathers donated clothes from local families and then offers them—in a store-like setting, but free of charge—to children in need. Ellen had years of experience in retail; she knew what she was doing. But when she appealed for donations and volunteers, "I was too clinical," she remembers. "I focused too much on our operations—'the business model,' 'the store,' 'the process.'"

Working together, we reimagined how she described her work—how she offers a "welcoming, fun, retail-like" setting for children to pick out "a season's worth of quality clothing," and how, "staffed entirely by local volunteers," The Clothesline "represents Arlington at our best—neighbors helping neighbors." Most of all, Ellen started telling a bigger, more human, story. "This is about more than giving a child a coat or a pair of shoes," she now says. "It's about kids feeling comfortable going to school so they can learn. It's about dignity."

"Instead of getting sidetracked by the operational details, our message now has more of a human touch. I speak about the heart of what we do, our larger purpose and mission." With *that* message,

Ellen has recruited a legion of volunteers, several part-time employees, and given free clothes to thousands of local kids, one of whom wrote a note to express her gratitude, saying, "You guys don't know how much you can change a life by just receiving clothes."

When you speak, get real. Avoid getting pulled into the weeds—the mechanics, processes, and *inputs* of your work—especially when you're making the case for why people should support your cause. Talk about real-world *outcomes*—the *people* you help and how you change their lives, even if it sometimes takes a few extra words.

Get Real

Instead of policies and programs . . .	Talk about people . . .
This program will generate economic impact.	We'll create new jobs for workers.
This initiative will reduce infant mortality.	We'll save children's lives.
This policy will alleviate food insecurity.	We'll help parents make sure their children have enough healthy food.

SWAP

Talking like a human also means avoiding acronyms. Sure, some acronyms are technically initialisms that are now widely used (NFL, NBA, IRS, PTSD, ADHD). Just about everyone knows them, so I say use them to your heart's content.

The problem is that sometimes acronyms can mean different things to different audiences. The Wisconsin Tourism Federation changed its name so it wouldn't be known as WTF. When Iowans were contemplating a new name for their elderly services agency, many worried that its Department of Aging would be referred to as DOA. If you're giving a speech about public transportation in Seattle, I wouldn't recommend using the acronym for the South Lake Union Trolley.

Acronyms are especially dangerous when you're talking about technical matters and not everyone in your audience shares the same level of expertise. Maybe you work for a company that does a lot of B2B. Or B2C. Maybe some of your audience WFH. Maybe, as you read this, you're confused too. That's my point. No matter how knowledgeable you think your audience is, there will always be someone who doesn't understand the acronyms you're using. Maybe you're thinking, *Well, I'll just explain it*. Here's another good public speaking rule: if you have to explain it, don't say it. Stop With Acronyms that Perplex.

Be Careful with Contractions

As we've discussed, good speakers think about how words *sound* when we say them *out loud*. It's why effective communicators don't write for the page; they *speak for the ear*. Case in point: contractions.

Sometimes, contractions can be your enemy. When we're speaking, "can't" can sound like "can." "Shouldn't" can be misheard as "should." "Didn't" can come across as "did." When our audience hears the opposite of what we mean, we're not speaking clearly. Whenever possible, avoid negative contractions. Spell it out. Say what you mean—"cannot," "should not," "did not."

Other times, contractions can be your friend. "I am excited to be here" does not sound like you're excited to be here. "Now is the time to take action" sounds like a sentient machine ordering its robot army to rise up against humankind. When you're speaking—especially about how you feel—contractions can help you sound less like a robot and more like a human: "I'm excited . . . ," "I'm happy . . . ," "Now's the time to protect humanity from runaway technology."

Don't Not Banish Double Negatives

Got that? You probably had to read it twice. Now imagine being in an audience and *hearing* it. *Wait, "don't not banish double negatives"? What?*

Double negatives are the enemy of clarity. They force our audience to figure out what we mean, which also means they're not listening to the next thing we have to say. Worse, the only word they often remember is the very opposite of what we intend. During Covid, some public health officials told us what to do if we were "not asymptomatic." Well, "asymptomatic" sounds a lot like "symptomatic," and I bet a lot of people, like me, often misheard it, which left me even more confused.

I generally don't like ironclad rules because there's almost always an exception. But here's a pretty good rule to follow when you're delivering a presentation: banish double negatives. There's always a better, more direct way to say it.

Begone, Double Negatives

Instead of being negative . . .	Stay positive . . .
It's not uncommon to hear this.	It's common to hear this.
The cost of this program is not insignificant.	The cost of this program is significant.
We can't not invest in our communities.	We need to invest in our communities.

Avoid Legalese

If you're speaking on behalf of a business or organization, it's some-times a good idea to run your remarks by your lawyers. More than once, the eagle-eyed attorneys at the White House spotted language in my drafts that could have triggered a diplomatic incident and got me fired. Thank you, lawyers!

That said, even the best lawyers can sometimes take things too far. In a draft speech on military drones, a White House attorney took most of the references to "Americans" and changed them to "U.S. persons." When one of my fellow speechwriters wrote that the United States had "won" a trade dispute with China, one law-yer instead suggested: "We achieved a favorable result." Seeing a draft speech in Vietnam in which Obama quoted Thomas Jeffer-son praising Vietnamese rice, one trade lawyer grew apoplectic. He was convinced that American farmers would take offense at a two-hundred-year-old quote praising another country's rice and torpedo negotiations over a trade deal with Asia. We kept it in. Did enraged American farmers march on the White House? No.

Yes, if you or your organization is ever slapped with a lawsuit, the things you say in public can and will be used against you in a court of law. So if your lawyers truly believe that your words could put you in legal jeopardy, work with them to find language that won't get you in trouble. Still, a speech is not a legal memorandum, and it shouldn't sound like one. As you prepare your remarks, write them for the broader court of public opinion, not a court of law. Make them clear and understandable for a general audience, most of whom are not lawyers. Now *that's* achieving a favorable result.

Let Us Not Get Too Lofty

There's a final way that we sometimes fail to speak like a human—when we try so hard to be eloquent that we end up sounding like a person from another century. I get why so many of us do this. Great speeches, we're taught, are lofty. Orators orate. In his second inaugural address—in the midst of the Civil War—Lincoln said, "Let us strive on to finish the work we are in." Kennedy, in his inaugural address, proclaimed, "Let the word go forth from this time and place, to friend and foe alike, that the torch has been passed." Beautiful. Alliterative. Soaring. And entirely appropriate for a president giving an inaugural address.

But we're *not* a president giving an inaugural address, and we shouldn't sound like one. Even Obama—a president who gave inaugural addresses—knew there was a time and place for lofty language. Once, I sent him a draft in which I'd started several paragraphs with "Let us . . ." When the draft came back, he had crossed out every one and replaced them with "Let's . . ." I got the message: let's only use "let us" during the most solemn occasions.

Obama's Selma speech is instructive. It was a historic occasion— the fiftieth anniversary of the landmark civil rights marches. But the event itself was not a solemn occasion. The thousands of spectators who were in the crowd were pumped up. Even as it was a day of remembrance, it was a celebration of America, and Obama wanted his remarks to resonate with the folks in the crowd.

"Look at that speech," Cody Keenan, who worked on the remarks with the president, says. "The Selma speech is not lofty. It's colloquial." Sure enough, Obama did not say "Let us go forth, united as one people, and summon the will to meet the tasks of our time." He said, "We have to recognize that one day's commemoration, no matter how special, is not enough. If Selma taught us anything, it's that our work is never done." Again, not speaking *at* his audience, speaking *with* them.

As you craft your remarks, don't write for the history books. Just speak. Talk to the human beings right in front of you in language they can understand and relate to.

Bring Lofty Language Down to Earth

Instead of being formal . . .	Be colloquial . . .
Let there be no doubt . . .	Clearly . . .
We shall . . .	We will . . .
We must . . .	We need to . . .
Let me be clear . . .	Without a doubt . . .

The Download

As you prepare your presentation, avoid jargon and technical language that risks confusing your audience. Talk like a human.

» **Remember the BBQ Rule.** Avoid the Curse of Knowledge. Just talk like you'd talk to a friend or family member at a BBQ, including your thirteen-year-old niece in the eighth grade. Use everyday words. Look at every sentence and every word and ask yourself: Will *everyone* in my audience understand this? What's a simpler way to say it?

» **Talk about people, not programs.** Instead of focusing on vague concepts, inputs, programs, and processes, talk about the *people* you're trying to help and the difference you can make in their daily lives.

» **SWAP.** Not everyone in your audience will know the acronyms you know. Stop With Acronyms that Perplex.

» **Be careful with contractions.** Avoid negative contractions that leave your listeners uncertain about what you *did* say and what you *didn't*. Use contractions when talking about how you feel.

» **Banish double negatives.** They're the enemy of clarity.

» **Avoid legalese.** A speech is not a legal memorandum and it shouldn't sound like one.

» **Don't get too lofty.** You're not a president delivering an inaugural address. Just talk to the human beings in front of you; instead of speaking *over* them, speak *with* them.

All that said, talking like a human ought to be the bare minimum when we speak. If we really want to touch the hearts of our audience, we can strive for something more—we can speak in a way that's truly music to their ears.

CHAPTER 10

Make It Sing

Wherever you find a sentence musically worded,
of true rhythm and melody in the words, there is
something deep and good in the meaning, too.

—Samuel Taylor Coleridge

In the early 1970s, an Italian pop star named Adriano Celentano put out a new song—a catchy mix of funk and Europop with a pulsating rhythm. It got people dancing from Rome to West Berlin. The thing was, though, no one understood what Celentano was singing. Most listeners apparently thought the lyrics were in English.

In fact, they weren't in any language at all.

Celentano had made up just about every word. The song was gibberish. Even the title—"Prisencolinensinainciusol"—was a jumble of letters that meant absolutely nothing.

It was an experiment. The words didn't matter. Celentano knew that his fans loved American music, and he wanted to see if he could create a song that *sounded* like something an American would perform. Even if it made no sense.

He was right. It became the top song in Italy and across Europe. (Go online and listen. It's trippy.)

Why am I telling you about a fifty-year-old song from Italy?

Because just like there's more to a song than its lyrics, there's more to a speech than its words. I learned this early in my career— the hard way.

As a White House intern during college, I was assigned to help President Bill Clinton's foreign policy speechwriters. I spent most of my time doing research in the White House library or on the computer trying to figure out how to use a funky new thing called the internet.

One day, we got word that the president would be hosting the king of Morocco for a state visit, and he'd need to make a toast. Swamped with more pressing remarks, the speechwriters asked me to take a stab at a first draft. I couldn't believe it. I was twenty-two years old, and I was writing a speech for the president of the United States!

I went all out. I plunged into my research and learned everything I could about the king and Morocco. I worked and wrote for days. Then I rewrote what I wrote. Then I rewrote it again. Finally, my draft was ready, and I turned in what I was sure would go down in history as one of the most memorable toasts ever delivered by a U.S. president.

Then one of the speechwriters, Bob Boorstin, called me into his office. I saw my draft on his desk. It was covered, almost entirely, in red ink.

"You did a good job," he said kindly, which made me wonder how much red ink it took to correct a bad job.

"What I want you to learn, though, is that a speech needs to move, it needs cadence."

I nodded that I understood.

I didn't. I hadn't studied rhetoric. I didn't play an instrument. I wasn't a singer.

Later, I cracked open the dictionary.

ca-dence (noun) *1: fall of the voice in speaking 2: inflection or modulation in tone 3: any rhythmic flow of sound 4: measured movement, as in dancing or marching, or the beat of such movement.*

I'd written for the eye—words to be read. Bob wanted me to write for the ear—words to be heard.

Bob took over and finished the draft. At the state dinner a few nights later, the president raised his glass and began his toast, "Your Majesty, Your Royal Highnesses, members of the Moroccan delegation, distinguished guests . . ." It was about the only part of my draft that had survived.

Still, I learned an important lesson: like a good song, a good speech has cadence. A beat. A tempo. A rhythm. It makes the audience *feel* something. Like Adriano Celentano's song in Italy, a good speech makes an audience want to *move*—maybe lean in, sit on the edge of their seat, clap, cheer, holler back, pump their fists in the air, stomp their feet, or get out of their chairs and give a standing ovation.

You don't have to be musically inclined to bring a beat to your remarks. Gorillaz was right when they sang, "Rhythm, you have it or you don't / That's a fallacy." Here are a few ways you can make *your* speech sing.

BE UNPREDICTABLE

"You campaign in poetry," the former governor of New York, Mario Cuomo, famously said, "but you govern in prose." Cuomo was a brilliant orator, and I know what he meant. Still, I've never cared for this quote. Yes, when we're campaigning or advocating for a cause we believe in, our rhetoric tends to be more aspirational—the grand hopes and dreams we want to make real. And yes, once we get down to business—leading organizations, running teams, governing—our soaring exhortations often come crashing down to earth. Visionary rhetoric devolves into vapid five-point plans.

But do our day-to-day speeches and presentations really have to be so . . . prosaic? Why *can't* we bring more variety—even a sense of poetry—to our toasts and eulogies for our loved ones, our presentations at work, and our comments at community meetings?

I read somewhere that perhaps 80 percent of the language that we use and hear in a given day is based on roughly the same few thousand words. I don't know if that's true, but I wouldn't be surprised. As you've probably noticed, most of us tend to use the same words over and over. On the one hand, it's good. As I explained earlier, we *should* speak in everyday words that are familiar to our audience. On the other hand, we don't want to be so prosaic that we become predictable.

Driving home from the White House at night, I sometimes listened to C-SPAN on the radio as it rebroadcast that day's political speeches (what can I say, I'm a glutton for punishment). I played a little game with myself that I called Finish That Sentence. Play along with me.

Politician: "We shouldn't be *dividing* people, we should be _____."

The answer? You got it: ". . . *uniting* people!"

Politician: "We shouldn't be *holding people down*, we should be _____."

Yup: ". . . *lifting people up!*"

I hate to brag, but I got it right. Every. Single. Time. You probably got them right too. Because sentences like these are not original. They're how a lot of politicians think they're *supposed* to talk. Because politicians have been talking like that forever. Which is exactly my point. Sure, lines like these have something going for them—the parallelism, the juxtaposition, their rhythm—and they can get a cheer at a political rally. But, by now, they're also totally predictable.

Obama didn't like being predictable. As he told me, he didn't *want* to be a conventional politician. "He has an allergy to applause lines," said Jon Favreau. And if we slipped up and wrote something that he felt sounded too contrived or packaged, he'd strike it out.

Whenever we speak, we have an opportunity to grab our listeners and hold their attention with language that's fresh, unexpected, even elegant. I learned this from an unlikely teacher—the secretary of defense.

TURN YOUR PROSE INTO POETRY

Before taking over the Defense Department, William Cohen had been a longtime U.S. senator from Maine and a respected voice on national security issues. He was also a student of the classics and a lover of language. In college, he earned degrees in classical Latin and Greek literature. Even as he served in Washington, he wrote two books of his own poetry. The several years that I wrote for him at the Pentagon—my first speechwriting job, in my twenties—were a crash course in how to elevate speeches to the sublime.

"Speeches are an auditory experience. Your audience is *listening* to you," he told me, like an audience listens to a poem. "Poets are said to pinch words until they hurt"—until you feel them. "There's an elegance and grace to the language." He wanted his remarks to have those same qualities. "Speeches can be beautiful. They can be lyrical," he said. "A phrase can mesmerize the audience, but you have to squeeze the words and give your listener something different to remember."*

Cohen pinched and squeezed his words in every speech, whether with his own lyricism or when borrowing from the best. Fallen service members, he said, quoting Pericles's Funeral Oration, "gave their bodies to the commonwealth and received, each for his own memory, praise that will never die." Veterans could look back on their service and know, as the Civil War veteran and jurist Oliver Wendell Holmes, Jr., had said, that "in our youth our hearts were touched with fire." Freedom is not free, Cohen said, because— borrowing the words of the journalist Walter Lippmann during World War II—"for every good that you wish to preserve, you will have to sacrifice your comfort and your ease."

Praise that will never die. Hearts touched with fire. Sacrifice your comfort and your ease. These weren't just words. They were lyrics. And when I heard them, I learned that, yes, speeches can be beautiful too.

Years later, I watched Obama do it as well. "There's a poetry to great speaking," he told me once. He talked about the "majesty" of America's national parks, the "nobility" of Memorial Day, and how the nation needs to uphold its "sacred covenant" with its veterans. We're bound together as human beings, he declared in his Nobel Prize address, by "that spark of the divine that still stirs within each of our souls."

Who talks like this in their daily lives? Well, no one, really. And that's precisely the point. Even as we should use everyday words as much as possible in our speeches and presentations, a touch of

---

* I learned another important lesson from Cohen. He did something that's all too rare in politics: a Republican, he crossed the aisle and served in the administration of a president from the other party—Bill Clinton, a Democrat. Which made me a Democratic speechwriter writing for a Republican serving a Democratic president. It was tricky, but it worked, and it was an example of how government *should* function— country before party.

elegance every so often can be nice too. In the auditory experience that is a speech, elegant words are unexpected. They surprise us. And, as a result, they remain tucked in our hearts and minds. A presentation that could have been mundane becomes memorable.

You can do it too. As you develop your remarks, look for words that are monotonous and—here and there—replace them with words that are mellifluous. Here are a few of my favorites:

Use Mellifluous Words

Alluring	Glorious	Onerous
Bliss	Graceful	Opulence
Cascade	Idyllic	Panacea
Celestial	Illustrious	Passion
Cherish	Imbue	Picturesque
Destiny	Incandescent	Pristine
Effervescent	Incendiary	Quintessential
Elegance	Ineffable	Resplendent
Eloquence	Iridescent	Sanguine
Ephemeral	Labyrinth	Scintilla
Epiphany	Love	Serenity
Eternity	Luminous	Solitude
Ethereal	Magnificent	Sublime
Euphoria	Miraculous	Sumptuous
Glittering	Nefarious	Tranquility

As you experiment with mellifluous words like these, don't just read them. Say them out loud. Hear how they *sound*—soft, soothing, melodic. How a word like "graceful" sounds, well, graceful. Audiences love elegant words too. In fact, many of the words above appear in surveys of what people consider the most beautiful words in the English language.

Need help finding some elegant words for your remarks? Go online and search for "beautiful words." Or, like I sometimes do, ask a bot: "What are 30 synonyms for _____?" Add a touch of elegance, and you'll be praised for your eloquence.

BRING ON THE RHYTHM

"There's a rhythm to speaking," Obama told me one time, "whether it's just you and a bunch of friends sitting on a porch or you're in front of a million people. The church tradition also embodies a lot of that—not just the Black church, but the white church as well."

That's why, during his eulogy for the nine Black parishioners who were murdered at their church in Charleston, South Carolina, in 2015, Obama was able to slide so effortlessly into singing "Amazing Grace," with the audience singing right along. His eulogy—both the words on the page and his delivery at the pulpit—was already infused with poetry and rhythm. His rendering of the beloved hymn was not *separate from* his speech, it was a seamless *extension of it*.

Here are a few ways you can bring some rhythm to your remarks.

Write Your Speech Like a Script

On the night he lost the New Hampshire primary during the 2008 campaign, Obama nevertheless went on to deliver one of the most memorable speeches of his career, recounting how Americans have always responded to moments of challenge "with a simple creed." If you go online and read it today, it will look like this:

It was a creed written into the founding documents that de-clared the destiny of a nation: Yes, we can. It was whispered by slaves and abolitionists as they blazed a trail towards freedom through the darkest of nights: Yes, we can. It was sung by immigrants as they struck out from distant shores and pioneers who pushed westward against an unforgiving wilderness: Yes, we can. It was the call of workers who organized, women who reached for the ballot, a president who chose the moon as our new frontier, and a king who took us to the mountaintop and pointed the way to the promised land: Yes, we can, to justice and equality.

When written that way, however—like an essay or an article—it fails to capture how Obama actually *delivered* it. He paused every few words, allowing his words to hang in the air. For longer passages, he spoke faster, his voice rising. For shorter passages, he slowed down. There was a beat, a rhythm.

That's why, whenever possible, I try to write speeches like a *script*— every new sentence starting on the left margin and a space between each line. Written this way, a draft of Obama's speech could have looked something like this:

It was a creed written into the founding documents that declared the destiny of a nation:

Yes, we can.

It was whispered by slaves and abolitionists as they blazed a trail towards freedom through the darkest of nights:

Yes, we can.

It was sung by immigrants as they struck out from distant shores and pioneers who pushed westward against an unforgiving wilderness:

Yes, we can.

It was the call of workers who organized, women who reached for the bal-lot, a president who chose the moon as our new frontier, and a king who took us to the mountaintop and pointed the way to the promised land:

Yes, we can, to justice and equality.

I first learned to write speeches like this back at the Pentagon, for the poet–secretary of defense. I don't know who came up with it, but I think it's brilliant. Every sentence is set off on its own. You can actually *see* the flow of the language right there on the page. You can see how "Yes, we can" stands alone—three syllables, three beats. You can see how each sentence grows a little longer, building to a crescendo.

What's more, when you *deliver* this passage this way, you're forced into the rhythm of the speech. Try it. Take a moment and read the version above out loud. Seriously, read it out loud.

Amazing, right? You just delivered a passage of a moving speech the way it was meant to be *heard*—because of how it was *written on the page.*[*]

What's going on?

Build in Your Breaths

If we want to maintain our rhythm and pace as a speaker, we have to breathe—at the right time. When we do, we can deliver each word and each line with the energy they deserve. When we breathe at the *wrong* time, it can disrupt the flow of an otherwise smooth sentence.

Writing our remarks like a script can help. Take the first line of

---

[*] At the White House, we didn't write speeches in this script-like format. It just would have been too unwieldy as we shared drafts with fellow staff and across the bureaucracy.

the passage from Obama's New Hampshire speech. Read it again out loud.

It was a creed written into the founding documents that declared the destiny of a nation:

Yes, we can.

After "destiny of a nation" and before "Yes, we can," did you take a quick, ever-so-slight breath? When I give my clients scripts like this—or ask people in my workshops to practice this—I find that they often take a little breath. You see, at the end of each line, our eyes have to dart back to the left. And in that split second, we often take a quick breath, instinctively. We're better at the podium when—by writing our remarks like a script—we build in our breaths on the page.

See Your Sentence Structure—and Vary It
When we write out our remarks like a script, we can also immediately spot long sentences.

And short ones.

It's a great reminder that our speeches are more interesting—and more musical—when we vary the lengths of our sentences.

So mix it up.

Like Obama did in New Hampshire.

He had a long sentence like:

"It was whispered by slaves and abolitionists as they blazed a trail towards freedom through the darkest of nights."

Immediately followed by something short:

"Yes, we can."

If one of our sentences starts to get too long, with too many words, and starts to run onto a second line of the page (like this), we'll see it right away.

We can try again and break it into a shorter, punchier sentence.

Today, I write like this for all my clients.

Maybe it will work for you too.

Give it a try.

Please.

Loosen It Up
After reviewing a draft of his State of the Union address one year, Obama called Cody Keenan to the Oval Office.

"Here's the thing," Obama said. "Everything is in here. Every sentence says something. Every word means something."

Now, maybe you're thinking, *What's the problem? Every sentence and word should mean something, right?* Obama explained, holding his hand in the air.

"The entire speech is up here at a ten. I need some of it down here," he said, lowering his hand, "at six, seven, eight. You following me?"[1]

Back in our office in the basement under the Oval Office—the Speechcave, we called it—Cody shared Obama's feedback. I wasn't following. Cody compared the speech to a sweater.

"He's saying it fits, but it's too tight. There are no gaps between the threads, no way for it to breathe. He wants me to loosen it up, make it more comfortable."

Now I got it.

Cody went to work. He turned bold, declarative sentences—the kind that might end with an exclamation point—into lines that were more conversational, that might end, more softly, with a period. Instead of forcefully proclaiming the president's policies, line after line, he took time to explain them, even if it took a few more words. When sharing the story of a young couple from Minnesota— Rebekah and Ben Erler—who embodied the financial struggles of so many Americans, he told their story with short sentences and simple words, which Cody likened to a John Mellencamp song: "She waited tables. He worked construction. Their first child, Jack, was on the way. They were young and in love in America. And it doesn't get much better than that."

Less intense. More relaxed. More of a comfortable six, not an intense ten.

Every sentence in a speech doesn't have to be a barn burner. Every passage doesn't have to build to a rapturous applause line. It's often good to slow it down. Stretch it out. Let your remarks breathe. Loosen up the threads so your audience can feel comfortable in the speech that you've so skillfully stitched together.

Create Rhythm with Repetition

Like a good song, a good speech can have a refrain—a line or phrase that repeats and creates some rhythm. (The fancy word for starting several sentences in a row with the same word or phrase is "anaphora." But if you're thinking *It's all Greek to me*, don't worry. I confess I never heard that word either until after I became a speechwriter.)

When we write our remarks like a script, it's easier to see how and where a refrain might work. You can try a refrain at the beginning of each section, like Obama's second inaugural address:

We, the people, still believe that every citizen deserves a basic measure of security and dignity . . .

We, the people, still believe that our obligations as Americans are not just to ourselves, but to all posterity.

We, the people, still believe that enduring security and lasting peace do not require perpetual war.

Or, if you want to get really creative, you can try two refrains at the same time, like Obama did in his New Hampshire speech. Every sentence *begins* with "It was . . ." ("It was a creed . . ." "It was whispered . . ." "It was sung . . .") and every sentence *ends* with "Yes, we can." In the final sentence, there's even a bit of parallelism ("the workers who organized . . . women who reached . . . a president who chose . . . a king who took us to the mountaintop . . ."). When written like a script, you can't miss it. The patterns jump off the page. And if you *don't* see any refrains, then that's a cue that maybe your remarks could use some.

How many? Many speakers and speechwriters love the Rule of Three. Ideas and phrases that come in three (like Lincoln's "government of the people, by the people, for the people") can be more pleasing to the ear. Hitting a point three times creates a nice beat. There's a rhythm to it.

That said, don't let the Rule of Three tie you down. If you have four examples of something or four important points to make, I say make them. Your audience can handle it. And if you've got a good refrain going, don't feel like you have to hold back just because you've already hit it three times. In his New Hampshire speech, Obama began four sentences in a row with "It was . . ." He said "Yes, we can" about a dozen times—and it was still a great speech.

Amplify with Alliteration, but Avoid an Avalanche

Like many great speakers throughout history, you can also lift up your language with a little alliteration. Similar-sounding words are melodic, and studies show that, like repetition, alliteration can make an idea more memorable.[2] In his second inaugural address, for instance, Obama said Americans' founding belief that we are all created equal is the "the star that guides us still, just as it guided our forebears through Seneca Falls, and Selma, and Stonewall."

I worry, though, that too many speakers—especially a lot of politicians—take alliteration to an extreme. You see, abundant alliteration, while an admirable and audacious artistic attempt to articulate and allure, can also appear as an absurdly assembled antic—an artificial and awkward appeal that amounts to an aggressive auditory assault that can agitate, alienate, and antagonize an audience.

I'm exaggerating. But you get my point. Used to excess, alliteration can come across as contrived and inauthentic—because we don't speak that way in our daily lives.

My recommendation: keep any rhyming and alliteration to a minimum. If you do it, I suggest no more than three alliterative words in a sentence. Four or more—or worse, sentence after sentence of alliteration—and you look like you're showboating, which can agitate, alienate, and antagonize your audience. Which makes the old joke about writing a pretty good rule to follow: Always avoid annoying alliterations.

Turn Your Speech into a Song

When giving Cody Keenan his feedback on that State of the Union address Obama also wanted him to do something else.

"Find me some silences."

It was another example of how a speech can resemble a piece of music, even jazz.

"You know what they say about Miles Davis?" Obama asked Cody. "It's the notes you don't play. It's the silences. That's what made him so good. I need a speech with some pauses, and some quiet moments, because they say something too. You feel me?"[3]

We all need some pauses in our presentations. There's power in a pause. Pauses—the words we don't say—help us connect with our audience. A pause lets our words hang out there for a moment, lets the audience ponder them, lets their meaning sink in. A pause adds emphasis, signaling to your listeners that you've just said something important. A pause adds drama, creating a moment of anticipation as your audience waits for what comes next.

But how, as speakers, do we "find" our silences?

For me, it's in the writing. Sometimes, I don't just write speeches like a script, I write them like a poem or a song. I break each line where I want the speaker to pause, even if only for a moment, to create a little silence. For example, when you *listen* to Obama's speech in New Hampshire, you can hear him pause, ever so slightly, every few words. Written more like a song, it would look more like this:

It was a creed written into the founding documents
That declared the destiny
Of a nation:
Yes, we can.

It was whispered by slaves and abolitionists
As they blazed a trail towards freedom
Through the darkest of nights:
Yes, we can.

It was sung by immigrants as they struck out from distant shores
And pioneers who pushed westward
Against an unforgiving wilderness:
Yes, we can.

It was the call of workers who organized,
Women who reached for the ballot,
A president who chose the moon as our new frontier,

And a king who took us to the mountaintop
And pointed the way to the promised land:
Yes, we can, to justice and equality.

Can you see it? More importantly, can you *hear* it? Between the last word of every line and the first word of the next, there's a silence, ever so slight. And together, those silences helped create a sense of rhythm. That's how Obama actually *delivered* it—almost like a song. Which is why will.i.am of the Black Eyed Peas was able to take the speech and turn it into an actual song.

If you want your remarks to have rhythm, write them out like a piece of music.

The Download

Never speak gibberish. But if you want, try a little Prisencolinensinainciusol. Bring some lyricism to your language. Give it a beat. Give it rhythm. Make it sing.

» **Be unpredictable.** Instead of using the first word or phrase that comes to mind, surprise your audience with language they might not expect.

» **Turn your prose into poetry.** Remember that speeches and presentations are auditory experiences. Give your audience something pleasant to *listen* to. Use mellifluous words.

» **Write your speech like a script.** When you write out your remarks like a script—each sentence starting on a new line and a space between each sentence—you can actually see the flow of the language right on the page, which will also help you deliver it better.

» **Vary your sentence structure.** A few sentences of the same length, or words with the same number of syllables, can create a nice beat. But too many sentences that are the same length can get monotonous. Mix it up. Longer sentences here, shorter sentences there.

» **Loosen it up.** Every sentence doesn't have to end with an exclamation point. Every passage doesn't need an applause line. Slow it down. Loosen it up. Let it breathe.

» **Create rhythm with repetition.** Bring some rhythm to your remarks by starting a few sentences or paragraphs with the same phrase, using the Rule of Three, or sprinkling in a *little* alliteration.

» **Turn your speech into a song.** Create silences and pauses in your presentation and add a sense of rhythm by writing out your remarks like the verses of a poem or a song.

Of course, for any presentation to be effective, it has to be more than musically worded. It also has to be true.

The End

Wow 'em

CHAPTER 11

Tell the Truth

To be persuasive, we must be believable;
To be believable, we must be credible;
To be credible, we must be truthful.

—Edward R. Murrow

For President Obama, enough was enough.

It was his final year in office, and for months, Donald Trump—by then the Republican nominee for president—had been blasting Obama for not using the words "radical Islamic terrorism" to describe the ISIS terrorists who had taken over parts of Iraq and Syria and inspired attacks around the world, including in the United States.

Then, on June 12, a gunman who had pledged allegiance to ISIS massacred forty-nine people and wounded dozens more at Pulse, a gay nightclub in Orlando. It was, at the time, the deadliest mass shooting in American history.

"Appreciate the congrats on being right on radical Islamic terrorism," Trump tweeted after the attack, even as families were still learning that their loved ones had been killed.

As the magnitude of the slaughter became clear, Obama addressed the nation, condemned the "act of terror," pledged to stand with the families and people of Orlando, and affirmed the resolve of the United States "to defend our people."

Soon, Trump was at it again. "In his remarks today, President Obama disgracefully refused to even say the words 'Radical Islam,'" Trump said. "For that reason alone, he should step down."

Two days later, Obama was scheduled to deliver one of his regular updates to the nation on the fight against ISIS, and I had worked on the remarks. But when I went to retrieve his edits outside the Oval Office, it was clear from his notes that there was something he wanted to get off his chest.

"Let me make a final point . . ." Obama had written. Overnight, he'd broken out his yellow legal pad and penned paragraph after paragraph—more than a page—about why he was so careful to avoid incendiary language like "radical Islamic terrorism." A few hours later, he stood at the podium, flanked by his military and national security advisors, and ripped into "politicians who tweet."

"Groups like [ISIS] and al Qaeda want to make this war a war between Islam and America," Obama explained. "That's their propaganda. That's how they recruit. And if we fall into the trap of painting all Muslims with a broad brush and imply that we are at war with an entire religion—then we're doing the terrorists' work for them." He went on, his anger building, noting that "the presumptive Republican nominee for president" had proposed to "bar all Muslims from immigrating to America."

"Where does this stop? . . . Are we going to start treating all Muslim Americans differently? . . . Are we going to start discriminating against them because of their faith?" That, he warned, would betray our basic freedoms, including freedom of religion, "the very things that make this country great . . . and we cannot let that happen."

It was one of Obama's most pointed rebukes of Trump during the entire campaign. Yet it was something else in his edits that has always stayed with me. On the top of the first page of the draft he'd written this:

Terry—I wrote out the changes on page 4 so they would be easier to track. Let me know if it's confusing, and make sure I'm precise in describing what Trump has already proposed.

Americans were reeling from the horrific attack in Orlando. Trump, in Obama's view, was using the tragedy to score political points. And Obama was clearly angry. And yet still, Obama was determined to be accurate: "make sure I'm precise." Even as he was excoriating a political opponent, he wanted to be sure he was telling the truth.

WHAT WE'RE UP AGAINST

Had I written this book a decade ago, I'm not sure I would have felt the need to devote an entire chapter to the importance of telling the truth. But it's often said that we now live in an Orwellian "post-truth" world. Politicians and their advisers dismiss criticism as "fake news," and when confronted by undeniable truths, offer their own "alternative facts." Social media—and now AI—turbocharges the spread of misinformation and conspiracy theories. Many of us, it seems, can no longer agree on basic facts.

It's no wonder that around the world public trust in institutions—governments, courts, law enforcement, the media—continues to plummet. The main reason, of course, is the *actions* of these institutions, specifically, their failure to uphold their obligations to their citizens, customers, viewers, and readers. Another factor driving this global crisis of trust, I believe, is what the leaders of our institutions *say*. At best, too many leaders shade the truth. At their worst, they outright lie.

Lies have always been shockingly easy to plant and spread. Tell a lie often enough—goes the saying, often attributed to Nazi propagandist Joseph Goebbels—and people will eventually believe it. Psychologists even have a fancy term for it: the illusory truth effect—the more we hear something, even if it's false, the more likely we are to believe it's true.

In the age of social media, lies travel especially fast. In one study, researchers at MIT examined millions of tweets on what was then Twitter. They found that "falsehood diffused significantly farther, faster, deeper, and more broadly than the truth."[1] Translation: lies often travel faster than the truth.

Worst of all, lies get people hurt—even killed. Lies and half-truths by U.S. officials across multiple administrations about the Vietnam War contributed to the deaths of more than fifty-eight thousand Americans and millions of people across Southeast Asia. The lie that the 2020 election was "rigged" led thousands of Donald Trump's supporters to storm Congress and attack police officers there, more than 140 of whom were injured. Most tragically, in the days and months that followed, five officers who'd been on duty at the Capitol died.

OUR CHOICE

I say all this because this is the world into which our words flow. Every time we speak—especially toward the end of our remarks as we lay out solutions or offer a way forward—we have a choice: stick to the facts or spread falsehoods, uphold trust or erode it, traffic in lies or tell the truth.

If you take away no other lesson from this book, I hope it's this: When you speak, tell the truth.

Now, perhaps like my Uncle Dan, you're no fan of Obama. So maybe you're reading this and screaming, *"Obama lied all the time! Why should I listen to one of his speechwriters?!"*

Here's what I can say: Across the hundreds of speeches that I worked on for President Obama, I always wrote what I believed to be the truth. I never included a fact or statement that I knew or feared was false. Same with my fellow speechwriters. We *wanted* to be accurate, because we wanted Obama to be believed. So did he. It's why Obama often began meetings, including our Downloads about upcoming speeches, by saying, "Let's start with what's true."

Moreover, we had an entire research team at the White House that, among other things, fact-checked every word in every draft before the president delivered it. And our fact-checkers were relentless. "If your presentation isn't based on credible arguments and facts," Ben Holzer, who ran the research team for several years, told me, "then how can your audience take you seriously?" Drafts of longer speeches might come back from the fact-checkers with dozens, sometimes hundreds, of corrections and comments such as "What you've written is true, but it could be misleading." And then we'd work together to come up with language that we agreed was both true and *not* misleading.

Did we make mistakes? Of course. During the debate over health-care reform in his first term, Obama frequently said versions of "If you like your [health care] plan, you can keep your plan." Then some Americans found out they *couldn't* keep their plan.

But had Obama *lied*? No. The mistake was speaking so unequivocally about a topic of incredible complexity. For the vast majority of Americans, reform worked—they kept their plan, and health-care coverage was *extended* to millions more people. When some Americans did lose their plan, Obama did what a responsible leader *should* do—he publicly acknowledged his mistake, apologized, and didn't say it again.[2]

My point is, even as we made mistakes, Obama and our team cared deeply about being truthful. I hope you do too. You won't always be perfect either. But the more truthful you are, the more credible and persuasive you'll be. To that end, here are what you might call Ten Commandments for Telling the Truth when it comes to public speaking.

THOU SHALT NOT STEAL

On a spring day in 2021, Robert Caslen, the president of the University of South Carolina, addressed his school's newest graduates. Toward the end of his remarks, he said this:

> *Know that life is not fair, and if you're like me, you'll fail often. But if you take some risks, step up when times are toughest, face down the cowardly bullies and lift up the downtrodden, and never, never give up—if you do those things, the next generation and the generations to follow will live in a world far better than the one we have today. And what started here, today, will indeed change the world for the better.*

It was beautiful. It was inspiring. It was also copied, almost verbatim, from someone else's speech. Admiral William McRaven, who oversaw the operation that killed Osama bin Laden, delivered those same words years earlier in his commencement address at the University of Texas at Austin.

Less than a week later, Caslen resigned.

Yes, a single speech—especially a plagiarized one—can cost you dearly.

As you collect material for your presentation, keep track of any quotes or content you might use. If you're going to borrow, or even paraphrase, someone else, *always* give them credit. If you do those things—to paraphrase Caslen stealing from McRaven—the words that start on your page will indeed change the world for the better.

THOU SHALT NOT MAKE SHIT UP

A few years ago, a candidate for Congress boasted about his biography. His Jewish grandparents, he said, had survived the Holocaust. His mother had survived the 9/11 attacks. He had attended Baruch College, where he was the star of the volleyball team. He'd worked at Goldman Sachs and Citigroup. Through a charity he started, he'd even rescued thousands of dogs.

None. Of. It. Was. True.

George Santos had made it all up.

He was only guilty, he argued later, of "embellishing" his resume. "I never claimed to be Jewish," he said with a straight face, only that "I was Jew-ish."

No one bought it. Federal investigators indicted Santos on nearly two dozen criminal charges, including fraud and lying to Congress. He was expelled from the House of Representatives, and by the time you read this he may have pled guilty or be on trial—or been convicted.

Don't be like George. Don't make shit up. It's a low bar, I know. But it's remarkable how many speakers—when pitching a proposal, policy, or product—embellish to the point of lying. Thanks to the internet, your audience *will* find out. And when they do, your credibility will be shot. As Alexandra Platkin, who led the White House research team at the end of Obama's presidency, put it, "Lying is bad. It's also stupid."

THOU SHALT GET THY FACTS RIGHT

In the early afternoon of December 7, 1942, a wave of Japanese aircraft descended on the American naval base at Pearl Harbor on the island of Hawaii. In the hours that followed, more than two thousand Americans were killed—the deadliest foreign attack ever against one of the fifty states. President Theodore Roosevelt called it "a date that will live in infamy," and when Congress responded by declaring war, it marked the start of World War II.

There are *eight* factual errors in the paragraph you just read. Did you catch them all? If you were speaking to an audience of veterans, they would have noticed immediately—and probably started to correct you. Or boo you. You don't want to get booed.

Even if it feels like sometimes we live in a "post-truth" world, facts still exist. Certain things *are* either right or wrong. For example, nouns—people, places, and things, including numbers. Good speakers get their facts right.*

As you prepare your presentation, double-check anything you get from Wikipedia, which can often be right but is sometimes wrong, or a chatbot, which can "hallucinate" and make up incorrect information. Be very, very skeptical of "facts" you see on social media platforms like X or TikTok.

Go through your draft, circle every fact, figure, and assertion. There are easy ways to check them:

- Primary sources, such as the reports or websites from government agencies or universities where the facts and statistics came from originally;

- Respected encyclopedias, such as Britannica;

- Independent fact-checking organizations, such as FactCheck.org and PolitiFact.com;

- Nonpartisan organizations, like Pew Research Center; and

---

* Of course, authors need to get their facts right too. For this book, I even hired some former White House fact-checkers who caught many mistakes in my draft manuscript. If you spot any that I missed, I'll be sure to correct them in any future editions.

- Reputable news organizations that have their own fact-checking process, such as the *Wall Street Journal*, the *New York Time*s, the *Washington Post*, the Associated Press, and Reuters. (Of course, even news organizations like these can sometimes get their facts wrong too, so it's always smart to check *multiple* sources.)

By using reliable resources like these, it's easy to spot and correct the eight mistakes in the passage above:

Mistake #1: "In the early afternoon"
Fact: the attack on Pearl Harbor started in the morning.

Mistake #2: "1942"
Fact: the attack occurred in 1941.

Mistake #3: "on the island of Hawaii"
Fact: Pearl Harbor is on the island of Oahu.

Mistake #4: "the deadliest foreign attack ever"
Fact: tragically, even more Americans were killed in the terrorist attacks of 9/11.

Mistake #5: "one of the fifty states"
Fact: at the time of the attack, Hawaii was not yet a state.

Mistake #6: "President Theodore Roosevelt"
Fact: the president at the time of the attack was *Franklin* Roosevelt.

Mistake #7: "a date that will live in infamy"
Fact: Roosevelt called it "a date *which* will live in infamy."

Mistake #8: "it marked the start of World War II"
Fact: the attack on Pearl Harbor marked the start of the *United States'* military involvement in the Second World War, but the war had started two years earlier with Germany's invasion of Poland.

THOU SHALT LOOK FOR THE SOURCE

While researching this book, I kept coming across a fascinating statistic: 73 percent of people are afraid of public speaking. It appears in countless news articles and online posts, but, oddly, most don't cite a source. Some claim it's from a study by the National Institute of Mental Health, but I could never find any such study. When I asked an author who included the statistic in one frequently cited article, he said he couldn't remember where he got it. To his credit, he quickly removed the reference.

Likewise, perhaps my all-time favorite quote is "I've learned that people will forget what you said, people will forget what you did, but people will never forget how you made them feel."

It's widely attributed to the author and poet Maya Angelou, and it captures everything I believe about communication and why we need to speak to people's hearts. But while fact-checking this book I learned that Angelou apparently never said it! Or if she did, others said it before her.

As Abraham Lincoln observed, "Don't believe everything you read on the internet."

Beware of statistics and quotes that everyone loves but no one can seem to verify. "If you're going to say it," says Kristen Barto-loni, the deputy director of the White House research team during Obama's second term, "prepare to defend it."

Always look for an authoritative source. For statistics, if you can't back it up, don't say it. For quotes, stick to collections that have been edited by experts, such as *Bartlett's* and the *Oxford Dictionary of Quotations*. Or check out one of my all-time favorite websites, QuoteInvestigator.com, run by a former researcher at Johns Hopkins University who uncovers the true origins of popular quotes.

Still not sure who said it? Perhaps just say, "As the old saying goes . . ." You'll always be right.

THOU SHALT BE HONEST ABOUT THE PAST

Soon after those nine Black worshippers were murdered in their church in Charleston in 2015, pictures emerged of the gunman, a white supremacist, posing with the Confederate flag. A few days later, South Carolina governor Nikki Haley, a Republican, gave a speech in which she called for the removal of the flag from the statehouse grounds.

"For many people in our state," she said, the Confederate flag stood for "traditions of history, of heritage, and of ancestry." At the same time, she said that many South Carolinians saw the flag as "a deeply offensive symbol of a brutally oppressive past." It was "a symbol that divides us . . . [and] causes pain to so many."

"It's time," she said, "to move the flag from the Capitol grounds."

Weeks later, after a debate and vote by the state legislature, the Confederate flag finally came down.*

---

* More recently, Haley seemed to struggle with telling the truth about the past. While running for president in 2023, she was asked by a voter what caused the Civil War. She failed to mention slavery. After facing a torrent of criticism, she added the next day: "Of course the Civil War was about slavery."

It's never easy to face painful truths, whether about our families, our communities, our companies, or our country. But that's what good speakers do. And it's not only the right thing to do. It's the smart thing. In a business context, it's called the blemishing effect— how sharing a little negative information about your product can sometimes help build a positive impression with your target audience.[3] It also works beyond business. When we tell the truth, including about our history, we convey humility, we acknowledge that we're all imperfect—which can build credibility and make people more likely to trust us and work with us.

THOU SHALT AVOID "HAPPY TALK"

Toward the end of his first term, Obama was getting ready to deliver the commencement address at the U.S. Air Force Academy. The draft I had worked on included a recitation of his foreign policy achievements. Apparently, I overdid it. The draft came back with a note from Obama:

> *This is really good—[my] only concern is that we need I think at least one paragraph acknowledging that the danger of terrorism still exists . . . don't want to have just happy talk.*

In my rush to accentuate the positive, I'd neglected to acknowledge the negative—the obvious truth that real challenges remained. At the podium the next day, Obama was clear-eyed. "We still face very serious threats," he declared, "from nations seeking weapons of mass destruction to the cell of terrorists planning the next attack, from the old danger of piracy to the new threat of cyber, we must be vigilant."

We should all be careful about slipping into "happy talk." Our credibility as a speaker depends upon us being honest about the complicated world we live in and the hard choices that we often have to make.

This is especially true during times of challenge or crisis. If you're a leader trying to guide your community, business, or organization through a difficult moment, be honest. Remember that first reports are usually wrong, so avoid jumping to conclusions. Be honest about what you do and don't know; when addressing the public after a terrorist attack or yet another mass shooting, some of the first words out of Obama's mouth were often "we don't yet know all the facts." And be honest about the road ahead. Complex problems rarely have easy answers, and speakers who overpromise by peddling quick fixes and painless solutions risk creating another crisis—a crisis of credibility.

THOU SHALT NOT HIDE FROM ELEPHANTS

Eleven months after taking office, Obama stood before an audience of dignitaries in Oslo, Norway, and accepted the Nobel Peace Prize. It was, in the words of the Nobel Prize committee, in recognition of his "efforts to strengthen international diplomacy and cooperation between peoples." But as he prepared to speak, there was an elephant in the room—a huge one.

Just days before, even as U.S. forces continued to fight in Iraq, Obama had ordered another thirty thousand American troops to Afghanistan. He was receiving a prize for peace even as he was stepping up a war.

Imagine if you were Obama in that moment. What would *you* say?

All too often, speakers simply avoid the elephant in the room, mention it only in passing, or try to hide it in the middle or end of their remarks. A community leader might refer vaguely to "the events of the past few days." A business leader, after a series of lay-offs, might allude to "recent difficulties." An elected official under scrutiny might note "the criticism of some."

But ignoring or downplaying the elephant in the room doesn't make it go away. On the contrary, it can make the speaker look out of touch—which only makes the elephant bigger. Worse, it's an insult to the audience, which knows, expects, and deserves the truth.

That's why, instead of avoiding the elephant in Oslo, Obama made the elephant the star of the show. The night before leaving for Norway, he stayed up late, took out his yellow legal pad, and wrote out much of the speech in longhand across seven pages. At the podium, he thanked his hosts, expressed his gratitude for the award, acknowledged the "controversy" of receiving it so early in his tenure, and then got right to it.

"But perhaps the most profound issue surrounding my receipt of this prize," he said, barely two minutes into his remarks, "is the fact that I am the Commander-in-Chief of the military of a nation in the midst of two wars. . . . I'm responsible for the deployment of thousands of young Americans to battle in a distant land. Some will kill, and some will be killed." He then made this tension—between war and peace, and the struggle to forge a just peace from the ashes of war—the centerpiece of his entire speech, often considered to be one of the best of his presidency.

If there's an elephant in the room when you're speaking—criticism, a controversy, a crisis—don't hide from it or mention it only as an afterthought. Face it squarely, honestly—ideally, right at the beginning of your remarks. Your audience will appreciate your candor. You'll enhance your credibility. It might even end up being one of the best presentations of your life.

THOU SHALT USE ABSOLUTES SPARINGLY

Even as some statements are demonstrably true or false, good speakers recognize that many things in life are not black and white. There's a whole lot of gray.

"Everyone in our community believes . . ."
"All companies are . . ."
"Conservatives always . . ."
"Liberals never . . ."

Absolute statements like these—or portraying reasonable disagreements as a contest between "right" and "wrong" or "good" and "evil"—may be comforting. They give us a sense of order in a complicated world. But life is rarely so cut and dry. And when we speak in absolutes or frame arguments in such stark moral terms that allow no room for nuance, we risk spreading falsehoods and undermining our own credibility. Worse, absolutist language too often becomes a license to use any means necessary to ensure that "right" and "good"—at least as the speaker perceives it—prevail no matter what the cost.

There's a better way.

Instead of saying . . .	Try saying . . .
All/Everything	Most/Nearly all
Always	Often
Everyone	A lot of people
Never	Rarely

Of course, words like "most" can raise questions too. Our speech-writing and fact-checking teams at the White House wrestled with quantitative terms like this all the time. Here's how I've come to think about it.

"Some" = less than 50 percent
"Most" = more than 50 percent
"Vast majority" = 70 percent or more
"Nearly/almost all" = 90 percent or more

Beware, however, of "many." It can be both entirely true and totally misleading. "Many" suggests a large number, but it doesn't necessarily mean a majority. Consider these two statements: "Many people love social media." "Many people hate social media." Both are totally accurate, yet neither tells us much. When you're dealing with numbers, saying "many" may only confuse many people in your audience.

THOU SHALT NOT FEAR NUANCE

Consider this commandment a corollary to avoiding absolutes. Good speakers step into the gray and acknowledge the complexities of the world as it is. Sometimes, this can make our language more complex, too, as Obama once explained to me. "I have too many commas, semicolons, parentheses, and codicils," he admitted. But he attributed this habit to "really worrying about accuracy and precision and nuance, because you've got to get that just right."

"My attitude is, I want to explain something. And I don't care if according to the political consultant's handbook this is too complicated or too verbose or I'm using too many big words or I'm trying to pull in too much history." There's often an "assumption that people aren't going to be able to follow all this," he said, but that's "sort of patronizing to the audience."

At times, this led to disagreements with his team.

"My political advisers, correctly, determined that their job was to get me to communicate as effectively as possible to get me the most number of votes possible so I could win an election," he told me. "My thinking was, I want to win the election, but I also want to see if I can get people to see some truths that maybe we don't talk about enough in our public lives and that compound some of the problems we have or prevent us from coming together to solve problems."

He pointed to his speech in Philadelphia during the 2008 campaign where—after incendiary comments by his pastor in Chicago—Obama grappled with the deeply ingrained complexities of race in America. There was "anger and bitterness" that lingers among some Black Americans, he said in Philadelphia, as well as "a similar anger [that] exists within segments of the white community."

"I take pride," Obama told me, "in being accurate and being able to see both sides of an argument. My natural inclination when I'm speaking and when I'm communicating to audiences is to say, 'This is true, but this is also true.' And it may seem contradictory, but it's not. It's not always the most effective form of communication. But I'm acknowledging reality."

Acknowledge reality and the nuances of our complicated world, even if it sometimes takes a few more words. That's a pretty good lesson for us all.

THOU SHALT SPEAK HARD TRUTHS

In the final months of the 2008 campaign, the Republican nominee, John McCain, took questions from a crowd of voters in Minnesota.

"I can't trust Obama," one woman said. "I have read about him, and he's not, um, he's an Arab."

McCain quickly grabbed the mic.

"No, ma'am," he said. "He's a decent family man [and] citizen that I just happen to have disagreements with on fundamental issues . . . He's not [Arab]."

It wasn't the ideal answer. You can be a "decent family man" *and* Arab American; they're not mutually exclusive. And I suspect that if he'd had more time to consider the question, McCain might have formulated his answer differently. Still, in a high-stakes moment, McCain chose to tell the truth about Obama's background, even if some in his audience didn't want to hear it. In fact, when McCain defended Obama another time at the same event—telling his supporters that they didn't have to be "scared" of Obama—some in the crowd booed and jeered him.

Good speakers don't just tell their audiences what they *want* to hear, they tell them what they *need* to hear. During one speech, Obama looked into an audience of Wall Street executives and said their industry had presided over "a dangerous erosion" of "rules and principles," including throwing "lavish birthday parties with company funds." In his speech in Cairo to the world's Muslim communities, he forcefully defended "Israel's right to exist" and said that "Hamas must put an end to violence." In an address to the people of Israel, he declared that "neither occupation nor expulsion [of Palestinians] is the answer" and that "Palestinians have a right to be a free people in their own land."

When you speak, speak the truth. It's not always easy. It takes courage, especially if you're an ordinary citizen speaking truth to power.

In the fall of 2016, Rachael Denhollander—an attorney and married mother of three young children—was leading a quiet life in Louisville, Kentucky. But for many years, she'd been carrying a secret. As a fifteen-year-old gymnast, she had been sexually abused, repeatedly, by the longtime doctor for USA Gymnastics and Michigan State University, Larry Nassar.

After seeing other gymnasts come forward to reveal similar abuse by their coaches, Rachael decided it was time to go public with her own story. She filed a police report, gave an interview to the press, and became the first woman to publicly accuse Nassar, who would emerge as one of the worst pedophiles in American history.

Speaking out came with a heavy price. "I lost every shred of privacy," she said.[4] One university official smeared victims like Rachael and their lawyers as ambulance chasers looking for a "pay day." But Rachael refused to be silenced.

Ultimately, hundreds of women and girls—including several U.S. Olympic medalists—came forward to say that Nassar had sexually abused them too. After his conviction, 156 of those women stood up at his weeklong sentencing hearing and, one by one, told their stories to the world. Nassar was ordered to prison for up to 175 years. Officials at USA Gymnastics and Michigan State—some of whom allegedly knew about the abuse but failed to stop it—resigned in disgrace, one was convicted and served time in jail,[5] and the victims won historic financial settlements with USA Gymnastics and Michigan State. All because a brave band of women—"sister survivors" they call themselves—had the strength to raise their voice, starting with Rachael Denhollander.

In her statement at the sentencing hearing, Rachael addressed the packed courtroom for thirty-six minutes. She spoke with the grit of a survivor, the precision of a lawyer, and the fierce resolve of a mother determined to protect her daughters and girls around the globe from the horror she suffered. And she repeatedly asked the court and the world:

"How much is a little girl worth?"

Toward the end of her remarks, she answered her own question.

"We are worth everything, worth the greatest protection the law can offer, the greatest measure of justice available."

I hope you never experience the kind of trauma that Rachael and so many young women endured. But whatever the issue, I hope that—like Rachael—you always have the courage to speak truth to power. Especially when it's hard and those in power don't want to hear it.

Because the truth demands it.

And you're worth it.

The Download

In a world where falsehoods can travel faster than lies, stick to the facts. Your credibility depends on it. Remember the Ten Commandments of Telling the Truth:

» **Thou shalt not steal.** Don't plagiarize. If you borrow from others, give them credit.

» **Thou shalt not make shit up.** It's wrong, you'll get caught, and your credibility will be shot.

» **Thou shalt get thy facts right.** Check every fact and figure against reputable sources.

» **Thou shalt look for the source.** Found it on the internet? Try to find the original source.

» **Thou shalt be honest about the past.** It shows humility and builds credibility.

» **Thou shalt avoid "happy talk."** Even as you accentuate the positive, don't forget to acknowledge the negative.

» **Thou shalt not hide from elephants.** Make the elephant in the room the main event.

» **Thou shalt use absolutes sparingly.** Because most issues aren't black and white.

» **Thou shalt not fear nuance.** Acknowledge the gray of our complicated world.

» **Thou shalt speak hard truths.** Because the change you want often depends on speaking truth to power.

CHAPTER 12

Turn Your Words into Deeds

Talk alone doesn't cook rice.

—A Chinese proverb

By the time Barack Obama took office, the world was in the depths of the worst economic crisis in nearly eighty years. Millions of Americans had lost their jobs, homes, or businesses. Major banks had collapsed, and there were fears of another Great Depression.

Enter Timothy Geithner, Obama's Treasury secretary. Several weeks into Obama's presidency, Geithner stood at a podium in the Treasury Building and outlined "a new Financial Stability Plan" to shore up the financial sector. News channels carried his address live. The whole world was watching—and, unfortunately, the world did not like what it heard.

As Geithner spoke, the stock market dropped. By the end of the day, the Dow Jones Industrial Average had plummeted nearly 400 points. (How's that for real-time feedback on a speech?!) "It's fair to say the speech did not go well," Geithner admitted later.[1] Obama was more direct. He called the speech a "disaster."[2]

What went wrong?

Part of the problem was Geithner's delivery. "Ever since high school, I had dreaded public speaking," he explained. He didn't practice ("I kept putting off" rehearsing the speech and only did "a couple of halfhearted run-throughs" the night before). At the podium, he kept shifting back and forth on his feet ("like an unhappy passenger on an unsteady ship").[3] None of which inspired confidence.

The bigger problem with Geithner's speech, though, wasn't *how* he said it, but *what* he said—or more accurately, what he *didn't* say. The day before, Obama had told the press that Geithner would announce details about the administration's strategy for rescuing the financial sector, including a plan to address the housing crisis. Instead, Geithner said in his speech, "We will announce the details of this plan in the next few weeks."

The world wanted specifics. Geithner offered vague generalities. As a result, a speech intended to reassure the public and the markets did the exact opposite. Like Obama said, a disaster.

As a speechwriter, I believe deeply in the power of words to inspire change. But Geithner's speech reminds us of the limits of language. Sometimes, talk *is* cheap. Words alone don't heal our families, build our communities, grow our companies, unite our countries, stop wars, or cure diseases. "A speech—even an elevated, eloquent speech—is still just a speech," Ted Sorensen, John F. Kennedy's speechwriter, acknowledged. "Saying so doesn't make it so."[4]

Words without deeds are empty rhetoric. If we describe a problem without offering a solution, our words ring hollow. That's why effective speakers don't simply make a diagnosis, they offer a prescription—a way forward, especially if you're trying to rally your audience around a shared challenge.

"You have to make your language empowering," says Michele

Gelfand, the cultural psychologist from Stanford we met in chapter 6. You have to lay out the concrete actions that your audience can take to deal with that challenge—changes your company can implement to become more efficient; proposals your community can adopt to improve public safety; laws your state or country can pass to uphold the rights of every person.

As you speak, it can be helpful to give your audience a road map so they know exactly what actions you're calling for: "I believe we need to take four steps . . ." And remember, your audience can't *see* your speech, so give them little signposts to let them know you're moving from one idea to the next: "First, we should . . ." "Second, let's . . ." "Third, we can . . ." "Finally . . ."

Ultimately, however, any speaker—no matter how eloquent—is only one person. We're speaking to a group of people because we want *them* to *do something*. Which is why Obama said to his audiences, "I'm asking you to believe. Not in my ability to bring about change—but in yours." Here are some ways to turn your words into deeds and inspire your audience to bring about change you want.

SHARE SOME LESSONS

There was no excuse for Robert Caslen, the now *former* president of the University of South Carolina, to steal those lines from Admiral William McRaven's speech at the University of Texas at Austin. You've got to hand it to Caslen, though, he knows a good speech when he sees one. McRaven's commencement address remains one of the best speeches of recent decades.

Why? McRaven's remarks had all the elements of a great speech. With anecdotes from his training as a young Navy SEAL, he told stories only he could tell. He spoke in short, crisp sentences. (On the trainees who failed uniform inspection: "Those students didn't make it through training. Those students didn't understand the purpose of the drill.") He painted vivid pictures with his words. (On spending the night in the mud: "bone-chilling cold . . . chattering teeth, and shivering moans of the trainees.")

Yet what truly set McRaven's speech apart, in my view, is that he gave his audience a gift—something they could actually *use* in their own lives. He offered the graduates "ten lessons I learned from basic SEAL training"—each lesson rooted in his personal experience, yet universal in its application. Among them: starting every day by completing a simple task ("making your bed"), surrounding yourself with people to help you in life ("find someone to help you paddle"), taking risks ("sometimes you have to slide down the obstacle headfirst"), and facing down dangers ("don't back down from the sharks"). It was brilliant.

As you develop your presentation, think about the lessons you've learned in your own life that your audience might use to improve theirs. Every one of us has something to share.

- Are you a parent? What lessons have you learned from raising your children?

- Are you an entrepreneur? What have you learned from building your business?

- Are you a new citizen? What have you learned by becoming part of a new country?

- Are you an advocate? What have you learned about how to make lasting change?

- Whatever your path, what have you learned along the way that's given you a sense of pride and accomplishment? It could be as simple as "making your bed."

HAVE AN ASK, *EVERY* TIME

If our audience leaves our presentation scratching their heads—unsure of what we want them to do next—our talk has missed the mark. Badly. We've wasted everyone's time and missed an opportunity to bring people to our cause or to our point of view. Which is why every good presentation needs to have a clear call to action—what we want our audience *to do*.

Think of the speeches you've learned about in this book. Every single one had some sort of ask. Sometimes it was something tangible. Nancy Brinker asked her audiences to give their time and money to support breast cancer research and treatment. Alphonso Davies asked FIFA to award the World Cup to North America. Ellen Moy asked her neighbors to donate clothes to help a child go to school with dignity.

It can be equally powerful to ask for something *in*tangible.

What are we doing when we honor a colleague at their retirement? We're asking our coworkers to celebrate and emulate their example—a job well done.

A wedding toast? We're asking family and friends to celebrate the newlyweds, bless them with a lifetime of love, and to be there when they need us through life's ups and downs.

Even eulogies—good ones—have a call to action. We're asking our grieving family and friends not simply to remember the person we loved, but to honor them by carrying on their work and embracing the values that defined their life.

A call to action can take many forms.

Be Specific
If you're appealing to an audience for help, don't just ask for their "support"—that's too vague. They won't know what you want them

to do. Instead, ask them to *do something specific*. It shouldn't be earth shattering. Just like big problems can seem overwhelming and numb your audience, big asks can be intimidating. Often, the best call to action is a small action.

"I'm asking you to sign our petition."

"I'm asking you to volunteer an hour of your time."

"I'm asking you to become a member of our group."

"I'm asking you to donate ten dollars."

"I'm asking you to make this one change at work."

"I'm asking you to try our product."

"I'm asking you to march with us."

"I'm asking you to call your member of Congress."

"I'm asking you to vote."

What specific thing will you ask *your* audience to do?

List Your Demands

On the morning of May 24, 2022, Kimberly Mata-Rubio kissed her daughter Lexi goodbye and dropped her off at elementary school. Later that morning, Kimberly was back, along with her husband, Felix, for an award ceremony. Lexi, a fourth grader, had earned straight As and a good citizen award. After the ceremony, Kimberly and Felix headed home, told Lexi they loved her, and said they'd have ice cream that night to celebrate.

They never got the chance.

Soon after, a gunman entered Lexi's school in Uvalde, Texas, killing her, eighteen other children, and two teachers.

Lexi was just ten years old.

As a parent, I cannot even begin to imagine the agony of losing a child. I'm in awe of parents who, stricken with grief, somehow summon the will to stand up at a vigil, funeral, or memorial, speak clearly, and honor the child who was their everything. Yet that's exactly what Kimberly and Felix did.

Two weeks after the tragedy—before their little girl was even laid to rest—they shared their story with the world. Sitting side by side in their home, they testified by video to Congress. Speaking through her tears, her voice almost breaking, Kimberly described the horror of that day—how she and Felix desperately ran to the school, she in her bare feet; how she kept thinking of the last time she saw Lexi after the awards ceremony: "She turns her head and smiles back at us."

Lexi, Kimberly said, was "intelligent, compassionate, and athletic. She was quiet. Shy, unless she had a point to make." She shared how Lexi—with five brothers and sisters—loved softball and dreamed of majoring in math in college and going to law school. "That opportunity," Kimberly said, "was taken from her."

But Kimberly wasn't speaking simply to let the world know who her daughter was. Toward the end of her remarks, she laid out, in no uncertain terms, what she wanted to be done in her daughter's memory.

> *Today, we stand for Lexi, and, as her voice, we demand action. We seek a ban on assault rifles and high-capacity magazines. . . . We seek to raise the age to purchase these weapons from eighteen to twenty-one years of age. We seek red-flag laws, stronger background checks. We also want to repeal gun manufacturers' liability immunity.*

With their impassioned call for action, Kimberly and Felix joined a movement for gun safety that had been building for years. And in the weeks that followed, their campaign reached a tipping point. Americans outraged by endless mass shootings raised their voices, too, flooding the phone lines of members of Congress to demand change. It worked. A month after Lexi's death, Congress passed—with bipartisan support—and the president signed the first major gun safety legislation in nearly thirty years, including stronger background checks. It wasn't everything that families like the Rubios wanted. Far from it. But it was one step forward that, for decades, had seemed unimaginable.

When you speak—especially if you're calling on leaders to take action on a cause you care about—don't be mealymouthed. Don't issue vague appeals for "progress" or "reform" or "change." Alone, those words can mean anything—and therefore nothing.

Be like Kimberly. Say *exactly* what you want. Lay out your demands. List them, one by one. Leave no doubt about what you expect from the leaders who are supposed to have your best interests at heart. Because the more specific you are, the harder it is for leaders and institutions to shirk their responsibilities—and, over time, progress that once seemed impossible becomes possible.

ISSUE A CHALLENGE

Here's how those of us at the White House *expected* Obama's final foreign trip as president to unfold. In the election that November, voters would reject Donald Trump, who had said that protesters at his rallies deserved to be "roughed up," who spread the lie that "voter fraud is very, very common," and who in the final weeks of the campaign refused to say whether he'd accept the results if he lost. Days after the election, with Trump defeated, Obama would travel to Athens, Greece—the birthplace of democracy—and, with the ancient white marble columns of the Parthenon as a backdrop, celebrate the enduring strength of democracy in America.

Then Trump won.

Two days after the election, President Obama welcomed President-elect Trump to the Oval Office to begin the transition. That afternoon, Obama called Ben Rhodes and me into his private dining room in the West Wing. His lunch—some kind of salad, I think—was half-eaten. He wanted to talk about the speech in Athens. It had to be, we all knew, less . . . triumphant.

"We're considering moving the event indoors," Ben said. Obama agreed.

"We can still affirm the strengths of democracy," the president told us. "But we'll need to be clear-eyed about the challenges."

I worked on the speech over the next few days, sent a draft to Obama, and then waited. We flew across the Atlantic. No edits. We landed in Greece. Still no edits. Then Ben pulled me aside in our hotel lobby in Athens. Obama, he said, was wrestling with the speech.

"He wants to go deeper on the threats to democracy," Ben explained. In Ben's hotel room, we reworked the speech late into the night and sent another draft to Obama.

The next morning—the day of the speech—I expected to wake up to the president's edits. Again, nothing. After breakfast, he strolled the Acropolis, the rocky, ruin-strewn hill overlooking Athens. He toured the Acropolis Museum, taking in the ancient statues and sculptures. By now, the speech was only an hour or so away, and I was beginning to panic. *When is he going to give us his edits?*

At the museum, I waited anxiously in the hall as Obama and a few top aides ate lunch in a private room. Now the speech was in less than an hour. Finally, the door cracked open, and Ben popped his head out.

"He's ready."

Obama remained seated, his lunch—another salad, I think—

once again half-eaten. I stood there, leaning over his shoulder, as he calmly walked us through his changes. I was stunned. I thought he'd been playing tourist all morning. Turns out he'd been rethinking his remarks the whole time and rewriting during breaks. And he didn't simply have edits. He'd restructured much of the draft—circling sentences and moving them to different paragraphs; marking entire paragraphs and moving them to other pages; reshaping the back half of the speech.

That last hour was a heart-stopping blur. I still don't know how we made all his changes. At one point—with the audience already in their seats and Obama waiting backstage—catastrophe struck. I lost my connection to the internet. The speech was trapped on my laptop. I was on the sidewalk outside the arena, on my hands and knees, desperately trying to get a connection. For several minutes, nothing. Finally, I got a signal and sent the speech to the teleprompter. A short while later, listening to Obama speak to a packed auditorium, I finally realized what he'd done in his blizzard of edits.

Speaking for nearly an hour, he never mentioned Trump by name once. But there was no doubt that Obama felt democracy itself was on the line. Diverse societies require "equality before the law," Obama said, "not just for the majority, but also the minority." He rejected "the belief that some are superior by virtue of faith or ethnicity." He warned against leaders who "maintain order through violence or coercion or an iron fist," and said that "democracy depends on a peaceful transition of power, especially when you don't get the result you want."

But his speech wasn't just some academic dissertation on democracy. Obama wanted his audience—those in the room and people watching around the globe—to *do something*. With his edits, he'd transformed the second half of the speech into an unmistakable call to action. He challenged the people of the world to "defend democratic values." With globalization leaving too many workers behind, he called for "building more inclusive economies." In the face of rising nationalism and sectarianism, he challenged people everywhere to uphold "a common creed that binds us together" in "our diverse, multicultural, multiracial, multireligious world."

And if there was any doubt about what he was asking, he ended his speech by speaking directly to the citizens of the world, especially young people.

> Because in the end, it is up to us. . . . That's why the most important office in any country is not president or prime minister. The most important title is "citizen." And in all of our nations, it will always be our citizens who decide the kind of countries we will be, the ideals that we will reach for, and the values that will define us.

It was a summons to citizenship—one that Obama made repeatedly during his final months in office. Over the four years that followed, people across America and around the world rose to the moment, taking to the streets in massive numbers to stand up for women's rights, to protest racial injustice, and to demand action on climate change. In the United States, voter turnout—including among young people—surged. American democracy, though battered, endured.

Every family, community, company, and country faces its challenges. None of them can be solved by rhetoric alone. In the end, our speeches and presentations can only have an impact if our audience turns our words into action—and if we, the speaker, challenge them to do so.

As you near the end of your presentation, how can *you* challenge *your* audience to think or act differently?

LEAD BY EXAMPLE

Of course, it's easy to ask *your audience* to do something. You say it, they do it. That's one kind of call to action. Here's another: back up your words with deeds of your own.

Step Up and Do Something
Effective speakers, like effective leaders, don't say "Do as I say." They say "Do as I do." That's why, when Obama called on Americans to do more to help young men of color succeed, he spent time visiting with and talking to young men himself. When Michelle Obama and Dr. Jill Biden challenged more Americans to help support military families, they gave their own time at schools and summer camps serving military kids.

When social media CEOs were hauled before Congress in 2024 after their platforms were accused of allowing the sexual exploitation of children, some CEOs used their testimony to announce their support for new legislation to protect kids online.

Whenever possible, back up your comments with a commitment.

- Calling on your family, employees, or neighbors to volunteer more? Use your remarks to make a personal pledge to volunteer a certain number of hours yourself.

- Trying to inspire your employees to put in longer hours on an important project? Commit to working extra hours too.

- Are you an executive who has to pause bonuses, cut pay, or lay people off? Probably a good idea to announce that you're taking a pay cut yourself.

- Speaking at an event on diversity and inclusion? Don't show up empty-handed. In your remarks, make a specific, measurable commitment, perhaps that you will hire, mentor, and promote more people from communities that are underrepresented in your sector.

Put Your Money Where Your Mouth Is

On a spring day in Atlanta, the investor and philanthropist Robert F. Smith addressed the commencement ceremony at Morehouse College, the nation's only historically Black liberal arts college for men. Smith commended the graduates on their achievement, recounted his own family's inspiring journey across eight generations, and shared his own "rules to live by." Then, toward the end, he stunned everyone.

"On behalf of the eight generations of my family who have been in this country, we are going to put a little fuel in your bus," he told the graduates. "This is my class—2019. And my family is making a grant to eliminate their student loans."

The shocked graduates exploded in cheers and jumped up and down in celebration. Smith—a billionaire and the wealthiest Black American—kept his word. He ultimately donated $34 million to pay off the student loans for some four hundred members of the class. It was a life-changing gift that, with their new savings, allowed the graduates to support their families, launch new businesses, and start nonprofits to help their communities.

But Smith didn't intend his gift to be a one-off. He said his donation was a "challenge" to people to take action "through our words, and through our deeds" to "make sure every class has the same opportunity." Indeed, his extraordinary deed helped renew a national debate and spark new proposals to deal with the mountains of student debt that saddle so many young people.

Few of us will ever be able to cough up the kind of cash Smith did. Still, his example is instructive, and you don't have to be a billionaire to make a difference.

In the early days of Covid, six-year-old Sophia Myers of Perkasie,

Pennsylvania, made a video in which she asked her community to donate to a local hospital because "the nurses are working very hard." Sophia got the ball rolling by donating her own pink-and-white unicorn piggy bank, filled with her life savings: $14.70 from chores. Inspired by Sophia's example, families across the community contributed more than $60,000 to the hospital, bringing some of those hardworking nurses to tears—all because one person, a little girl with a unicorn piggy bank, led by example.

Want to inspire your audience to action? Don't just urge your listeners to support a noble cause. Do it yourself. Put your money—or your organization's money—where your mouth is.

OFFER A VISION

Perhaps the single most effective way to motivate your audience, however, is as simple as it is timeless: give them a goal—a vision to imagine in their minds, carry in their hearts, and steel their souls for the work ahead. Show your listeners how, if they heed your words, life will be better.

A vision of the world that awaits is at the center of many great religions, from Christians' conviction that—as Jesus promised in the Sermon on the Mount (a speech!)—they'll be welcomed to "the kingdom of heaven," to Muslims' faith that a life of belief and good deeds will be rewarded with eternal paradise.

The Declaration of Independence laid out a vision—"All men are created equal"—that Americans have strived to fully realize for more than two hundred years. Abolitionists risked life and limb for their vision of an America without slavery. Suffragists like Susan B. Anthony were harassed and jailed for their vision of an America where women could vote. The labor leader Cesar Chavez spoke of his "one dream, one goal, one vision: To overthrow a farm labor system in this nation which treats farm workers as if they were not important human beings." Martin Luther King, Jr.'s dream—for which activists marched and gave their lives—was of

> *that day when all of God's children, Black men and white men, Jews and Gentiles, Protestants and Catholics, will be able to join hands and sing in the words of the old Negro spiritual: Free at last! Free at last! Thank God Almighty, we are free at last!*

Ronald Reagan, adapting the words of the Puritan colonist John Winthrop, spoke of America as "a shining city upon a hill." Barack Obama said he was working for a future where "no matter what you look like, no matter where you come from, no matter who you love, no matter what your last name is, no matter how you worship, you can make it here in America if you try."

Visions are crucial in business as well. With the iPhone, Steve Jobs wasn't just introducing a new device, he had a vision to "reinvent the phone." Nike executives talk about their vision to "bring inspiration and innovation to every athlete." Workers at Tesla aren't just assembling cars, they come to work to build "a world powered by solar energy."

Visions of a better future push activists and advocates to roll up their sleeves every day. Habitat for Humanity strives for "a world where everyone has a decent place to live." The online Khan Academy seeks "a free, world-class education for anyone, anywhere." Advocates for nuclear disarmament speak of "a world without nuclear weapons."

Why are big, bold visions so powerful? For the same reason that President Kennedy said America needed to send astronauts to the moon—"because that goal will serve to organize and measure the best of our energies and skills." Even if it's a goal that may not be achieved right away, offering your vision of the world as it ought to be can challenge your audience, unite them, and inspire them for the hard work ahead.

Anyone can do it.

~

In the winter of 2007, nine-year-old Felix Finkbeiner stood before his fourth-grade class and delivered a report on the environment. He'd read about Wangari Maathai, the Kenyan activist who was awarded the Nobel Peace Prize for her campaign to plant thirty million trees across Africa, which gave Felix an idea of his own.

"I said to my class," he told me years later, "that every country in the world should plant one million trees."

How, I asked him, did he decide, as a nine-year-old, on a million trees per country?

"It just made sense to me," he said with a laugh.

It made sense to a lot of people. A few weeks later, Felix and his classmates planted their first tree—a crab apple tree—at their school outside Munich, Germany. Other teachers invited him to speak to their classes. Other towns invited him to speak at their schools. Before long, with the support of his parents, Felix was traveling around the country for tree-planting events and launching a new initiative—Plant-for-the-Planet. Three years later, they'd planted one million trees.

Felix became something of a sensation. When he was ten years old, he was invited to speak at the European Parliament ("I was too young to be scared"). When he was thirteen, he addressed the United Nations ("By then I was super nervous"), and he decided to set a new goal.

"We [can] combine our forces," he declared at the UN, dressed in a T-shirt and gray hoodie with world leaders looking on, "old and young, rich and poor, and together we can plant a trillion trees." Soon after, the United Nations put Felix and Plant-for-the-Planet in charge of the campaign to get it done, a role that earned him—though still just a teenager—recognition as one of the world's leading environmentalists.

Today, Felix is in his mid-twenties. He gives dozens of speeches a year to raise awareness and donations for his organization, which has grown to a staff of 150 people and, in cooperation with partners, has helped restore and plant nearly one hundred million trees around the world.

"I know some people resist simple slogans like 'one trillion trees,'" he told me by phone as he inspected rows of young saplings at a nursery in Mexico's Yucatán Peninsula. "But it was the right goal then. At the beginning of a movement, you have to make your goal catchy and simple so that people understand and get excited."

By exciting people, Felix helped bring new energy to the global forest movement, especially the hundred thousand young people his group has recruited in seventy-five countries to plant trees and protect forests—a global mission that began with the audacious goal of a nine-year-old boy.

What vision can you offer to inspire *your* audience? Think big. Be bold. Then boil it down. Keep it simple. Be specific. Make it catchy so people understand, get excited, and then get to work. Need some help? Try filling in the blank:

"Our vision is a community where every person is _____."

"Our vision as a company is to _____."

"Our vision is a society where every child _____."

"Our vision is a world free from _____."

The Download

Words are no substitute for action. As you wrap up your presentation, make sure your audience knows exactly what you want them *to do* after your speech is over.

» **Share some lessons.** No matter who you are or what you do, sharing lessons from your own life and work can help your listeners improve theirs.

» **Have an ask.** Every good speech has a call to action. Be specific about the steps or actions you want your audience to take. If you're calling for change, list your demands, one by one.

» **Issue a challenge.** Perhaps you're speaking because there's a sense of urgency. Issue a bold challenge to your audience to think or act differently.

» **Lead by example.** Back up your words with deeds of your own. Motivate your audience to take action by showing them that you're stepping up yourself.

» **Offer a vision.** Inspire your audience with a big idea or goal for your community, company, country, or the world as it ought to be.

CHAPTER 13

The Only Way
to End a Speech

Believe.

—Ted Lasso

The morning after the 2016 election, I arrived at the White House in stunned disbelief. Even in the final days of the campaign, with the polls tight, I knew a win by Donald Trump was possible. But I didn't think it was probable. *The same country that elected Barack Obama twice was going to turn around and elect his polar opposite?* I just couldn't wrap my mind around it.

That morning, about forty of us—speechwriters, press aides, communications staff—gathered in the press secretary's office in the West Wing. Most were young, still in their twenties or early thirties. Some had been with Obama for over a decade, since his first presidential campaign. They were Black, brown, white, gay, and straight, from every corner of the country, and they'd given years of their lives to realizing Obama's vision of a more inclusive America.

We huddled together—crammed on couches, sitting cross-legged on the floor—mostly quiet, many of us with our eyes red from a night of crying. One young woman, a Muslim American, was distraught, knowing that Trump had pledged to ban people like her from coming to the United States. Everything that we'd worked so hard for over eight long years suddenly seemed at risk.

Down the hall in the Oval Office, Obama was getting his daily intelligence briefing when someone told him that we were all gathered nearby. Word came that he wanted to see us, so we all quietly filed in. Obama stood by the large Resolute Desk, Vice President Biden by his side.

I don't remember everything Obama said that morning. I was struggling to process what was happening. I do recall him saying that he knew it was a hard day, that he was proud of us, and that we should hold our heads high, proud of the work we'd done. America has been through tough times before, he said. "History doesn't move in a straight line," he said, but instead "zigs and zags."

"We're going to be okay."

I wasn't so sure. Trump had vowed to undo everything we'd accomplished and steer the country in a radically different direction.

A few hours later, we gathered again, in the Rose Garden, as Obama addressed the nation. I watched from the side, behind a white marble column along the West Colonnade. Again, Obama tried to strike a positive tone. He said he was "heartened" by his phone call overnight with Trump, and he said that, as Americans, "we are now all rooting for his success in uniting and leading the country." Then he spoke to all the young people watching.

Sometimes you lose an election, he said, "And then if we lose, we learn from our mistakes, we do some reflection, we lick our wounds, we brush ourselves off, we get back in the arena. . . . We try even harder next time." And that, he said, is "why I'm confident that this incredible journey that we're on as Americans will go on."

For me, that wasn't cutting it. And for the first time in all the years I'd worked for Obama, I started to feel myself getting angry with him. Looking back, I now realize I just needed to direct my fury over the election results toward . . . someone. But in that moment, Obama wasn't, I felt, speaking for me—what was in my heart. I was distraught; he was keeping the faith. I was scared; he seemed almost optimistic.

On one level, I understood what Obama was doing. He had committed himself, like every president before him for more than two hundred years, to a peaceful transition of power. He *had* to stay positive. Still, part of me wanted Obama to show, even if just a little, that, like me, he was worried too. We hadn't just lost an election. We were losing, I felt, the country that I thought I knew. Back in my office, I closed the door, sat down at my desk, and broke down.

During his final two months in office, Obama did it again and again. At a convention hall in Chicago, in his farewell address, I stood in the back of the crowd as he spoke directly, once more, to young people. "You know that constant change has been America's hallmark; that it's not something to fear but something to embrace," he declared. "You are willing to carry this hard work of democracy forward. You'll soon outnumber all of us, and I believe as a result the future is in good hands."

Finally, on Inauguration Day, I stood in a cold aircraft hangar at a military base in Maryland along with hundreds of other staff. Back in Washington, Trump had just been sworn in. Now *former* president Obama, Michelle at his side, took the stage, and thanked us one last time.

Our democracy's not the buildings; it's not the monuments; it's you being willing to work to make things better, and being willing to listen to each other and argue with each other and come together and knock on doors and make phone calls and treat people with respect. And that doesn't end. This is just a

little pit stop. This is not a period. This is a comma in the con-
tinuing story of building America.

And with that, he and Michelle walked past the honor guard, up the stairs to the awaiting plane (no longer designated Air Force One), turned, gave us one last wave, and flew off.

The Obama presidency was over.

Standing there in the hangar—as Obama's plane taxied away and the crowd began to disperse—I was still afraid of what was to come. And I still struggled to make sense of his parting words over those last months.

"I am confident"?
"The future is in good hands"?
"This is just a little pit stop"?

Watching his plane fade into the distance, it finally dawned on me what he'd been doing. Obama wasn't speaking *for* me, he was speaking *to* me—and to everyone else who was so anxious about what lay ahead. He was ending his presidency the same way he had ended every speech he'd ever given—including that first speech I'd heard him deliver at the convention in Boston all those years ago—with the most powerful message that any speaker can impart to their audience.

He was trying to give us hope.

THE DANGER OF FEAR

Every day, it seems, we're told to be afraid. Demagogues tell us to fear people who look, live, love, or pray differently than us. Social media algorithms bombard us with posts that stoke our fears and outrage. News outlets feed us an endless stream of conflict and negativity. Some candidates build their campaigns around the notion that, if the other person wins, everything we hold dear will be lost forever.

Why do so many people try to stoke our fears? Well, because it often works. When we're afraid, neuroscientists tell us, the older, more primitive part of our brain—our amygdala, which helps regulate our emotions—kicks in and can overtake our more advanced prefrontal cortex, which controls higher-level thinking and rational judgment.[1] Research also shows that we tend to remember negative information and traumatic events more vividly than positive ones.[2] So, yes, appealing to people's fear *can*, at times, work. It can win votes, get more clicks online, and boost viewership. Sometimes, appealing to people's fears can even be harnessed for good—like getting people to wear their seat belt, quit smoking, or rally together to meet a legitimate danger.

Peddling fear, however, is playing with fire. Cry wolf too many times and you risk being dismissed as an alarmist. Or paint too dark a picture of the world and you risk leaving your audience feeling overwhelmed and helpless. Righteous indignation can fire up a crowd, but anger without answers can be off-putting, and too much pessimism can lead to fatalism.

If we give the impression, for example, that our community is condemned to a future of addiction or violence, why should our audience support interventions and treatments that can save lives?

If we declare that an apocalyptic future of catastrophic climate change is inevitable, why bother with the hard but necessary transition to clean energy?

In short, if we deny our audience a sense of agency—the belief that they *can* make things better—what's the point of speaking in the first place?

Fear, in the end, is also self-defeating. The fear-driven rash judgments that ensured our ancestors' survival in the jungle can threaten our collective survival in our diverse, modern world. I still think Master Yoda said it best: "Fear is the path to the dark side. Fear leads to anger. Anger leads to hate. Hate leads to suffering."

There's actually an easy way to tell if a speaker is engaging in fearmongering. When they're done talking, is their audience more afraid? More angry? More suspicious of others? More interested in vengeance and retribution? More inclined toward violence? If the answer is yes, then that speaker has started down a dark path.

There's a better way, especially when it comes to the end of your presentation—your grand finale—the part that your audience will often remember most.

In fact, I believe there's only one way.

THE POWER OF HOPE

Remember what we learned in chapter 3—a speech is not like most other forms of communication. That goes for the end of your presentation too. A news article or policy paper can focus exclusively on a rising threat. In the last scene of a book, your favorite character may die, breaking your heart. A movie or TV series can have an ambiguous ending. What *did* happen to Tony Soprano in that diner after the screen cut to black?

A speech is different. Your remarks *cannot* end on a downer or leave your audience confused—because the whole point of your presentation is to convince your audience to do something. And the only reason to do something is if you believe that the progress is possible—that your goals and vision are achievable. It's why I believe there's only one way to end a speech.

You have to end with hope.

Never underestimate the power of hope.

After all, why do we go to school for years and study and learn new skills? Because we hope to make a living, support our families, and contribute to our communities.

Why do entrepreneurs start new ventures? Because they hope to develop new products, deliver new services, and change the way we live and work.

Why do we donate to causes we care about? Because we hope to alleviate suffering, cure a disease, or save a life.

Why do prisoners of war, jailed dissidents, and hostages hold on for another day under unspeakable conditions? Because—like Vice Admiral James Stockdale, a naval aviator who was shot down over North Vietnam and survived nearly eight years of brutal torture as a prisoner of war—they hope that one day they'll finally be free. "I never lost faith in the end of the story," Stockdale said. "I never doubted . . . that I would get out."[3]

In our everyday lives and in the face of seemingly insurmountable odds, hope sustains us. Hope inspires us to survive, to strive, to imagine, to build, and to reach. Want to be a great speaker? Be a hopeful speaker who taps into the faith and aspirations of your audience.

WE'RE HARDWIRED FOR HOPE

Why is hope so powerful? Some researchers believe hope is wired deeply in our brains.

Tali Sharot—the neuroscientist who warned us about the limits of statistics in chapter 8—has spent years studying how people think about the past and future, and she's found that, as we look ahead, most of us tend to be hopeful. We "overestimate the likelihood of good events happening to us," like getting a promotion at work, she explains, "and underestimate the likelihood that bad events will come crashing down," like getting in a car accident.[4]

Sharot and others call this the "optimism bias": "the belief that the future will probably be much better than the past and present."[5] As much as 80 percent of people, according to studies, experience this bias toward optimism across countries, cultures, genders, and socioeconomic backgrounds, even in dark and difficult times.[6] Which means that most of us, Sharot argues, may be "hardwired for hope."[7] In fact, based on studies that have examined what actually causes people to change their behavior, she says that, compared to fear, "hope is a better motivator, on average, for motivating action."[8]

I hope Sharot is right because I absolutely love this idea. If we humans are biased toward optimism, then, as communicators, we have an extraordinary tool at our disposal. When you're preparing a presentation, remember that most of your audience may be hardwired for hope. They *want* an optimistic, positive vision of the future where their hopes trump their fears. They *believe* that good things can happen. And they're ready to do the work—the deeds you ask of them—because they're optimistic that tomorrow can be better than today.

WHAT HOPE REALLY IS

Of course, hope is not a strategy—in life or in public speaking. So I want to be clear about what I mean by hope—and what I don't mean. I don't mean wishful thinking or Pollyannaish optimism that's divorced from reality. That was the charge that critics and opponents leveled at Obama when he first ran for president. On the night he won the Iowa caucuses, he offered his response:

For many months, we've been teased, even derided for talking about hope. But we always knew that hope is not blind optimism. It's not ignoring the enormity of the tasks ahead or the roadblocks that stand in our path. It's not sitting on the sidelines or shirking from a fight. Hope is that thing inside us that insists, despite all the evidence to the contrary, that something better awaits us if we have the courage to reach for it and to work for it and to fight for it.

There are two parts of this passage that I encourage you to remember. First, hope is "not ignoring the enormity of the tasks ahead or the roadblocks that stand in our path." If you want to inspire an audience, your vision can't be delusional. Your hopes need to be realistic. Don't be a speaker who promises all gain and no pain—the leader who says that the war will be quick, the entrepreneur who boasts of a "revolutionary" technology that hasn't even been tested yet, the self-help guru who promises to "change your life!" . . . if you just pay for his six-step course.

When asked about his fellow prisoners of war who didn't survive the camps, James Stockdale said it was often the ones who had unrealistic expectations—that they'd be released by Christmas or Easter—only to have their hopes dashed. "You must never confuse faith that you will prevail in the end—which you can never afford to lose—with the discipline to confront the most brutal facts of your current reality, whatever they might be."[9]

So, too, when you speak to an audience. Be disciplined. Don't make promises you probably can't keep or set goals that are not attainable. Don't gloss over the hardships that your audience may face along the way. Confront the facts of your reality. That's why even as Obama called for a world without nuclear weapons, he also said, "I'm not naïve. This goal will not be reached quickly—perhaps not in my lifetime. It will take patience and persistence." Effective speakers prepare their audiences for the hurdles that stand in the way of their hopes.

The second thing I want you to remember from the passage above is how a goal or vision can only be realized "if we have the courage to reach for it and to work for it." Hope alone is not enough. Hope without action is indeed false hope. For hope to have meaning, it has to be matched by the deeds that you're asking of your audience.

As you paint a picture of the future that's possible, make sure your audience knows that nothing is inevitable. Success isn't guaranteed. Their hopes will only be realized if they *act*.

HOPE WORKS

"Hope is not just an idea. Hope is not simply an emotion," explain Casey Gwinn, cofounder of the Alliance for HOPE, and Dr. Chan Hellman, a psychologist at the University of Oklahoma, in their book, *Hope Rising*. "Hope is about goals, willpower, and pathways"— the steps we take to realize our hopes.[10] In fact, Hellman argues that hope "is a leading predictor of success" across virtually every aspect of our lives.[11] Numerous studies—what you might call the Science of Hope—seem to back him up.

Students who report feeling more hopeful are more likely to attend class, earn higher grades, and graduate.[12] Employees who are more hopeful often miss fewer days of work, are less likely to burn out, and perform better at their job.[13] People with a greater sense of hope report healthier behavior and outcomes, including fewer chronic conditions and more satisfaction with their lives.[14] In short, hopeful people are happier people who achieve more and live longer.[15]

It makes perfect sense, right? When we're consumed with despair about what tomorrow will bring, we're less likely to try to build the future we want. On the other hand, "hope, whether internally generated or coming from an outside source," explains Tali Sharot, "enables people to embrace their goals and stay committed to moving toward them." And this hopeful behavior "will eventually make the goal more likely to become a reality."[16]

As speakers, *we* can be the "outside source" that helps generate hope in our audience and makes our goals more likely to become reality. Think about the speeches you've learned about in this book. Every single one, in the end, has been about hope.

Naiara Tamminga spoke up at her city commission meeting in Michigan because she hoped her community would take action so she could walk the streets of her neighborhood without fear.

Amanda Jones raised her voice in Louisiana because she hoped that her parish would allow her to make her library a welcoming place for all children.

Olivia Vella delivered her poem to her Arizona classmates because she hoped that they would open their hearts and accept her for who she is.

Greta Thunberg—even as she told world leaders in one speech, "I don't want your hope . . . I want you to feel the fear I feel every day"—was, in her own way, expressing her hope that our leaders will finally take real action on climate change.

BE A HOPE-MONGER

When critics slammed him for talking so much about hope during his first presidential campaign, Obama had a pretty good comeback. "They call me a hope-monger," he joked. I've always loved that phrase. If our choice is between stoking pessimism or optimism, fear or hope, I say be a hope-monger. Great communicators are optimists, not pessimists. And there's never a wrong time to be hopeful, especially as you end your remarks.

Hope After a Setback

If you lead any kind of organization or business, the question is not *if* you'll face a failure, but *when*. Despite your best efforts, a new initiative might flounder, quarterly earnings sometimes miss the mark, a new product might tank. If you're running for office—or trying to pass a new law—you might not win. Great speakers, like great leaders, keep their teams focused on the long game.

When he was the CEO of Roche, a leading maker of cancer drugs, Severin Schwan would pop open a champagne bottle with his team to celebrate the end of a research project—even if it failed. "We need a culture where people take risks because if you don't take risks, you won't have breakthrough innovation," he said. "From a cultural point of view, it's more important to praise the people for the nine times they fail, than for the one time they succeed."[17]

If *your* organization fails to meet a goal, take a page from Schwan's playbook. Don't condemn failure and risk-taking. Celebrate it. Maybe even toast it. Remind your team that we have to learn from our mistakes, pick ourselves back up, dust ourselves off, work even harder, and keep striving until we achieve our next big breakthrough.

That's what Hillary Clinton told her supporters after Donald Trump won the 2016 election. "I know we have still not shattered that highest and hardest glass ceiling," she declared, "but some day someone will and hopefully sooner than we might think right now."

Even the most devastating of setbacks, as one soldier learned, can be a source of hope.

Hope Is Contagious

Cory Remsburg is lucky to be alive.

On patrol in Afghanistan in 2009, the elite Army Ranger was nearly killed by a massive roadside bomb that sent a storm of shrapnel ripping into his body and head. In the explosion and the surgeries that followed, a third of his brain was damaged or removed. He spent three months in a coma, his parents watching over him, praying for his recovery. When, miraculously, he slowly opened his eyes, he still couldn't speak for another six months.

Even today—after years of painstaking rehab, speech and physical therapy, and more than thirty surgeries—Cory is blind in one eye, largely deaf in one ear, mostly paralyzed on one side, and can't safely stand or walk on his own. He can understand what his family and friends are saying, but he struggles to get his own words out, sometimes just five or six words at a time.

Most Americans first heard about Cory when President Obama honored him as a symbol of American resilience during his 2014 State of the Union address. Recounting his years of therapy and relentless determination to stand and speak again, Obama intoned, "Sergeant First Class Cory Remsburg never gives up, and he does not quit."

Cory was sitting in the balcony. Despite his injuries, he pulled himself up, stood tall and proud in his Army uniform, and waved to the audience, which gave him a standing ovation that went on for nearly two minutes. With millions of Americans watching at home, Cory was suddenly one of the most well-known veterans in the country. Over the course of his presidency, Obama met with Cory from time to time and updated the American people on Cory's progress.

I came to consider Cory a friend and constantly marveled at his perseverance in the face of unimaginable odds. We came from vastly different backgrounds—him, the hard-charging soldier from Missouri; me, the liberal from Massachusetts—and our friendship felt like a small, unlikely bridge in a country where too few civilians truly understand the sacrifices made by our men and women in uniform and their families.

A few months after I left the White House, Cory asked me to help him with a speech of his own. His high school in St. Louis was inducting him into their hall of fame, and he had a message he wanted to share. Over the phone, I asked Cory questions about his life, the explosion, and his plans for the future. Like working with Alphonso Davies on the World Cup bid, it was one of the easiest speeches I've ever been involved with—because just about every word in the draft came straight from Cory's mouth.

But there was a problem. The draft was more than a thousand words long. Most of us could deliver that in about seven minutes. But when he practiced reading it aloud, with his speech impairment, it took Cory more than twenty minutes. Moreover, he wanted to stand up and give his speech at a podium.

I was nervous.

"Has Cory ever stood up and given a speech for that long?" I asked his dad, Craig, the night before the ceremony.

"Nope," Craig replied nonchalantly.

"Maybe we can get Cory to shorten his remarks?" I suggested.

Craig found Cory, asked him, and quickly came back with his answer.

"Nope. He says he's going to deliver the whole thing."

It seemed like an accident waiting to happen. I imagined Cory losing his balance, stumbling, and falling at the very moment when he was determined to show his resilience.

"Don't worry, Terry," Craig told me, "you'll be there to hold him up."

True, Cory had invited me to come to the ceremony, stand beside him, and steady him while he spoke. It was an honor to be asked. Still, it all seemed too much. I consider myself a hopeful person. I'd like to think I have the optimism bias too. But this seemed delusional—the kind of unfounded hope that could get Cory hurt.

The night of the ceremony in his old high school auditorium, I pushed Cory onstage in his wheelchair, stood to his left, and grabbed the gait belt around his waist as he hoisted himself up to the podium to the cheers of family and friends. On Cory's right, his older brother, Chris, also an Army veteran, held the leash of Cory's service dog, Leo, a large brindle Dutch shepherd.

Cory had been a bit of a class clown in high school, and even with his injuries he never lost his wicked sense of humor. He started his remarks by saying how unlikely it was that he was being inducted into their hall of fame.

"I never thought I'd be standing here. Most of my teachers never thought it either!"

Standing in his dark blue Army dress uniform, his medals and ribbons gracing his chest, Cory shared the story of his service—enlisting in the Army on his eighteenth birthday, deploying ten times to Iraq and Afghanistan. He paid tribute to one of his best friends who'd been killed in the explosion, Sergeant Robert Sanchez. Cory thanked everyone who'd helped him persevere through years of recovery—family, friends, doctors, therapists, and his fellow Rangers, whom he called "my brothers for life."

Barely ten minutes into his remarks, however, I could feel Cory shifting his weight between his feet, trying to keep his balance. My right hand started to go numb, and I wasn't sure how much longer I could hold him up.

But Cory seemed unfazed. Reading from the script that he had refused to trim, he turned his speech into a celebration of other wounded warriors and their caregivers.

"We can never thank . . . them . . ." he said, at times closing his eyes in concentration as he pushed out each word between breaths, "or support them enough."

Fifteen minutes in, Cory's whole body seemed to be wobbling. Behind the podium, his left leg was shaking uncontrollably. Now my entire right arm felt numb. Before the speech, I'd worried that Cory wouldn't be able to stand up for so long. Now I wasn't sure I could.

"On that day in Afghanistan . . ." he went on, "I was some-how spared . . . and now I'm trying to make . . . the most of the extra . . . time I was given. As you can tell . . . it's hard for me to speak . . . but I have a voice, darn it . . . I will keep raising my voice for other veterans. . . . This is my new mission . . . and I'm just getting started."

"I hope my story can be an example," he said, coming to a close. "We all have challenges . . . everybody falls down. . . . But I'm here to tell you . . . if I could pick myself back up . . . and push on . . . then you can too. Nothing in life that's worth anything . . . is easy. Don't ever give up. Never quit."

Cory had managed to stand and speak for more than twenty-four minutes.

By the end, much of the audience, including his stepmom, Annie, was in tears. As he finished—"God bless America, and, of course, Rangers lead the way!" with his fist in the air—the crowd was on their feet, applauding, cheering, and whistling.

It was one of the most inspiring speeches I've ever heard.

Over the years, Cory has delivered a version of that speech to audiences across the country dozens of times. His hope—his resilience, his unshakable optimism, his hopes for himself and our country—has proven contagious. Moved by his message, more Americans have come to see the true costs of war. More people have donated to charities supporting veterans. More wounded warriors have been inspired to push on in their own recovery.

For Cory and his father, the frequent travel can be exhausting. But Cory wouldn't have it any other way. I asked him once why he does it, and why he always ends his remarks the way he does. He responded with three simple words:

"To give hope."

The Download

Just like you thought deeply about the opening of your presentation, think hard about your closing—your grand finale. No matter how great your speech is, your audience probably won't recall most of what you said, but they'll likely remember your ending and how it made them feel. Tap into their bias toward optimism. End your remarks with a message of hope. You'll empower your audience with a belief in their own capacity to push on, pick themselves up if they fall, and, just maybe, make tomorrow a little better than today. There are many ways to do it.

» **End by recapping your main points.** Quickly summarizing your key points can empower your audience with a to-do list that can inspire and motivate them for the hard work ahead.

» **End with your most hopeful story.** When you were researching your remarks, what was the story, anecdote, or quote that gave you the most hope? End with that. It's especially powerful in tributes, toasts, and eulogies. Like any good performer, save your best for last.

» **End by bookending.** Did you begin your remarks with a story? You don't have to tell it all at once. Perhaps save the end of the story for the end of your speech. It will keep your audience engaged and give them the emotional closure they've been waiting for.

» **End with a question.** If you're challenging your audience to think or act differently, perhaps end by speaking directly to your listeners: "What will *you* do?"

» **End with your vision realized.** If you've offered your audience a bold vision to inspire them, paint a hopeful picture of how your family, community, company, country, or world will be better once your vision is realized.

There, you've done it. You've prepared your presentation—a Beginning that grabs your audience, unites them around a shared purpose or idea, and speaks to their values; a Middle where you speak from your heart and to theirs in language that is clear and maybe even sings; and an End where you ask your audience to take action, perhaps in pursuit of a vision that gives them hope.

You're done!

Not quite . . .

Showtime

*Leave 'em wanting
more*

CHAPTER 14

Make It Better

For it is with words as sunbeams—the more
they are condensed, the deeper they burn.

—Robert Southey

There were six words that my fellow speechwriters and I never wanted to hear from President Obama after we gave him a draft:

"I could deliver this speech today."

Translation: he didn't want to deliver the speech today.

"We've got a few more days," he'd say. "So let's make it even better."

"You have everything in there," he might add, leaning back in his chair behind the large Resolute Desk in the Oval Office as we took notes. "But here's how I'd order it." He'd then proceed to lay out a new argument or restructure the whole speech. Or maybe, after breaking out his yellow legal pad overnight and adding hundreds of new words of his own, he'd remark, "Also, if we can trim a little, that would be helpful."

This is another reason why the 50–25–25 Rule works so well. If you spend about 50 percent of your time thinking and organizing your presentation and another 25 percent of your time writing it out, that leaves you 25 percent of your time to make it better.

Think of it like crafting a beautiful piece of woodwork. First, you imagine your piece and select the wood (you think through and research your remarks). Then you cut and carve the wood (you craft your remarks). Finally, you sand it (you smooth out the rough edges in your draft) and varnish it (you add the finishing touches, your final edits) so it truly shines. And when you build in time to make it shine, you can take any piece of work—wood or words—from good to great. Here's how.

STOP THE EARBASHING

Perhaps you've heard that the attention span of a typical audience is only ten to fifteen minutes—or that you only have just a few seconds to capture the attention of your audience. But research shows that it's not so simple.[1] Which makes sense. At one time or another, we've all been captivated by a great speaker who talked for twenty or thirty minutes, or longer.

Still, there are good reasons to keep our remarks as short as possible.

For one, it's always better to leave our audience wanting more than wanting us to shut up already. Sadly, too many speakers just don't get it. Your colleague's PowerPoint has a hundred slides. In a job interview, the overeager candidate drones on. Oscar winners won't stop talking, so the Academy cranks up the music—at times a song fittingly called "Too Long." At a conference a few years ago, one speaker went on for so long that conference organizers sent him a desperate message on the teleprompter: "PLEASE END NOW! (Seriously)."[2]

As he had as a younger politician, Obama sometimes struggled to keep it brief as president. "There are times when I am too long-winded," he admitted to me once, pointing to press conferences and debates, where he felt the format was "artificial and stilted" ("I was just never that good"). "He's going on way too long!" Obama said, comically impersonating frustrated advisers who urged him to be more succinct. "He's explaining too much stuff!"

"But most people never have to speak like that," Obama pointed out, noting that debates and press conferences are a "particular template of political speechmaking." Still, those experiences taught him the value of being succinct. "I definitely had to work hard on skinnying down, narrowing, and disciplining myself, and guard against my tendency to overexplain stuff, get into the weeds, and go off on tangents."

Australians have a wonderful phrase for too much talking—"earbashing." As speakers, we should raise our right hand and take an oath: "I do solemnly swear that I will never bash the ears of my audience."

Easier said than done, I know.

THE BEAUTY IS THE BREVITY

As speakers, we often feel a tension between being substantive and being brief. In our desire to be substantive and to show how much we know—especially at work or in job interviews—we tend to speak too much. When we try to keep our remarks short, we worry we're not being substantive enough. That's why it's often harder to prepare a short presentation than a long one. When we can't say *everything*, we have to work extra hard to say *anything*. Still, it's possible.

More often than not, the beauty is in the brevity. Abolitionist Sojourner Truth's forceful speech in 1851 on women's rights was less than four hundred words long. Ronald Reagan's moving address after the explosion of the space shuttle *Challenger* was just over four minutes. Lincoln's Gettysburg Address imagined a "new birth of freedom" for the United States in only 272 words—and just ten sentences. (In contrast, the featured speaker at Gettysburg— the famed orator Edward Everett—spoke for more than two hours, and his speech has been largely forgotten.) Though not a speech, Michael Jordan's statement upon returning to the NBA in 1995, sent by fax, showed how even just a few words can become iconic: "I'm back."

Many of the speeches you've learned about in this book—Brayden Harrington speaking through his stutter, Naiara Tamminga speaking her truth to her city commissioners, Alex Myteberi offering his home to the boy from Syria, Kimberly Mata-Rubio demanding that Congress take action on gun violence—were just a few minutes long. And they were powerful.

You don't have to talk a lot to say a lot.

It's a lesson that was drilled into me when a museum asked for my help writing the brief messages that would greet visitors as they entered each new exhibit. Entire books have been written about the sweeping topics covered by each exhibit—global events spanning years, rife with nuance and complexity. I had to boil them down to a few sentences—just seventy-five words.

Forced into generalities, my first drafts often said nothing. Editing and improving each seventy-five-word message—saying something without saying a lot, keeping what was truly essential, cutting what was not—ended up taking me several *hours*. It was hard. But it was worth it. Being brief forces us to think more deeply about our subject and express ourselves as simply and directly as possible.

HOW TO EDIT

So, yes, less truly is more. But how do you get to less?

Cut 15 Percent

On a flight from Brazil to Chile aboard Air Force One, I was in my seat making what I thought were the final edits to a speech Obama would give in Santiago and tossing back the sugary cocktail that kept me awake on long trips: handfuls of jelly beans washed down by swigs of Coke. (Healthy? No. But, for me, stronger than a Red Bull.) Suddenly, the president was standing over me, holding the draft in his hand.

"This is a good six-page speech," he said. "It would be a great five-page speech."

I thought he was messing with me. We'd already begun our descent into Santiago, and his speech was just a few hours away.

"See if you can shave a page off," he added, as he handed me the draft and walked back to his cabin to be with the First Lady and his daughters.

Shave off a whole page?! Was he serious?

He was.

I checked the draft to see if he had any suggestions on what to cut. He didn't.

Most of the time, I tried to approach editing like a surgeon with a scalpel, making precise incisions, carefully carving out unnecessary words and sentences, and gently stitching the speech back up, leaving no scars.

To lop off a whole page, I needed a machete. With Air Force One now in a rapid descent—the aircraft shaking, making it hard for my fingers to find the keyboard—I hacked away.

A sentence here? Too long. Gone.

A paragraph there? Too much detail. Bye-bye.

A whole section? The world could live without it. Adios.

It wasn't pretty. Language that had been carefully negotiated with our policy experts disappeared with the tap of my delete button. Initiatives that the president would have announced were now relegated to a press release. Where I had gouged out text, the remaining transitions were serviceable, but not always smooth.

But it worked. The speech was suddenly a page—about 15 percent—shorter.

A few hours later, Obama stood in the hall of Santiago's cultural center and delivered his address to diplomats from across the Western Hemisphere. He spoke for a little over thirty minutes. Had we not made all those cuts, he might have spoken for closer to forty minutes—not the end of the world, but also not necessary. None of the policy experts complained that something crucial had been cut. Obama's core themes remained intact, and his remarks were well received.

Obama did this *a lot*, often right before a speech. "See if you can trim a little." "See if you can cut a few paragraphs." No suggestions. No sense of what he thought was worth saving or scrapping. Just a vague, yet unequivocal, presidential order. And when the president tells you to cut, you cut.

It often sent me into a panic. Sometimes I got annoyed. *Why is he doing this to me? The speech is great the way it is!*

But over time, I realized what Obama was doing. He was teaching us—forcing us to decide what was truly necessary. And I have to admit, he was right. The cuts made the speech shorter, sharper, better—every time. You see, just because you *can* speak for fifteen, thirty, or forty minutes doesn't mean you *should*. You don't have to say everything, everywhere, all the time.

Done with a draft of your presentation? Take it, and as Obama would say, see if you can trim a little. Better yet, like the Santiago speech—see if you can cut 15 percent. Even if you can't shave off that much, you'll cut more than you thought possible—and your remarks will be better for it.

Slash Needless Words

Being in the audience when Obama addressed the 2004 convention in Boston was a thrill. But if I'm being honest, the real highlight for me, as a young speechwriter, was when our room of exhausted wordsmiths received an unexpected visitor—President Kennedy's legendary speechwriter, Ted Sorensen.

By then, Sorensen was in his mid-seventies, but with his bright eyes, square jaw, and neatly parted black hair, he still exuded the optimism and idealism of the Camelot years. On a personal level, it felt like my life had come full circle. Growing up in Massachusetts, as a kid fascinated with politics, I sometimes listened to an album of famous Kennedy speeches that my mum had given me as a gift. Now, here I was, with the writer who had helped JFK craft those very words. I couldn't believe it.

Even better, Sorensen turned his visit into a teachable moment. He told us a story about a sign outside a store selling fish. The sign read: "Fresh Fish for Sale Here Today."

"Are there any words on that sign that you can do without?" Sorensen asked us.

"Fresh," I thought to myself. *You don't need the word "fresh." It can just say "Fish for Sale Here Today."*

I caught myself.

No wait, you don't need "today" either. It can just say "Fish for Sale Here."

Other speechwriters chimed in with their own cuts. After a minute or so, Sorensen put his hand up, and we all fell silent.

"There's only one necessary word on that sign," he said with a smile. "'Fish.'"

We'd been schooled by the master. It was Sorensen's way of

teaching us the timeless lesson captured in *The Elements of Style*, the classic book on writing: "Omit needless words."

Presidents and prime ministers can often get away with long speeches. For the rest of us, good speeches are short speeches. Fewer pages. Fewer paragraphs. Fewer sentences. Fewer words. Fewer syllables.

Sometimes, it's just "fish."

As you edit your presentation:

- Look closely at each paragraph. Does it advance your story?

- Study each sentence, each anecdote, each detail, each adjective. Does it add anything new that you or others haven't already said? Are you saying what only you can say?

- Scrutinize each word. Is it *truly* necessary?

If the answer is no, let it go.

And when in doubt, cut it out.

It's not easy. If Obama was ever reluctant to trim down a long speech, Jon Favreau took it upon himself—even cutting out words that Obama himself had written.

"You've become very good at cutting," he told Jon, who wasn't sure if it was a compliment.

Want to be a good speaker? Get good at cutting. Break out the machete. Slash needless paragraphs, sentences, and words. Make it a game. Challenge yourself: I *will* cut two hundred words from this draft! And then cut some more.

Get a Second Opinion. And a Third. And a Fourth.

A few months before the 2008 election, Obama traveled to Berlin to deliver a major address on America's role in the world. The speech, drafted by Ben Rhodes and Jon Favreau, included a beautiful German phrase they had found: how people are connected by "a community of fate"—*schicksalsgemeinschaft*.

Like any good speechwriter, Ben did his due diligence. First, he googled *schicksalsgemeinschaft*, which turned up results in German he couldn't understand. So he asked the campaign's Europe experts, who didn't see any problem. Finally, he flagged it for the German translator who was reviewing Obama's remarks.

"Unfortunately, there is a link to the Nazis," the translator emailed back. "Hitler himself used the term '*schicksalsgemeinschaft*.'"

"It was terrifying," Ben remembers. Obama had almost echoed Hitler. In Berlin. Ben quickly deleted the phrase and reworked the passage, saving Obama from a catastrophe on the world stage— and the *schadenfreude* of his political opponents back home.

As you edit your remarks, share your draft with friends, family, coworkers, maybe even any experts you know. Ask for their *honest* feedback ("Is this clear? What am I missing? Anything I can cut? How can I make this better?"). Ask them what they think your main message or argument is. If they don't know—or if their answer is different from the 10-word summary that you wrote down when you started—that's . . . not good. Back to the drawing board.

At the White House, we shared drafts of Obama's speeches with dozens of people, sometimes more than a hundred. As you've seen in this book, some of the edits we got back were bonkers—too wordy and wonky. Invariably, though, someone somewhere would have a suggestion that we hadn't thought of—or a correction—that made the speech better.

You may not like all the critiques you receive. Some may hurt. But you asked for—and you *need*—honest feedback. That's the whole point of sharing your draft with others—so they can spot any weaknesses and you can make it stronger. Their honesty is a gift. Accept it with humility. Don't instinctively reject their critiques. In- stead, try this: assume they're right and ask yourself whether there's a way to incorporate their suggestions—especially if multiple people are telling you the same thing. Even if it means changing or cutting something you love.

In the end, though, no good speech has ever been written by committee. It's *your* speech. It has to be in your voice, from your perspective, the way you would say it. Don't let yourself get bullied into saying something that doesn't feel authentic to you. If you want to *be* yourself at the podium, you have to *trust* yourself as you edit. Go with what feels right and natural *to you*.

Ask a Bot

Having a hard time editing your remarks? This is another area where AI can help. In fact, this is one of my favorite ways to use a chatbot. Bots can be surprisingly good editors. Just paste a section of your draft into a bot and give its marching orders:

"Remove 50 words from the following text." Seconds later, your draft is 50 words shorter. I do it a lot and sometimes can't even tell what was removed—a sign that, whatever it was, it wasn't necessary.

"Make the following text more formal/less formal."

"Make the following text clear for a beginner/more suitable for a subject matter expert."

"Make the following text more engaging for an audience of [describe your audience]."

Again, a bot won't get it right every time. But neither will our friends and colleagues who are humans. Give it a try. Worst case, you ignore the edits and stick with what you have—and, unlike your human friends, you don't have to worry about hurting the bot's feelings.

HOW TO REHEARSE

Here's another way that Obama became a skilled orator after freezing up in that conference room as a young community organizer in Chicago.

"I would practice," he told me once, with a bemused look as if he were stating the obvious.

He rehearsed his speech for the 2004 convention many times. "I had never read off a teleprompter before," he said. David Axelrod watched him rehearse. "The more he practiced, the more he owned the words, the more organic they became," Axelrod said. "If the teleprompter had broken, he could have delivered his speech from memory."

Obama even practiced as president. In the lead-up to State of the Union addresses, staff would set up a teleprompter in the White House Map Room so Obama could read through every line. "I don't think those were fun sessions for him," Jon Favreau remembers with a laugh. "We nitpicked every sentence. But it allowed him to see where he was putting his emphasis, how fast he was speaking, where the rhythm was. Saying the words out loud beforehand made him an even better speaker at the podium."

Remember, a speech *is*, in part, a performance, and like any good performer, you have to rehearse. Practice builds muscle memory. Over time, as you start a new sentence, the rest of the sentence will come more naturally. The more times you say the words, the easier they'll be to pronounce later. Even if you've been speaking for years, the more you practice the better you'll be.

Here's how.

Print It Out

Rehearse with the same copy of your speech that you'll have when you deliver your remarks. Even if you don't plan to deliver your presentation word for word, *practice it* word for word. Print your script out in a format that's easy to see and read. For example:

- Enlarge the text (at the White House, we printed Obama's speeches in 24-point).

- Space out your lines (for Obama, we used 1.5 line spacing).

- Bold the entire speech, so every word pops off the white page.

- End every page with a period, so you're not flipping pages in the middle of a sentence.

- Leave the bottom quarter or third of the page blank, so you're not looking down at the bottom of the page—chin to chest—when you should be looking up at your audience.

Yes, this can sometimes create a *lot* of pages. But trust me, it works. Because the easier it is to see the words on the page, the easier it will be to deliver them. And if the thought of managing all those pages terrifies you, consider doing what we did for Obama—put them in a three-ringed binder, in plastic sleeves, with your pages on the front and back. You'll have fewer pages to flip, and, if the event is outside, your speech won't be blowin' in the wind.

Don't Try to Memorize It
Some people are blessed with a great memory. Obama told me that he memorized his first big speech at the *Harvard Law Review* dinner as well as a few other speeches during his career. Donovan Livingston committed to memory the entire spoken-word poem that he recited at his graduate school convocation. Olivia Vella memorized the slam poem she delivered to her Arizona classmates. If, like them, you think you can remember every word, have at it.

If you're like me, though, you can't remember where you put your car keys—never mind all the words in a speech. For us, trying to memorize a presentation can be a train wreck waiting to happen. Forget one word, and we risk losing our train of thought. Skip over a sentence, and our presentation goes off the rails. No need to court disaster. In my experience, I've found that most speakers don't memorize their remarks—and you don't have to either.

Hear Your Words

Practicing your remarks out loud is important for several reasons. For one, you'll immediately see how long your presentation will actually take. Too long? Cut it down. Too short? Maybe add some more meat. Just right? Keep rehearsing.*

By practicing out loud, you'll also see whether any words trip you up. Words like "inextricably" and "phenomenon" are easy to read on the page, but harder to pronounce. I can't seem to say "indefatigable." I was once working with a speaker who, during rehearsals, every time he came to the phrase "under*served* communities" pronounced it "un*deserved* communities." Yikes. No matter how hard he tried, he kept calling them "un*deserved*." So we changed the text to "marginalized communities," which he pronounced just fine.

Multisyllabic words can be . . . formidable; if you're stumbling over one, try using a one-syllable word instead. It's not as . . . hard.

Feel Your Fears

If you struggle with public speaking, practicing out loud can also help prepare you for any anxieties you might experience at the podium.

---

* Some speech coaches recommend practicing in front of a mirror or videotaping your rehearsal. I'm agnostic. On the one hand, some people find that recording and watching themselves is helpful. If it works for you, go for it. On the other hand, I worry that this puts too much focus on body language, which, while important, I think is often overrated (more on that in chapter 15).

"If you know that your heart will pound when you speak, practice speaking while your heart is pounding," explains Dr. Ellen Hendriksen, the psychologist from Boston University's Center for Anxiety and Related Disorders. She suggests, for example, rehearsing a presentation after doing some exercise, a form of what's called interoceptive exposure. "By exposing yourself to the internal sensations you'll feel when you give your speech later, you're trying to make your brain bored with the feared stimulus," she explains. "You're trying to build a tolerance."

In other words, practice feeling what it feels like to feel anxious. If you can, do some jumping jacks. Or go for a brisk walk or run. If you can't do that, wave your arms around. *Feel* your heart rate speed up, your chest tighten, your breath shorten. *Then* practice your presentation. The more you get used to feeling this way during practice, the less it may scare you when you speak.

STILL NERVOUS?

You've prepared your presentation. You've edited it. You've practiced it. Still, you might be anxious. It's alright. Here are a few other things I've learned to tell myself so that I can stay calm in the final days before a presentation.

- "I *will* make mistakes." Perfection is impossible. Mistakes are inevitable. Even the best speakers mispronounce a word or stumble over a sentence. I will too—and that's okay.

- "When I make a mistake, I will recover." We tend to catastrophize, even though our worst fears rarely come to pass. We *don't* trip going onstage and fall flat on our face. The audience *doesn't* burst out laughing at us. Dr. Hendriksen encourages us to make our fears "smaller and more specific"

(*I may lose my train of thought for a moment*) and have a plan to recover (*I will pause for a moment, take a breath, collect myself, find my place in my script, and keep speaking*).

- **"The audience won't see my nerves."** With our heart racing and our hands shaking, we assume our audience will see through us and spot our panic. Not necessarily. Psychologists call this the illusion of transparency.[3] As Dr. Hendriksen explains, "How we feel is often not how we look to our audience." After shaking and stammering while delivering my skit that night in the karaoke bar in Japan, I told a coworker who had been sitting right next to me how embarrassed I was about being so nervous. He had no idea what I was talking about. As you practice, try to remember what my coworker said to me—and what so many anxious speakers have heard from their audience afterward—"You didn't *look* nervous."

- **"I'll be better than I think."** It can be excruciating to watch a video of a presentation you gave. But if, like me, you've ever done it, you may have noticed something. The word you thought you butchered was actually quite clear. The pause that you felt went on forever only lasted a few seconds. Remember what a group of British researchers found when they asked people to watch videos of themselves speaking—an astonishing 98 percent said they came across better than they had predicted beforehand.[4] You will too.

Here are two other things you might try doing in the days before your presentation:

- **Visualize your success.** Like so many great athletes—for example, the batter stepping up to the plate—imagine yourself hitting a home run. Close your eyes. See yourself standing there in front of your audience, delivering your remarks with confidence, the audience smiling back, nodding along in agreement, applauding you when you're done. It works for a lot of people, including me. And it's not just in our heads. Studies show that visualization can help reduce stress and anxiety and prime our brains and bodies for the performance we want to deliver.[5]

- **Do a dry run.** Don't just see your success in your mind's eye; see it in person. If possible, go to the room where you'll be speaking. Go onstage. Stand at the podium. Look out at the room. Feel the space. Practice your presentation. Test any slides, audio, or video; better to catch any problems now than to have a tech meltdown in front of a crowd.

I tried a lot of these techniques as I prepared to give the first big speech of my adult life.

Several months after getting that phone call from Antti, the Finnish speechwriter, he welcomed me to his hometown of Hämeenlinna, about an hour's drive from Helsinki. The small Nordic city was as I expected—orderly, cold, and, by late afternoon, as dark as midnight. Antti welcomed me by paraphrasing a famous sign that had once greeted arriving tourists: "Nobody in their right mind would come to Finland in November. Except you, badass. Welcome."

I didn't feel like a badass.

In the months since Antti's call, I'd tried to remember all the lessons I'd learned as a speechwriter and that I've shared with you in this book. I thought about the stories that only I could tell—my experiences at the White House. I thought of my presentation as a performance and decided that, instead of slides full of words, I'd project photographs of working with President Obama.

I did my research, learning everything I could about my audience—Finland, its people, and their values. I wrote out every word, even though I knew I wouldn't have a podium. I practiced my draft out loud, over and over—not memorizing it, but internalizing it, getting comfortable with it. I timed myself, cut my script, then cut it some more. When I arrived in Hämeenlinna, I went out for drinks with some friendly Finns who taught me how to pronounce their favorite phrases (which got harder with every beer).

And still, I was nervous.

But I wasn't scared. Not only because I'd prepared so much. But because the night before my remarks, Antti took me to the theater where I'd speak. It was dark and empty. Then Antti flipped a switch, flooding the room with light. In that moment, it all became clear. I imagined the seats filled with people. I imagined Antti introducing me. I imagined taking the stage, standing there, giving the speech only I could give. I could see it.

I still didn't feel like a badass.

But, for the first time in my life, I thought, *Yeah, I can do this*.

The Download

Remember the 50–25–25 Rule: use the last 25 percent of your time to make your presentation even better and practice.

» **Cut 15 percent.** No matter how short your speech is, it can always be shorter. Go through your draft and try to cut it by 15 percent. Take a break. Come back. Cut some more.

» **Slash needless words.** Is every idea and word in your draft truly necessary? Probably not. Aim for fewer pages, fewer paragraphs, fewer sentences, fewer words, fewer syllables.

» **Share your draft.** Ask family, friends, coworkers, and experts for their honest feedback. Set aside your ego. Be open to their suggestions. But in the end, say what feels right *to you*.

» **Practice, practice, practice.** Print out your remarks in large font so they're easier to see and read. Hear your words; if you stumble, choose a different word. Feel your fears by getting your heart racing and practicing what it feels like to feel anxious.

» **Be kind to yourself.** Remind yourself: I will make mistakes, and that's okay. When I make a mistake, I will recover. The audience won't see my nerves. I'll be better than I think.

» **Get ready.** In the final days before your presentation, visualize your success. If you can, go to the room where you'll speak. Get to know the space. Do a dry run. The night before you speak, get a good night's sleep. Because when you wake up . . .

The day of your speech has arrived.

CHAPTER 15

Stand and Deliver

I get butterflies, don't get me wrong. I get
nervous and anxious, but I think those are all
good signs that I'm ready for the moment.

—Steph Curry

Lynne Benioff and her husband Marc, the CEO of Salesforce, are among the world's leading philanthropists. Together, they have donated more than one billion dollars to charitable causes and are invited often to fundraising galas. But Lynne calls herself "a lifelong introvert" who finds public speaking "terrifying." So, when—as cochair of a fundraising campaign—she had to speak at the opening of a new park in the Presidio of San Francisco overlooking the Golden Gate Bridge, we worked together to make sure she was ready.

Weeks before the event, we talked out what she wanted to say. We drafted every word, and Lynne rehearsed. "I practiced my speech out loud so many times," she said, "that my body and my mouth just *knew* what I needed to do at the podium. I was prepared for anything, including my intense nerves."

At the event, she stashed a protein bar under her seat, "in case I felt like I was low on blood sugar." As she approached the podium, she carried a bottle of water "in case my mouth dried up" and lozenges "in case I started to cough."

And when it came time for her to speak, Lynne stepped up and . . . hit it out of the park.

"I was present in the moment," she told me afterward. "I took deep breaths. I looked at my husband and kids in the audience to calm myself down. I tried to channel the joy and excitement of the audience, and it felt great. I felt like I was on fire. Afterward, I was totally drained. But for the first time in my life, I really enjoyed speaking!"

When the day comes to give your speech, here's how you can be on fire and enjoy it too.

GET IN THE ZONE

Remember, any presentation is, in part, a performance. On the day of yours, like any good actor or athlete, you need to get in the zone.

Let Your Clothes Do the Talking
Your attire shouldn't be an afterthought. What you wear can reinforce what you say. Think of the multicolored kente stole that Donovan Livingston wore at his graduation to affirm his identity as a Black graduate. Or how Alphonso Davies addressed FIFA wearing red and white to show his Canadian pride. In 1998, Kate Logan, a high school senior in Vermont, stunned her audience by stripping naked during her commencement address and delivering the rest of her remarks in the nude. She said it was to express her individuality. Gotta give her credit. Like any good speaker, she truly revealed herself.

There's no dress code for being a good speaker (although, as a general rule, I say keep your clothes on). Of course, dress for the occasion. Look the part. At the same time, don't be afraid to wear something a little different to reinforce your message—a pin to show solidarity with your audience, the colors of the school or country where you're speaking.

But don't overthink it. Most of the speakers you've met in this book stood up and spoke wearing their everyday clothes. And they were great. Because what you say is far more important than what you wear. Delivering her poem at school, Olivia Vella wore her favorite T-shirt because, she said, "It made me feel safe." Wear what feels safe and comfortable *for you*.

Make Some Friends

Thinking back to his days as a community organizer in Chicago, Obama told me that another reason it was so important to listen to folks in those church basements was because it made speaking to them later "less nerve-racking." Instead of speaking to "complete strangers," he said, "I was talking with people with whom I'd had a conversation. A relationship was formed and some baseline of trust."

You can do it too. If you can, use the hours before your presentation to mingle with people who will be in your audience. Strike up a conversation. Make some friends. Listen to what they're interested in. You might even tweak your presentation to make it even more personal: "Earlier, I was talking to Melissa, who's here today. She told me . . ."

Keep Correcting . . .

Until you start speaking, it's never too late to fix something in your presentation that's wrong.

One night, while out for pizza with my family, I got an urgent message on my BlackBerry from our White House fact-checkers. The speech that Obama was about to deliver had an awful mistake.

The fallen Marine who he planned to honor was killed in Afghanistan, not (as I had written) in Iraq. The Marine's family would be in the audience. They'd already suffered an unimaginable loss. Now, because of me, the president was going to screw up the story of their son's service.

I sent a frantic message to staffers at the speech, on the other side of the country. It was too late, they said. Obama was already speaking.

I felt sick to my stomach.

Standing offstage, Marvin Nicholson, the president's tireless trip director, had an idea. The president was using a teleprompter, and his tribute to the Marine didn't come until the end of his remarks. There was still time. But not much.

Marvin ran over to the teleprompter operator, who—even as Obama was speaking—pivoted to a second screen, popped open the script, corrected the mistake, and closed the speech back up.

Moments later, Obama—unaware of the mad scramble backstage—told the story of the Marine the way it deserved to be told: accurately.

On the other side of the country, staring down at my pizza, I breathed a sigh of relief.

In the hours before your remarks, keep practicing out loud. Keep scrutinizing every word. And if you catch a mistake, correct it. Until you say it, there's always time to make it right.

. . . but Stop *Editing*

When you're the president, the audience waits for you. The speech doesn't start until you start giving it. Which I guess is why Obama was usually so nonchalant in the final moments before a speech. He'd sometimes edit. And edit. And edit. Until. The. Very. Last. Minute. The audience would be in their seats, cheering or stomping their feet with anticipation. And Obama would be sitting backstage, maybe sipping his tea with honey and lemon, and calmly handing us last-minute changes, which we'd have to race over to the teleprompter operator to frantically type in, word by word.

Every time this happened, it took years off my life.

I do not recommend doing this.

Yes, keep practicing your remarks. Make little tweaks if you want to. Change a word here, delete a sentence there. But in the final hours and minutes before you speak, don't attempt any major surgery. Don't rewrite your presentation.

At the White House, the most satisfying email our team of writers sent before every speech had this header: "This is final." Or, if someone caught a mistake that we had to fix and send it again: "This is final final."

Make your remarks final final. Stop editing. And just practice.

Count Your Pages

"Hello, Vegas!"

And with that, Obama was off, delivering a fiery campaign speech. He thanked his hosts, expressed his gratitude to his supporters, and proceeded to make his case. Several minutes in, however, he turned a page of his script and saw . . .

Nothing.

Someone had forgotten to put the rest of his speech in the binder.

Obama was on his own.

"What did you think of the speech?" he asked Marvin Nicholson afterward.

"It was great, boss," Marvin replied, unaware of the snafu.

"I'm glad you liked it, because I had to make most of it up!"

Number your pages. And count them to make sure they're all there.

Also, "carry the speech with you," Obama told me once, "even if you have it memorized. Just in case you have a brain freeze. That's helpful," he said with a chuckle. It's especially helpful if you plan to read your remarks off your phone or tablet, which could glitch or die in the middle of your presentation.

Not planning to deliver your remarks word for word? It's still a good idea to bring a cheat sheet—a one-page outline or a few key points . . . just in case your brain starts to freeze.

Remember: Your Nerves Are Natural

Still anxious as you're getting ready to speak? Tempted to run away? Starting to sweat? Here's the good news—there's *nothing* wrong with you. It's just our body and brain doing what they've always done when we sense a threat.

"We go into one of four modes," Dr. Hendriksen told me. "Fight, flight, freeze, or appease. We try to fight like a cornered animal, flee, freeze to avoid danger, or try to people-please ourselves out of our predicament. Our adrenaline surges. We start to sweat, so we don't overheat. We breathe faster, drying out our mouths. Our hands get cold and clammy as blood rushes back to our heart, which pumps harder, pushing blood to the bigger muscles we'll need to fight or flee."

Don't fight. Don't flee. Remember: if you're shaking and sweating, it's your body doing exactly what it's *supposed* to do—preparing you to survive, to succeed. Maybe think of it this way: *the more I sweat, the more I'll succeed.*

Just Breathe

Last-minute butterflies happen to even the most accomplished singers, actors, and athletes. It happened to Obama. Even as he confidently entered the arena for his 2004 convention speech in Boston—telling a reporter, "I'm LeBron, baby"—he later admitted that, yes, he felt "a tad bit nervous."[1]

If you're anxious, it's because you care. And that's a good thing. What's not good is if your nerves paralyze you. Like a lot of speakers, I've found that one of the best ways to stay calm in the final moments before a speech is also one of the easiest—just breathe. For me, it's box breathing:

Inhale for four seconds.
Hold your breath for four seconds.
Exhale for four seconds.
Hold for four seconds.
Repeat a few times.

Find an exercise that works for you. You'll breathe easier too.

Channel Your Anxiety into Excitement

If trying to calm your nerves doesn't work, consider embracing them. "Anxiety and excitement feel the same physically," explains Dr. Hendriksen. "Instead of trying to change what you're feeling physically, try changing your mindset and rechanneling your anxiety into excitement."

It's called emotional reappraisal, and in a fascinating experiment, Alison Wood Brooks, a professor of business administration at Harvard Business School, showed how it works. She asked 140 people to prepare, deliver, and be evaluated on a two-minute speech.[2] Before their presentations, some speakers were instructed to tell themselves "I am calm." Others told themselves "I am excited." The result? "Stating 'I am excited,'" explained Wood Brooks, "caused individuals to feel more excited, to speak longer, and to be perceived as more persuasive, competent, confident, and persistent."*

* In another experiment, Wood Brooks asked study participants to say "I am anxious" or "I am excited" before singing Journey's "Don't Stop Believin'." Same result. Those who said "I am excited" sang the song better. It can work for anyone, even if you're "just a small town girl livin' in a lonely world."

Want to be a better speaker? Don't count on someone else to get you excited. Tell yourself!

Get Pumped

One last thing before you take the stage: crank up the music.

Before a big speech, Obama sometimes got into the zone with Eminem's "Lose Yourself"—maybe the best hype song ever. I like House of Pain's "Jump Around." Whatever your style, there are tons of great ones. AC/DC's "Thunderstruck." Carrie Underwood and Ludacris's "The Champion." Sia's "Unstoppable." Wiz Khalifa's "We Dem Boyz."

Have your own hype song. Before you speak up, turn it up—and get pumped.

NAIL IT

It's Go Time.

The audience has gathered. It's your turn to speak. All the work you've put in, all the words you've written, all the practice you've done has prepared you for this moment. Here's how to own it.

Smile!

However you greet your audience—"Hello!" "Good afternoon!" "Good evening!"—say it with a smile. It's so easy. It's also easy to forget, especially if you're nervous. Of course, don't flash a big grin as you begin a eulogy or if you're an executive announcing layoffs. That's creepy. In most cases, though, it's smart to start with a smile.

Like saying hello, smiling signals to your audience that you're a friend, which can be good for your credibility. Studies show that smiling can often make you come across as more likeable, trust-worthy, intelligent, and competent.[3] And flashing those pearly whites is good for your audience because, as studies have now confirmed, smiling really is contagious.[4]

Write it down in all caps at the top of your remarks so you remember: SMILE! Soon, your audience will be smiling with you and more likely to see you as a likable, trustworthy, intelligent, and competent speaker worth listening to.

Look 'em in the Eyes

The floor. Your slides. Your watch. These are just a few of the things that you should *not* be looking at when you speak. There's only one place you should be looking—at your audience. Little or no eye contact can make you appear insecure or uncertain about what you're saying. Good eye contact shows confidence and builds trust.[5*]

If you took my advice and printed your remarks out in large font—keeping the bottom portion of your pages blank—it's easier to look up every line or so and visually connect with your listeners.

Find those friends in the audience that you made earlier. Speak *to them*. As you pause and prepare to move on to your next point, shift your gaze to someone else. Over the course of your remarks, slowly move back and forth across the room. It's easier to talk to one person at a time than to many.

Vary Your Voice

As you speak, pay attention to your pace, pitch, and volume. Talk too fast or too loud and you'll sound like a breathless used car salesman. Too quiet or too slow—or too many long pauses—and you'll put your audience to sleep. Or you'll look contrived. "I have absolutely nothing to say whatsoever," said a *Saturday Night*

---

* Good eye contact is especially important if you're presenting by Zoom, where your face takes up most of the screen. If you're not looking at your audience, they'll know it. Consider covering up your screen so you don't get distracted by others on the screen. Put a sticker next to your camera to remind yourself to look into the lens.

Live writer in one of the great parodies of TED Talks. "And yet, through my manner of speaking, I will make it seem like I do."[6] Have something to say? Just speak the way most people actually speak in their daily lives—again, around 150 words a minute.

And since you're a human, be careful not to slip into the monotone voice of a robot. "The modulation of your voice, your tone, your volume," Obama said to me once, "all that is communicating emotion."

Here are a few dos and don'ts to help you communicate what *you* want:

- *Don't yell.* "If you're at ten decibels the entire speech, you lose people," Obama told me. "People scream into the microphone not realizing it's a good mic. People can hear you. That's the whole point of having a mic!" he said, laughing. "We're not in the 1800s."

- *Have a conversation.* "If you were just speaking to a friend," Obama pointed out, "you would not holler at them the entire time." Listen to how you talk with your friends and family— "not constrained," Obama said, "by self-consciousness or feeling judged or being afraid of failing." Bring that same comfort level and voice to your presentation. Natural, not noisy. Smooth, not strident. As if you're having a conversation with family or friends.

- *Lower your voice* when you want to pull your audience in, for example, when telling a story. "If you really want to make a point," Obama said, "you might actually bring it down to a whisper."

- *Raise your voice* (but don't scream) when you want to stress an important point or when building up to a line you think might get applause or cheers.

- *Slow down*—as if every word is its own sentence—When. You. Want. Your. Audience. To. Remember. Every. Single. Word.

- *Speed up* to bring some energy to your remarks or as you build to a great line.

- *Enunciate* your words clearly, because your audience won't hear or remember what you mumble. But . . .

- *Don't <u>overenunciate</u>,* like the speaker I heard once who enunciated every syllable of every word ("We stand for pros-per-i-ty! For o-ppor-tu-ni-ty! And for se-cur-i-ty!"). It can sound ro-bo-tic.

- *Pause* for effect—and take a breath—when telling a story, when you want your audience to reflect on what you just said, or as you move on to your next point.

- *Be okay with a moment of silence* if you lose your train of thought. Just pause for a second or two while you find the next word in your script. It's, um, better than, ah, filling the silence with, er, too many filler words that, you know, make you sound like you don't, um, know what you're, like, talking about.

That's a lot to remember. Fortunately, you don't have to. These are goals to strive for, not marks you *have* to hit every time you speak. Lots of people, even Obama, sometimes fall into long pauses or use too many filler words—and they're still great speakers. Just do your best. Be yourself. Talk the way *you* talk.

Body Language: Don't Overthink It

It's also important to be yourself when it comes to body language. Unfortunately, we're bombarded with advice from what's been called a "multimillion-dollar body-language industry" that tries to sell us "hidden codes" to succeed in work and life.[7] *Stand like this. Plant your feet like that. Move your hand just so. Pause. Take a few steps. Make your point. Pause again. Take a few more steps. Make your next point.*

It's all too much. We're giving a speech, not dancing the salsa.

I believe the importance of body language is sometimes exaggerated. For example, maybe you've heard that 93 percent of our communication is nonverbal. It's one of the most commonly cited principles of communication. It's rooted in the 7–38–55 rule, from a famous study.[8] Only 7 percent of our communication is based on our words, we're told, and the other 93 percent is based on the tone of our voice (38 percent) and our body language (55 percent).

But that's *not* what the study said. Which is obvious if you think about it. You're giving a presentation, but 93 percent of your communication is . . . *not* the words you speak? It doesn't make sense. Turns out, the study was focused narrowly on how listeners identify a speaker's *emotions*—like whether they're expressing love, where body language is obviously a pretty big clue.[9] In fact, so many people misinterpreted the study that its author issued a clarification: "Unless a communicator is talking about their feelings or attitudes," the 7–38–55 rule is "not applicable."[10] So, no, 93 percent of communication is *not* the tone of our voice and our body language.

Or maybe you've heard that standing in a "power pose"—like Superman or Wonder Woman—can *cause* the release of hormones so we feel less stressed and more confident on stage. It's from a popular TED Talk that was, in turn, based on a study that concluded "that a person can, by assuming two simple 1-min[ute] poses, embody power and instantly become more powerful."[11] But other researchers couldn't replicate those findings.[12] The lead author of the original study also later conceded that its "data are flimsy," declaring, "I do not believe that 'power pose' effects are real."[13]

I'm not saying body language doesn't matter at all. Of course it does. *How* you say it can amplify *what* you say. Certain nonverbal displays—for example, how we stand—have been shown to make speakers *appear* more powerful to their audience.[14] And if standing in a "power pose" makes you feel more confident (whether or not it's actually triggering the release of any hormones), go for it.[15]

I'm saying that when it comes to body language, don't overthink it. You can't be relaxed and authentic in front of an audience if you're obsessing over your every move. Plus, you can still give a good speech without perfect body language, but good body language will never save a bad speech. Because, in the end, *what* you say matters far more than *how* you say it.

Two Rules for Body Language

If I could boil down my advice on body language, it would be this:

- *Relax.* Just carry yourself like you would in a conversation with family and friends. Stand up straight (A, because you'll look better, and B, because it will help you breathe). Stay loose and don't lock your knees (because you might pass out). Don't wave your arms wildly (because it's distracting, and you'll look unhinged). Don't pound the podium with your fist (because you're not a dictator).

- *Let your body match your words.* If you're comfortable doing it, just let simple gestures reinforce your message. When you say something like "Welcome, everyone!" maybe open your arms or hands as if to welcome them. "We all need to come together"—perhaps pull your arms in or clasp your hands together. "We need to lift everyone up!"—raise your hands in a lifting motion. "Thank you, from the bottom of my heart"—maybe place your hand over your heart, like Alphonso Davies did when he said it was an honor to speak to FIFA.

Yeah, you're acting out your words. But I bet you already do this every day without even realizing it when you talk with family and friends. Need some inspiration? Go online and watch Donovan Livingston deliver his spoken-word poem at his graduation. It's a master class in great body language. Every gesture is so genuine, every move is so natural. Do it like Donovan and let your body lift your message.

Keep Calm and Carry On

Even as you try to do everything right, be ready if things start to go wrong.

Make sure there's some water close at hand. If your mouth starts to dry up, you'll need it. If you lose your train of thought, taking a sip is a great cover for the moment you need to collect your thoughts and get back on track.

Mispronounce a word or stumble over a sentence? It's okay. Your audience may not even notice it. Don't apologize, which will only draw even more attention to it. Take a breath. Check your script, find your place, and carry on.

Feel like you're losing your audience? Get them involved. "There were times during the campaigns when you could tell the crowd was a little flat," Obama told me once. "If you know something's not working, maybe try something else. I just ad-libbed to see if I could get folks energized. That's how something like 'Fired Up! Ready to Go!' comes in."

Your audience a little flat? Mix it up. Raise—or lower—your voice. Ditch your script for a moment and try something different. Ask the audience a question. Tell a story.

Technical fail? Maybe your slides get stuck. Maybe your video doesn't play. Don't get frazzled. Acknowledge what's happening; own it so it doesn't own you. Ask for some assistance. Smile. And have some fun with it. One time while Obama was speaking, the presidential seal fell off his podium and hit the floor with a thud.

"That's all right, all of you know who I am," he joked, to laughter from the audience. "But I'm sure there's somebody back there," he went on, nodding to staff backstage, "that's really nervous right now." And then he got back on track, to even more laughter: "Where were we?"

WHAT MATTERS MOST

So, yes, what you do at the podium—your delivery and how you carry yourself, including your body language—can sometimes help. But here's the truth: you can be a great communicator even if you can't stand or deliver. Or even speak.

For the first year or so of her life, Elizabeth Bonker was "a typical toddler," her mother, Virginia, told me. Then, at fifteen months old, everything changed. "One day she was happy and talking," her mother said, "the next day she was screaming and banging her head on the floor, unable to speak."

Elizabeth was diagnosed with autism. She endured a daily horror. She was imprisoned in her own body—able to hear and understand everyone around her, but unable to communicate back. The few moments of respite came when her mother held her in her arms and read to her. "Elizabeth would lie quietly," Virginia remembers, "and blink her eyes slowly to tell me she was understanding what I was saying."

For years, Elizabeth's mother took her to every specialist they could find. When Elizabeth was five years old, they found another mother who had taught her autistic son and other children to express themselves by pointing to letters. She agreed to teach Elizabeth too. Before long, Elizabeth was pointing to letters and spelling out words, even sentences. "I was freed," Elizabeth told me years later by email. "My life went from hopeless to hopeful."

Elizabeth began writing poetry, went to her local public school in Byram Township, New Jersey, and graduated high school. She was accepted into the honors program at Rollins College in Florida and started a nonprofit to help other nonspeakers with autism learn to communicate by typing, like she did. She earned a 4.0, graduated as a valedictorian, and was selected by her classmates to give the commencement address.

Her classmates knew Elizabeth wouldn't be able to do most of the things usually associated with being an effective speaker—smiling, modulating your voice, standing still, making eye contact, using your hands to make a point. And yet, Elizabeth went on to give an extraordinary speech. Because, in the end, what matters most—far more than your body language—is the message you're delivering. And Elizabeth had a powerful message to deliver.

"I thought a lot," she told me by email, "then I wrote it"—her mother holding her keyboard as she slowly tapped out each letter with the index finger of her right hand. "Once I got it all out of my head, I polished every word and phrase." All told, it took her "more than a month . . . maybe fifty hours total." And she practiced, which in her case meant playing her text-to-speech software over and over. (Her advice to other speakers: "Record it ahead of time. Ha. Ha.") The day before her speech, she went to the stadium to practice walking up to the podium. "That helped me know I could do it."

The next day, in front of a crowd of thousands, Elizabeth—with blue and pink flowers adorning her cap and gown—approached the lectern, and a computer-generated female voice began to speak.

"Greetings to my fellow members of the elated class of 2022 and to the relieved parents . . ."

Elizabeth celebrated her classmates' achievements and then gave the speech only she could give. She shared how learning to type "unlocked my mind from its silent cage" and how "I have struggled my whole life with not being heard or accepted." She recounted how her high school principal had said that, despite Elizabeth's high grades, "The retard can't be valedictorian."

"Yet today," Elizabeth said, "here I stand," as the crowd broke into cheers.

Like one of her heroes, Hellen Keller, Elizabeth said she was dedicating her life to service—to the estimated "thirty-one million nonspeakers with autism in the world . . . relieving them from suffering in silence and to giving them voices to choose their own way." As she finished, the crowd burst into a standing ovation and her mother watched with tears of joy. Elizabeth's parting message—a call to action to her audience—hung in the air.

"God gave you a voice. Use it."

Elizabeth hadn't *spoken* a word, but her speech went viral, captivating people around the world. "I wrote from my heart," she told me, "and it resonated in theirs. We all want to feel our lives have meaning and purpose." Nonspeakers with autism flooded her with messages of gratitude, including a teenage girl who called Elizabeth "my role model" because by learning to type "I can finally show the world how smart I am."

Maybe, like Elizabeth, you can't do all the things that other people think a great communicator should do. So what! Even if you can't speak, you still have a voice. Even if you can't see or hear, you can still look ahead and imagine the future you want. Even if you can't stand on your own or fully control your body, you can still stand up for what you believe and for a more just and equal world. Because in the end, as Elizabeth teaches us all, we can only find our voice if we're willing to use it.

~

In Finland, backstage, moments before my speech, I was finally ready to use mine.

Offstage, I could hear the previous speaker finishing up. I was still practicing out loud, still cutting words from my script. I felt my heart racing but remembered it was natural. I told myself that if I made a mistake—no, *when* I made a mistake—it would be okay. The audience might not even notice. And my worth as a person was not going to be defined by whatever I did or did not do on that stage.

Then it was time.

A keynote address.

Three hundred people.

No podium.

No turning back.

Before I took the stage, I played a short video to warm up the crowd—that montage of Obama saying hello in different languages around the world. Then I jogged onstage, trying to create a little energy. I smiled. I greeted the audience in Finnish ("Hei!"), and they greeted me back. I attempted a phrase that my new Finnish friends had taught me over beers—a curse about the terrible weather in November—and the crowd laughed and cheered.

I made mistakes. I said "um" and "ah" way too many times. I waved my hands—and the notes I was holding—too much. I stumbled over a word here and there—in Finnish and in English. Without a podium to settle me, I often rocked back and forth on my heels. I sometimes called up the next slide too soon. At one point, a video clip took too long to load, leaving me standing in silence.

Still, things were beginning to click. My voice was steady. The words came naturally, and I started to find my rhythm. I looked for my new friends in the audience and spoke directly to them, then shifted my gaze and spoke to someone else. I tried to talk in short sentences, pausing to breathe, visualizing my next sentence.

And that's when I felt it—a sensation I'd never experienced in front of an audience. My heart stopped racing. A wave of calm washed over me. I wasn't outside myself, floating above, looking down, second-guessing my every move and word. I was present. At ease. I *wanted* to be there. And I was actually enjoying it.

The audience seemed to be enjoying it too. They were smiling, listening, and nodding along in agreement. And the more I sensed they were receiving what I had to offer, the more I wanted to give them—that kind of moment between a speaker and an audience that Obama had talked about. A physical feeling. A current of emotion passing back and forth. An *experience* we were sharing together.

With the time I had, I tried to give the speech only I could give—taking the audience on a journey inside the White House, on my trips with Obama around the world, sharing the lessons I'd learned along the way, and playing clips of his speeches. I tried to speak to their values—a progressive people known for their commitment to social and economic equality.

I shared the story of little Alex Myteberi offering to take care of Omran in Syria, and when I did, I unexpectedly started to choke up. Pausing to collect myself, I noticed a woman in the audience dabbing away tears as well.

I built up to a call to action—the hope that, in the face of

296 Say It Well

demagogues who spread lies, hate, and fear, we can use our voices to create a world of more honesty, civility, and empathy.

And I ended, in Finnish, with four words that can be the perfect ending for any presentation: thank you very much.

I'd been asked to speak for twenty minutes. Without realizing it, I'd spoken for nearly fifty minutes. As I finished, I wasn't sure what to expect. Had I gone on too long? Had I lost the audience? Another attempt at public speaking down in flames?

But the audience started applauding.

Then they started cheering.

Then they rose from their seats in a standing ovation.

And the ovation went on—for twenty seconds, then thirty seconds, then a full forty-five seconds.

I couldn't believe it.

I'd actually done it. Something I'd been afraid of and avoided for so many years. Something I had thought I didn't have in me.

Standing there, looking at the applauding crowd, I felt . . . free. Finally free from that Voice of Doubt that I'd been listening to for so long. Free from the worry that I didn't have something worthy to share. Free from the fear of what would happen if I stood up and spoke.

There, on that stage, thousands of miles from home—taking a chance, finally putting myself out there—I'd proven to myself that I could do it.

In urging others to raise their voice, I'd finally found my own.

The Download

In the final hours before your presentation, get into the zone.

» **Let your clothes do the talking.** What you wear can reinforce what you're saying. Are there clothes, colors, or accessories that can help you connect with your audience? At the same time, wear what makes you feel safe and comfortable.

» **Make some friends.** If you can, mingle with your audience before the event. Make a friend who you can speak to later when you're at the podium.

» **Keep correcting . . . but stop editing.** As you practice your remarks a few last times, keep looking to make sure everything is accurate. If not, fix it. But resist the urge to keep rewriting. You worked hard on your draft. Trust your gut. Just keep practicing.

» **Your nerves are natural.** Palms sweaty? Knees weak? The anxiety you feel is normal. It's your body preparing you to succeed. Try box breathing. Tell yourself "I'm excited!" Get pumped with your favorite hype song.

» **Count your pages.** Make sure they're all there!

When you get to the podium . . .

» **Smile!** In most cases, it's the easiest way to connect with your audience. If it helps you remember, write SMIILE! at the top of your draft.

» **Look 'em in the eyes.** Good eye contact shows confidence and builds trust. Speak to your new friends in the audience. As you move on to your next point, shift and talk to someone else. Over the course of your remarks, move across the room.

» **Vary your voice.** Keep it conversational, the way you might talk with friends or family. If you want, lower your voice and slow down to make a point. Raise your voice or speed up to convey momentum and energy. Pause for effect. If you lose your place for a moment, that's okay; a little silence is better than lots of "ums" and "ahs."

» **Two rules for body language.** First, keep it real by carrying yourself like you would in a conversation with family and friends. Second, just let your body match your words by using simple, natural gestures that reinforce your message.

» **Keep calm and carry on.** Be ready if things go wrong. Bring some water in case of dry mouth. Stumble over a word? Don't apologize. Keep going. Losing your audience? Tell a story or ask a question. Tech or prop fail? Make a joke.

» **Remember what really matters.** You can still give a good speech without perfect body language, but good body language will never save a bad speech. In the end, what matters most is not your body language but the message you're delivering.

» **End with four words.** The final words out of your mouth are one last chance to express your gratitude to your audience for their time and attention. You also need to make it clear that you're finished; it's their cue to applaud! You can do it with four words that work for just about every kind of presentation: "Thank you very much."

Epilogue

After the Applause

Congratulations!

You did it. You spoke in front of a group of people—a toast to a friend, a tribute to a loved one, a presentation at work, a comment at a community meeting, or maybe an impassioned appeal for a cause you care about. And since I've encouraged you to always tell the truth, let's be honest.

Were you perfect?

Probably not.

Did you make mistakes?

Almost definitely.

Did every quip get a chuckle? Was every person in your audience swayed by your logic?

Unlikely.

And that's alright. A speech is just a speech. The important thing is that you put yourself out there—and you did it.

"You're not always going to be on point," Obama said to me once. "But if you've done your job, if you're a professional—even when the magic's not there, even if the audience isn't getting the same high that they were hoping for—it will be okay. Your audience is still getting information."

And if you weren't totally on point this time, how do you get better for next time? Just *keep* doing it. Because the more you speak, the better you'll be. "It doesn't matter whether it's a big business presentation or talking at Parents Day at your kid's school," Obama said. "Like anything else, it requires some practice. That's when you're going to be at your best."

I asked him, reflecting on his career, when he thought he was at *his* best as a speaker. He ticked off a few of his earliest speeches—at a rally in Chicago when he was still a state senator and spoke out against the invasion of Iraq, his keynote at the convention in Boston, his speech on race in Philadelphia.

"It's those moments," he answered, "when your heart and your head, the emotion and the idea, the passion and the logic come together, when you are speaking both out of sufficient experience and having enough reps. You know that you have prepared and that you have written it, but that you're also loose and in the moment as you're talking. There's a certain freedom that comes with that. That's when I felt I was at my best."

How will *you* know when *you're* at your best—and that your voice made a difference?

You'll know.

You'll know your voice made a difference because—as you're speaking—your audience will show you how it made them feel.

When you greet them and smile, they greet you right back. When you make a little quip about a connection you share, they chuckle, maybe even laugh. When you make a compelling point, they nod in agreement. When you share a moving story, they listen in rapt attention and lean in, eager to hear how the story ends.

Perhaps they applaud because you've given voice to a value they cherish. Maybe they shed a tear because your words touched their soul. Perhaps there even comes a point in your speech when they get up out of their seats and applaud and cheer, because you've said something so true, you've shared something so powerful, you've tapped into that collective spirit so deeply, that they want to stand up and move and share in the moment too.

You'll know your voice made a difference because, after you're done speaking, you'll see a change in the world around you.

Your audience answers your call to action and turns your words into deeds—family and friends carry on the legacy of a loved one; a colleague goes the extra mile at work; a company selects your firm to do business with because of your product *and* your values; voters pass the new law you called for; a concerned citizen signs your petition; a neighbor donates their clothes so someone else's child can go to school with dignity and a smile.

Even if the progress you want doesn't come right away, you'll know your remarks had an impact as the hearts and minds of your audience begin to open. Perhaps they start to see the world differently. Or they acknowledge, for the first time, that an old problem needs a new solution. They share your hope. They embrace your vision. Suddenly, the idea that you spoke up for becomes less of a dream and more of a reality.

You'll know your voice made a difference because you'll see a change in yourself, just like speaking up changed the lives of the people you've met throughout this book.

"It boosted my confidence in myself," says Naiara Tamminga, who credits addressing her city commissioners in Grand Rapids, Michigan, with a newfound belief in her own ability to advocate for her community. "I carry myself differently now." Her advice to others: "Don't self-sabotage. Don't dim your own light. Never doubt the power of what you have to say."

Since the video of him reading his letter about Omran went viral, Alex Myteberi has been invited to speak to groups around the world, including five thousand young people in Texas, where he stood on a stool to reach the podium. "You'll be surprised how loud your voice can be," Alex says. "The more you show that you care, the more people you can help."

Olivia Vella says that sharing her most intimate emotions in her slam poem with her English class "helped me be more vocal about how I'm feeling." And she has a message for anyone who's afraid to be vulnerable in front of an audience. "You're only preventing yourself from reaching a deeper level of healing. The feelings that we leave unexpressed never really leave us. They just become physical tensions. The only way to let go of the tension in our lives—and to create deeper connections with other people—is to honor our feelings by expressing them."

Since giving my first real speech in Finland, I've changed too. For the most part, the Voice of Doubt is gone. I still hear it sometimes. But it's quieter. When I'm invited to speak somewhere, I no longer make up excuses for why I can't do it. I remember that I have a story to share. I follow the 50–25–25 Rule. I plan and prepare and write and rewrite and practice and practice and practice. Don't get me wrong, I still get nervous. I still stumble over a sentence here or there. And maybe I always will. But I know I can do it. Today, in workshops and training sessions—and at American University where I teach a class on speechwriting—I'm able to take audiences on a journey to becoming a better speaker because I've made that journey myself.

For other speakers in this book, raising their voice has given them new opportunities to reach audiences they could have never imagined. After Zander Moricz's graduation speech about his curly hair, donations poured into a nonprofit he had created, the Social Equity and Education Initiative, which works to defend marginalized communities across the United States. "I always wanted to be a teacher," he says, explaining why he switched his college major to political science. "Now I want to change the system."

Elizabeth Bonker says that her speech going viral "changed my life." Her nonprofit, Communication 4 ALL, now has a global following. She travels the world—her mom holding her keyboard as she types—urging governments and schools to give all nonspeakers the tools to express themselves. "Life without communication is not a life," Elizabeth says. "Everyone wants to be seen and heard."

After speaking out against attempts to remove books from her school library, Amanda Jones started an alliance to support other librarians, and she continues to draw strength from her faith. "God," she says, "has given me this purpose." Today, she's a leading advocate for the freedom to read, traveling the country and delivering a simple message to communities and leaders: "Trust your librarians."

Since speaking on national television, Brayden Harrington has been invited to talk to groups of young people about having the courage to do what scares us, like speaking with a stutter. He dreams of becoming a speech pathologist to help kids like himself. He even wrote a children's book about the speech he gave from his bedroom to an audience of millions—a book that ends with advice for us all.

"Don't be scared to speak up," Brayden wrote. "Speak out, and use your voice. You are amazing just the way you are!"

Finally, you'll know your voice made a difference because people who heard you speak will tell you. Maybe right away. Maybe weeks or even years later.

"You touched my heart."

"You changed my mind."

"You gave me hope."

And the *next* time you have the opportunity to speak—to your family, your neighbors, your colleagues, or your community— you'll have the confidence and the skills to do it. Because you won't only know what to say . . .

You'll know how to say it well.

Acknowledgments

Writing a book, I've learned, is a lot like writing a speech. It's a journey—sometimes thrilling, sometimes overwhelming. From conception to completion, this book was a nearly three-year journey that I never could have made alone. I'm profoundly grateful to so many family, friends, and colleagues who encouraged and supported me every step of the way.

When I first approached Bridget Matzie of Aevitas Creative Management with the idea for this book, all I could offer was a vague concept. "Alright," she said, "the next step is turn this into a book proposal." To which I replied, "What goes in a book proposal?" For the next year, Bridget was my guide, forcing me to scope it out, think it out, figure it out, and write it out. Her edits, along with those from Elena Steinert, helped me tell the story that only I could tell. Thank you, Bridget and Elena, for helping me turn my idea into a proposal. Thank you to the entire team at Aevitas—including Vanessa Kerr and Erin Files—as well as the extraordinary Liz Biber and her tireless team at The Lede Company, including Emmy Chang, Mia Jacobs, Alex Rabney, and Brianna Sasson, for helping to bring this book to readers in more than fifty countries and territories around the world.

I realized this book would become a reality when I saw Hollis Heimbouch's enthusiasm for my proposal. Every author should be so lucky to work with an editor like Hollis. "I'm offering ideas," she told me, "but this is your book. You have to be proud of it." Over multiple iterations, she, along with James Neidhardt, offered ideas on how to make my chapters shorter, sharper, and better. When I submitted a manuscript that was too long, she said with a smile, "I've heard you can cut any draft by fifteen percent." Thank you,

Hollis, James, and everyone at HarperCollins—including Jessica Gilo and Rachel Molland—for helping me turn my proposal into a book that I am proud of.

I'm forever grateful to the Obama White House speechwriting team for eight years of camaraderie and friendship and to those who shared their memories for this book: Jon Favreau, Cody Keenan, Ben Rhodes, Adam Frankel, Sarah Hurwitz, Jon Lovett, Kyle O'Connor, Tyler Lechtenberg, David Litt, Sarada Peri, Stephen Krupin, Dave Cavell, Laura Dean, Susannah Jacob, and Zev Karlin-Neumann.

Thank you, David Axelrod, for sharing your memories of Barack Obama's historic 2008 campaign with the same joy and generous spirit with which you always welcomed our speechwriting team to your West Wing office: "Hello, Wordsmiths!"

Thank you, President Obama, for being the best boss a speechwriter could ask for. If a draft I wrote missed the mark, you gave me the chance to "make it better." You used each draft not simply to edit us, but to teach us what our words can achieve when we speak with civility, honesty, and empathy.

It would have been impossible to write a book that celebrates the speeches of people from so many different backgrounds without the candor and cooperation of people who've actually done it, including Ashley All, Lynne and Marc Benioff, Elizabeth Bonker, Nancy Brinker, William Cohen, Rachael Denhollander, Felix Finkbeiner, Brayden Harrington, Amanda Jones, Donovan Livingston, Kimberly Mata-Rubio, Zander Moricz, Ellen Moy, Alex Myteberi, Cory Remsburg, Naiara Tamminga, Olivia Vella, and Evan Wolfson. I'm honored that you allowed me to share your stories.

I'm indebted to the many researchers, scholars, psychologists, and neuroscientists who spoke with me or responded to my inquiries about the science behind effective communication, including Sinan

Aral, Chris Bail, Jonah Berger, Dana Carney, Matthew Feinberg, Dan Fessler, Michele Gelfand, Jack Gorman, Uri Hasson, Chan Hellman, Ellen Hendriksen, Alisa Lehman, Katherine Milkman, Deb Roy, Tali Sharot, Almog Simchon, Deborah Small, Jay Van Bavel, Soroush Vosoughi, Robb Willer, and Alison Wood Brooks.

Once I had a manuscript, I tried to practice what I preach by sharing it with friends and colleagues. When I asked for their honest feedback, they didn't hold back, and this book is better for it. Thank you, Rumana Ahmed, Tom Becherer, Bob Boorstin, Nahida Chakhtoura, Kim DeMott, Julie Eill, Dan Farber, Edward Felsenthal, John Gibson, Lisa Fine, Chris Haugh, Darby Hopper, Sarah Hurwitz, Rashad Hussain, Zev Karlin-Neumann, Cody Keenan, Naseem Khuri, Sera Koulabdara, Stephen Krupin, Peter Mahoney, Antti Mustakallio, Alex and Val Myteberi, Kyle O'Connor, Sarada Peri, Joe Plenzler, Kevin Varney, and Meredith and Lance Wade.

When it was time to check my facts, there was only one place to go: Silver Street Strategies. Kristen Bartoloni, Alex Platkin, and Allison Kelly subjected this book to the same relentless fact-checking with which they scrutinized President Obama's speeches at the White House. They saved me from many, many mistakes. If any remain, it's because I didn't heed their wise advice.

This book was largely finished by the time I started teaching speechwriting at American University. But in every class, I learned from my students as we explored the world through their younger eyes. More than once, their insights and idealism led me to revisit my manuscript and, I hope, make it even more relevant for the next generation of speakers and leaders as they raise their voice for the change they want.

I'm eternally grateful to my family, who tolerated me obsessing over this book for nearly three years, read drafts, offered feedback, and blessed me with their love and support: my parents, Stach and

Peggy; my sisters, Erica and Kay; my brother-in-law, Ben Allsup; my brothers- and sisters-in law, Charlie and Haneen Abdella and Anibal and Diana Abdella; and my mother-in-law, Samia Abdella.

Finally, I owe everything to the three people who were on this journey with me every single day. Jack and Claire—I wrote this book for everyone, but especially for young people like you. Nothing gives me more pride or happiness in life than watching you find your voice, speak your mind, and inspire everyone around you. I can't wait to see what you do next.

Most of all, my wife, Mary. This book simply would not exist without your endless love and support—and patience. You endured my brainstorms when I wasn't sure what to write and my doubts when the words wouldn't come. You read early drafts and made them better, and final drafts in which you caught things everyone else missed. You once gave me a collection of poems by Kahlil Gibran, including his reflections on love: "When love beckons to you, follow him."

Thank you, Mary, for allowing me to follow you, and love you, all these years.

Notes

Chapter 1: Love Your Sacred Story

1. Barack Obama, *Dreams from My Father: A Story of Race and Inheritance* (New York: Three Rivers Press, 1995), 107–8.

Chapter 2: Say What Only You Can Say

1. Gordon Bower and Michal Clark, "Narrative Stories as Mediators for Serial Learning," *Psychonomic Science* 15, no. 4 (April 1969): 181–82, https://doi.org/10.3758/BF03332778; Chip Heath and Dan Heath, *Made to Stick: Why Some Ideas Survive and Others Die* (New York: Random House, 2007).

Chapter 3: What a Speech Really Is

1. Barack Obama, *A Promised Land* (New York: Crown, 2020), 52.
2. Greg J. Stephens, Lauren J. Silbert, and Uri Hasson, "Speaker-Listener Neural Coupling Underlines Successful Communication," *Proceedings of the National Academy of Sciences* 107, no. 32 (August 10, 2010): 14425–30, https://doi.org/10.1073/pnas.1008662107; Lauren J. Silbert, Christopher J. Honey, Erez Simony, David Poeppel, and Uri Hasson, "Coupled Neural Systems Underlie the Production and Comprehension of Naturalistic Narrative Speech," *Proceedings of the National Academy of Sciences* 111, no. 43 (September 29, 2014): E4687–96, https://doi.org/10.1073/pnas.1323812111.

Chapter 4: The 50–25–25 Rule

1. "President Obama to Bob Woodward: 'Mistake' to Dress Down Paul Ryan to His Face in Budget Speech," ABCNews.Go.com, September 6, 2012, https://abcnews.go.com/Politics/obama-bob -woodward-mistake-dress-paul-ryan-face/story?id=17171273.
2. Ryan Lizza, "Battle Plans," *New Yorker*, November 8, 2008, https:// www.newyorker.com/magazine/2008/11/17/battle-plans.
3. Zachary C. Irving, Catherine McGrath, Lauren Flynn, Aaron Glasser, and Caitlin Mills, "The Shower Effect: Mind Wandering Facilitates Creative Incubation During Moderately Engaging Activities," *Psychology of Aesthetics, Creativity, and the Arts* (2022), https://doi.org/10.1037/aca0000516.

Chapter 5: Have 'em at Hello

1. Emmanuel Ponsot, Juan José Burred, Pascal Belin, and Jean-Julien Aucouturier, "Cracking the Social Code of Speech Prosody Using Reverse Correlation," *Proceedings of the National Academy of Sciences* 115, no. 15 (March 26, 2018): 3972–77, https://doi.org/10.1073/pnas.1716090115.
2. "Modeling the Future of Religion in America," Pew Research Center, September 13, 2022, https://www.pewresearch.org/religion/2022/09/13/modeling-the-future-of-religion-in-america/.

Chapter 6: Be a Uniter

1. Virginia Choi, Snehesh Shrestha, Xinyue Pan, Michele Gelfand, and Dylan Pieper, "Threat Dictionary," www.michelegelfand.com/threat-dictionary.
2. German Lopez, "Research Says There Are Ways to Reduce Racial Bias. Calling People Racist Isn't One of Them," *Vox*, July 30, 2018, https://www.vox.com/identities/2016/11/15/13595508/racism-research-study-trump.
3. Almog Simchon, William J. Brady, and Jay J. Van Bavel, "Troll and Divide: The Language of Online Polarization," *PNAS Nexus 1*, no 1 (March 10, 2022): 1–12, https://doi.org/10.1093/pnasnexus/pgac019.
4. Daniel L. Byman, "How Hateful Rhetoric Connects to Real-World Violence," Brookings Institution, April 9, 2021, https://www.brookings.edu/articles/how-hateful-rhetoric-connects-to-real-world-violence/.
5. "Threats to American Democracy Ahead of an Unprecedented Presidential Election," Public Religion Research Institute, October 25, 2023, https://www.prri.org/research/threats-to-american-democracy-ahead-of-an-unprecedented-presidential-election/.
6. Daniel Druckman, "Nationalism, Patriotism, and Group Loyalty: A Social Psychological Perspective," *Mershon International Studies Review* 38, no. 1 (April 1, 1994): 43–68, https://doi.org/10.2307/222610.
7. James Devitt, "Bridging Divides in an Age of Identity," New York University, September 7, 2021, https://www.nyu.edu/about/news-publications/news/2021/september/bridging-divides-in-an-age-of-identity.html.
8. Yarrow Dunham, "Mere Membership," *Trends in Cognitive Sciences* 22, no. 9 (September 2018): P780–93, https://doi.org/10.1016/j.tics.2018.06.004.

9. Matthew S. Levendusky, "Americans, Not Partisans: Can Priming American National Identity Reduce Affective Polarization?," *Journal of Politics* 80, no. 1 (October 2017): 59–70, http://dx.doi.org/10.1086/693987.

10. Niklas K. Steffens and S. Alexander Haslam, "Power Through 'Us': Leaders' Use of We-Referencing Language Predicts Election Victory," *PLOS ONE* 8, no. 10 (October 23, 2013): e77952, https://doi.org/10.1371/journal.pone.0077952.

11. Christopher J. Bryan, Gregory M. Walton, Todd Rogers, and Carol S. Dweck, "Motivating Voter Turnout by Invoking the Self," *Proceedings of the National Academy of Sciences* 108, no. 31 (2011): 12653–56, https://doi.org/10.1073/pnas.1103343108.

12. Jonah Berger, *Magic Words: What to Say to Get Your Way* (New York: HarperCollins, 2023), 8.

Chapter 7: Appeal to Values

1. Matthew Feinberg and Robb Willer, "From Gulf to Bridge: When Do Moral Arguments Facilitate Political Influence?," *Personality & Social Psychology Bulletin* 41, no. 12 (December 2015): 1665–81, https://doi.org/10.1177/0146167215607842.

2. "Empathy Is Key to Political Persuasion, Shows New Research," University of Toronto, Rotman School of Management, November 11, 2015, https://www.rotman.utoronto.ca/Connect/MediaCentre/NewsReleases/20151111.aspx.

3. Christopher A. Bail, Lisa P. Argyle, Taylor W. Brown, Alexander Volfovsky, "Exposure to Opposing Views on Social Media Can Increase Political Polarization," *Proceedings of the National Academy of Sciences* 115, 37 (August 28, 2018), https://www.pnas.org/doi/full/10.1073/pnas.1804840115.

4. Peter Ditto and Spassena Koleva, "Moral Empathy Gaps and the American Culture War," *Emotion Review* 3, no. 3 (June 28, 2011): 331–32, https://doi.org/10.1177/1754073911402393.

5. Jonathan Haidt and Craig Joseph, "Intuitive Ethics: How Innately Prepared Intuitions Generate Culturally Variable Virtues," *Daedalus* 133, no. 4 (Fall 2004): 55–66, http://dx.doi.org/10.1162/0011526042365555.

6. Jesse Graham, Jonathan Haidt, and Brian A. Nosek, "Liberals and Conservatives Rely on Different Sets of Moral Foundations," *Journal of Personality and Social Psychology* 96, no. 5 (May 2009): 1029–46, https://doi.org/10.1037/a0015141; Spassena P. Koleva, Jesse Graham,

Ravi Iyer, Peter H. Ditto, and Jonathan Haidt, "Tracing the Threads: How Five Moral Concerns (Especially Purity) Help Explain Culture War Attitudes," *Journal of Research in Personality* 46, no. 2 (April 2012): 184–94, https://doi.org/10.1016/j.jrp.2012.01.006.

7. "Starts With Us: American Values Poll," *NORC at the University of Chicago*, May 11–15, 2023, https://startswith.us/wp-content/uploads/Report-and-Methodology-For-Website.pdf.

8. Barack Obama, *A Promised Land* (New York: Crown, 2020), 143.

9. Obama, *A Promised Land*, 145.

10. Richard Edelman, "Companies Must Not Stay Silent," Edelman, February 3, 2023, https://www.edelman.com/insights/companies-must-not-stay-silent#:~:text=Business%20leaders%20must%20not%20only,and%20lead%20on%20societal%20issues.

11. "The 2022 EY US Generation Survey: Addressing Diverse Workplace Preferences," Ernst & Young LLP, https://www.ey.com/en_us/diversity-inclusiveness/the-2022-ey-us-generation-survey.

12. Giusy Buonfantino, "New Research Shows Consumers More Interested in Brands' Values Than Ever," *Consumer Goods Technology*, April 27, 2022, https://consumergoods.com/new-research-shows-consumers-more-interested-brands-values-ever.

13. Dame Vivian Hunt, Lareina Yee, Sara Prince, and Sundiatu Dixon-Fyle, "Delivering Through Diversity," McKinsey & Company, January 18, 2018, https://www.mckinsey.com/capabilities/people-and-organizational-performance/our-insights/delivering-through-diversity; W. Malnight, Ivy Buche, and Charles Dhanaraj, "Put Purpose at the Core of Your Strategy," *Harvard Business Review*, September-October 2019, https://hbr.org/2019/09/put-purpose-at-the-core-of-your-strategy; "2020 Global Marketing Trends: Bringing Authenticity to Our Digital Age," Deloitte, https://www2.deloitte.com/content/dam/insights/us/articles/2020-global-marketing-trends/DI_2020%20Global%20Marketing%20Trends.pdf.

14. "The 2023 Axios Harris Poll 100 Reputation Rankings," Axios, May 23, 2023, https://www.axios.com/2023/05/23/corporate-brands-reputation-america.

15. "The 2023 Axios Harris Poll 100 Reputation Rankings."

16. "By the Numbers: Speaking Out," Axios, June 22, 2023, https://www.axios.com/newsletters/axios-communicators-b6251fd3-572d-4098-bf2a-e9d3a55ce6ba.html?chunk=1&utm_term=emshare#story1.

17. "Celebrating Pride at Disney," Life at Disney, June 1, 2023, https://sites.disney.com/lifeatdisney/culture-and-values/2023/06 /01/celebrating-pride-at-disney/; "LGBTQIA+ Team Members & Guests," Target, https://corporate.target.com/sustainability -governance/our-team/diversity-equity-inclusion/team-members -guests/lgbtqia#:~:text=We%20embrace%20our%20team%20 members,inclusive%2C%20safe%20employer%20and%20retailer; "Anheuser-Busch CEO Addresses Bud Light Controversy on 'CBS Mornings,'" Paramount, June 28, 2023, https://www.paramount pressexpress.com/cbs-news-and-stations/shows/cbs-mornings /releases/?view=106717-anheuser-busch-ceo-addresses-bud-light -controversy-on-cbs-mornings.

18. Jan G. Voelkel, Mashail Malik, Chrystal Redekopp, and Robb Willer, "Changing Americans' Attitudes About Immigration: Using Moral Framing to Bolster Factual Arguments," *Annals of the American Academy of Political and Social Science* 700, no. 1 (2022): 73–85, https://doi.org/10.1177/00027162221083877.

19. Feinberg and Willer, "From Gulf to Bridge."

20. "Poll: Obama's Speech Buoyed Public Support," CBS News, September 11, 2009, https://www.cbsnews.com/news/poll-obamas -speech-buoyed-public-support/.

Chapter 8: Speak from Your Heart . . . and to Theirs

1. Brendan Nyhan, Jason Reifler, Sean Richey, and Gary L. Freed, "Effective Messages in Vaccine Promotion: A Randomized Trial," *Pediatrics* 133, no. 4 (April 2014): e835–42, https://doi.org/10.1542 /peds.2013-2365.

2. Tali Sharot, *The Influential Mind: What the Brain Reveals About Our Power to Change Others* (New York: Macmillan, 2017), 7.

3. Daniel Västfjäll, Paul Slovic, Marcus Mayorga, and Ellen Peters, "Compassion Fade: Affect and Charity Are Greatest for a Single Child in Need," *PLOS ONE* 9, no. 6 (June 18, 2014): e100115, https:// doi.org/10.1371/journal.pone.0100115; Ezra M. Markowitz, Paul Slovic, Daniel Västfjäll, and Sara Hodges, "Compassion Fade and the Challenge of Environmental Conservation," *Judgment and Decision Making* 8, no. 4 (July 2013): 397–406, https://doi.org/10.1017 /S193029750000526X.

4. Deborah Small, George Loewenstein, and Paul Slovic, "Sympathy and Callousness: The Impact of Deliberative Thought on Donations to Identifiable and Statistical Victims," *Organizational Behavior and*

Human Decision Processes 102, no. 2 (March 2007): 143–53, http://
dx.doi.org/10.1016/j.obhdp.2006.01.005.

5. Deborah Small, "To Increase Charitable Donations, Appeal to
the Heart—Not the Head," Wharton School of the University
of Pennsylvania, *Knowledge at Wharton*, June 27, 2007, https://
knowledge.wharton.upenn.edu/podcast/knowledge-at-wharton
-podcast/to-increase-charitable-donations-appeal-to-the-heart
-not-the-head/#:~:text="It%27s%20easy%20to%20override%20
people%27s,to%20generate%20feelings%20toward%20statistics.

6. Jonah Berger and Katherine L. Milkman, "What Makes Online
Content Viral?," *Journal of Marketing Research* 49, no. 2 (April 2012):
192–205, https://doi.org/10.1509/jmr.10.0353.

7. John Tierney, "Will You Be E-Mailing This Column? It's Awe-
some," *New York Times*, February 8, 2010, https://www.nytimes
.com/2010/02/09/science/09tier.html.

8. William J. Brady, Julian A. Wills, John T. Jost, and Jay J. Van Bavel,
"Emotion Shapes the Diffusion of Moralized Content in Social
Networks," *Proceedings of the National Academy of Sciences* 114, no. 28
(June 26, 2017): 7313–18, https://doi.org/10.1073/pnas.1618923114.

9. Gloria Wilcox, "The Feelings Wheel: A Tool for Expanding
Awareness of Emotions and Increasing Spontaneity and Intimacy,"
Transactional Analysis Journal 12, no. 4 (1982): 274–76, https://doi
.org/10.1177/036215378201200411; Robert Plutchik, "The Nature
of Emotions: Human Emotions Have Deep Evolutionary Roots,
a Fact That May Explain Their Complexity and Provide Tools for
Clinical Practice," *American Scientist* 89, no. 4 (July-August 2001):
344–50, http://www.jstor.org/stable/27857503.

10. Thomas Sy and Daan van Knippenberg, "The Emotional Leader:
Implicit Theories of Leadership Emotions and Leadership Per-
ceptions," *Journal of Organizational Behavior* 42, no. 7 (September
2021): 885–912, https://doi.org/10.1002/job.2543.

11. Stephanie M. Ortiz and Chad R. Mandala, "There Is Queer Ineq-
uity, But I Pick to Be Happy: Racialized Feeling Rules and Diversity
Regimes in University LGBTQ Resource Centers," *Du Bois Review:
Social Science Research on Race* 18, no. 2 (2021): 347–64, https://doi
.org/10.1017/S1742058X21000096.

12. Tara Van Bommel, "The Power of Empathy in Times of Crisis and
Beyond," Catalyst, 2021, https://www.catalyst.org/reports/empathy
-work-strategy-crisis.

13. Paul J. Zak, "Why Inspiring Stories Make Us React: The Neuro

science of Narrative," *Cerebrum*, no. 2 (January-February 2015), http://www.ncbi.nlm.nih.gov/pmc/articles/pmc4445577/.

14. Pei-Ying Lin, Naomi Sparks Grewal, Christophe Morin, Walter D. Johnson, and Paul J. Zak, "Oxytocin Increases the Influences of Public Service Advertisements," *PLOS ONE* 8, no. 2 (February 27, 2013): e56934, https://doi.org/10.1371/journal.pone.0056934.

Chapter 9: Talk Like a Human

1. Christopher Ricks and Leonard Michaels, *The State of the Language* (Oakland: University of California Press, 1980), 257.
2. Colin Cramer, George Loewenstein, and Martin Weber, "The Curse of Knowledge in Economic Settings: An Experimental Analysis," *Journal of Political Economy* 97, no. 5 (October 1989): 1232–54, https://doi.org/10.1086/261651.
3. "Reading Level of State of the Union Addresses," University of California Berkeley School of Information, n.d., https://ischoolonline .berkeley.edu/blog/trump-state-of-the-union-analysis-reading -level-accessible/.

Chapter 10: Make It Sing

1. Cody Keenan, *Grace: President Obama and Ten Days in the Battle for America* (New York: Mariner Books, 2022), 156.
2. R. Brooke Lea, David N. Rapp, Andrew Elfenbein, Aaron D. Mitchel, and Russel Swinburne Romine, "Sweet Silent Thought: Alliteration and Resonance in Poetry Comprehension," *Psychological Science* 19, no. 7 (July 2008): 709–16, https://doi.org/10.1111/j.1467 -9280.2008.02146.x.
3. Keenan, *Grace*, 156.

Chapter 11: Tell the Truth

1. Soroush Vosoughi, Deb Roy, and Sinan Aral, "The Spread of True and False News Online," *Science* 369, no. 6380 (March 9, 2018): 1146–51, https://doi.org/10.1126/science.aap9559.
2. "With respect to the pledge I made that if you like your plan, you can keep it, I think—and I've said in interviews—that there is no doubt that the way I put that forward unequivocally ended up not being accurate. It was not because of my intention not to deliver on that commitment and that promise. We put a grandfather clause into the law, but it was insufficient," Barack Obama, "Statement by the President on the Affordable Care Act," November 14, 2013,

https://obamawhitehouse.archives.gov/the-press-office/2013/11/14
/statement-president-affordable-care-act.

3. Danit Ein-Gar, Baba Shiv, and Zakary L. Tromala, "When Blemishing Leads to Blossoming: The Positive Effect of Negative Information," *Journal of Consumer Research* 38, no. 5 (February 2012): 846–59, https://doi.org/10.1086/660807.

4. Rachael Denhollander, "Rachael Denhollander: The Price I Paid for Taking on Larry Nassar," *New York Times*, January 26, 2018, https://www.nytimes.com/2018/01/26/opinion/sunday/larry-nassar -rachael-denhollander.html.

5. A second individual was convicted and served time in jail, but her conviction was later vacated.

Chapter 12: Turn Your Words into Deeds

1. Josh Boak and Martin Crutsingerap, "Geithner Memoir: He Made Repeated Offers to Resign," Associated Press, May 9, 2014, https:// apnews.com/article/8f49426880b0426c87053bf39c2ddb5e.

2. Barack Obama, *A Promised Land* (New York: Crown, 2020), 282.

3. Timothy F. Geithner, *Stress Test: Reflections on Financial Crises* (New York: Crown, 2014), 11–12, 296.

4. Ted Sorensen, *Counselor: A Life at the Edge of History* (New York: HarperCollins, 2008), 142.

Chapter 13: The Only Way to End a Speech

1. Jack M. Gorman, M.D., "Many scientists have identified this higher-order, rational, slow-working part of the brain, which is basically the prefrontal cortex, and the more primitive parts of the brain that work faster or more automatically, and subserve emotions like fear," quoted in Olga Khazan, "Why People Fall for Charismatic Leaders," *The Atlantic*, October 13, 2016, https://www.theatlantic.com /science/archive/2016/10/why-people-fall-for-charismatic-leaders /503906/.

2. Daniel M. T. Fessler, Anne C. Pisor, and Carlos David Navarrete, "Negatively-Biased Credulity and the Cultural Evolution of Beliefs," *PLOS ONE* 9, no. 4 (April 15, 2014): e95167, https://doi.org/10.1371 /journal.pone.0095167.

3. Jim Collins, *Good to Great: Why Some Companies Make the Leap and Others Don't* (New York: HarperBusiness, 2001), https://www .jimcollins.com/concepts/Stockdale-Concept.html.

4. Tali Sharot, "Optimism Bias: Why the Young and the Old Tend

to Look on the Bright Side," *Washington Post*, December 31, 2012, https://www.washingtonpost.com/national/health-science /optimism-bias-why-the-young-and-the-old-tend-to-look-on-the -bright-side/2012/12/28/ac4147de-37f8-11e2-a263-f0ebffed2f15 _story.html.

5. Sharot, "Optimism Bias."

6. Tali Sharot, "The Optimism Bias," *Current Biology* 21, no. 23 (2011): R941–45, https://doi.org/10.1016/j.cub.2011.10.030.

7. Tali Sharot, "The Optimism Bias," *Time*, May 28, 2011, https:// content.time.com/time/health/article/0,8599,2074067,00.html.

8. "When It Comes to Politics and 'Fake News,' Facts Aren't Enough," National Public Radio, *Hidden Brain*, March 13, 2017, https://www .npr.org/transcripts/519661419?storyId=519661419.

9. Collins, *Good to Great*.

10. Casey Gwinn and Chan Hellman, *Hope Rising: How the Science of Hope Can Change Your Life* (New York: Morgan James Publishing, 2018), xvi.

11. "Hope Changes Everything," Hope Rising Oklahoma, https:// hoperisingoklahoma.org.

12. Jason Featherngill and Chan M. Hellman, "Nurturing the Hope and Well-Being of Oklahoma Students: The Role of Individual Career and Academic Planning," University of Oklahoma Hope Research Center and the Oklahoma State Department of Education, https://www.okedge.com/wp-content/uploads/2021/09 /DRAFT-2-Nurturing-the-Hope-and-Well-being-of-Oklahoma -Students-2.pdf.

13. Aamir Ishaque, Muhammad Tufail, and Naveed Farooq, "Psychological Capital and Employee Performance: Moderating Role of Leader's Behavior," *Journal of Business and Tourism* 3, no. 1 (June 30, 2017), https://www.semanticscholar.org/paper/Psychological -Capital-and-Employee-Performance%3A-of-Ishaque/6c25abb98f 47876807545ad43e28a6b5f65286e4.

14. "Health Benefits of Hope," Harvard University, T.H. Chan School of Public Health, 2021, https://www.hsph.harvard.edu/news /hsph-in-the-news/health-benefits-of-hope/; Holly Burns, "How to Change Your Mind-Set About Aging," *New York Times*, September 20, 2023, https://www.nytimes.com/2023/09/20/well/mind/aging -health-benefits.html.

15. Tali Sharot, *The Optimism Bias* (New York: Vintage Books, 2012), 57.

16. Sharot, *The Optimism Bias*, 58.

17. Caroline Copley and Ben Hirschler, "For Roche CEO, Celebrating Failure Is Key to Success," Reuters, September 17, 2014, https://www.reuters.com/article/us-roche-ceo-failure-idUSKBN0 HC16N20140917/.

Chapter 14: Make It Better

1. Neil A. Bradbury, "Attention Span During Lectures: 8 Seconds, 10 Minutes, or More?," *Advances in Physiology Education* 40, no. 4 (December 2016): 509–13, https://doi.org/10.1152/advan.00109.2016.
2. Dominic Gwinn (@DominicGwinn), X post, March 4, 2023, 3:07 p.m., "Mike Lindell went over his time during his speech at CPAC and the teleprompter displayed this message," https://twitter .com/DominicGwinn/status/1632110547150700544.
3. Thomas Gilovich, Kenneth Savitsky, and Victoria Husted Medvec, "The Illusion of Transparency: Biased Assessments of Others' Ability to Read One's Emotional States," *Journal of Personality and Social Psychology* 75, no. 2 (1998): 332, https://psycnet.apa.org/doi/10.1037 /0022-3514.75.2.332.
4. Emma Warnock-Parkes et al., "Seeing Is Believing: Using Video Feedback in Cognitive Therapy for Social Anxiety Disorder," *Cognitive and Behavioral Practice* 24, no. 2 (May 2017): 245–55, https:// doi.org/10.1016%2Fj.cbpra.2016.03.007,
5. Barbara L. Rees, "Effect of Relaxation with Guided Imagery on Anxiety, Depression, and Self-Esteem in Primiparas," *Journal of Holistic Nursing* 13, no. 3 (September 1995): 255–67, https://doi .org/10.1177/089801019501300307.

Chapter 15: Stand and Deliver

1. Barack Obama, *The Audacity of Hope* (New York: Crown Publishers, 2006), 359.
2. Alison Wood Brooks, "Get Excited: Reappraising Pre-Performance Anxiety as Excitement," *Journal of Experimental Psychology* 143, no. 3 (June 2014): 1144–58, https://doi.org/10.1037/a0035325.
3. Smiling can make a person seem more likable: Gemma Gladstone and Gordon Parker, "When You're Smiling Does the Whole World Smile for You?," *Australasian Psychiatry* 10, no. 2 (June 2002): 144–46, https://doi.org/10.1046/j.1440-1665.2002.00423.x; more trustworthy: Lawrence Ian Reed, Katharine N. Zeglen, and Karen L. Schmidt, "Facial Expressions as Honest Signals of Cooperative Intent in a One-Shot Anonymous Prisoner's Dilemma

Game," *Evolution and Human Behavior* 33, no. 3 (May 2012): 200–209, https://doi.org/10.1016/j.evolhumbehav.2011.09.003; more intelligent: Sing Lau, "The Effect of Smiling on Person Perception," *Journal of Social Psychology* 117, no. 1 (1982): 63–67, https://doi.org/10.1080/00224545.1982.9713408; more competent: Hyounae (Kelly) Min and Yaou Hu, "Revisiting the Effects of Smile Intensity on Judgments of Warmth and Competence: The Role of Industry Context," *International Journal of Hospitality Management* 102 (April 2022): 103152, https://doi.org/10.1016/j.ijhm.2022.103152.

4. Barbara Wild, Michael Erb, Michael Eyb, Mathias Bartels, and Wolfgang Grodd, "Why Are Smiles Contagious? An fMRI Study of the Interaction Between Perception of Facial Affect and Facial Movements," *Psychiatry Research: Neuroimaging* 123, no. 1 (May 2003): 17–36, https://doi.org/10.1016/S0925-4927(03)00006-4.

5. Helene Kreysa, Luise Kessler, and Stefan R. Schweinberger, "Direct Speaker Gaze Promotes Trust in Truth-Ambiguous Statements," *PLOS ONE* 11, no. 9 (September 19, 2016): e0162291, https://doi.org/10.1371%2Fjournal.pone.0162291.

6. Will Stephen, "How to Sound Smart in Your TEDx Talk," TedxNewYork, January 15, 2015, https://www.youtube.com/watch?v=8S0FDjFBj8o.

7. Miles L. Patterson, Alan J. Fridlund, and Carlos Crivelli, "Four Misconceptions About Nonverbal Communication," *Perspectives on Psychological Science* 18, no. 6 (2023): 1388–1411, https://doi.org/10.1177/17456916221148142.

8. Albert Mehrabian and S. R. Ferris, "Inference of Attitudes from Nonverbal Communication in Two Channels," *Journal of Consulting Psychology* 31, no. 3 (1967): 248–52, https://doi.org/10.1037/h0024648.

9. Tuvya Amsel, "An Urban Legend Called: 'The 7/38/55 Ratio Rule,'" *European Polygraph* 13, no. 2 (June 2019): 95–99, https://doi.org/10.2478/ep-2019-0007.

10. Albert Mehrabian, "'Silent Messages'—A Wealth of Information About Nonverbal Communication (Body Language)," kaaj.com, http://www.kaaj.com/psych/smorder.html.

11. Dana R. Carney, Amy J. C. Cuddy, and Andy J. Yap, "Power Posing: Brief Nonverbal Displays Affect Neuroendocrine Levels and Risk Tolerance," *Psychological Science* 21, no. 10 (September 20, 2010), https://doi.org/10.1177/0956797610383437.

12. Tom Loncar, "A Decade of Power Posing: Where Do We Stand?," *British Psychological Society*, June 8, 2021, https://www.bps.org.uk /psychologist/decade-power-posing-where-do-we-stand.

13. Dana R. Carney, "My Position on 'Power Poses,'" University of California Berkeley, Haas School of Business, October 2016, http:// faculty.haas.berkeley.edu/dana_carney/pdf_My%20position%20 on%20power%20poses.pdf.

14. Dana R. Carney, "The Nonverbal Expression of Power, Status, and Dominance," *Current Opinion in Psychology* 33 (June 2020): 256–64, https://doi.org/10.1016/j.copsyc.2019.12.004.

15. One of the researchers involved with the original study on power posing, Amy Cuddy, whose TED Talk made the concept famous, later updated her research. She argues that even if power posing does not release hormones to boost confidence, power posing still creates "postural feedback effects" that cause "people to feel more powerful." Amy J. C. Cuddy, S. Jack Schultz, and Nathan E. Fosse, "P-Curving a More Comprehensive Body of Research on Postural Feedback Reveals Clear Evidential Value for Power-Posing Effects: Reply to Simmons and Simonsohn (2017)," *Psychological Science* 29, no. 4 (2018): 656–66, https://doi.org/10.1177/0956797617746749.

Index

Abdella, Mary, 5, 76
absolute statements, 213–214, 219
Accenture, 127
AC/DC, 284
acknowledgements
  avoid starting with, 81–82
  how to do acknowledgements
    right, 87–89, 98
acronyms, 172–173
advocacy, 39
Ahmed, Rumana, 68
Air Force One, xviii, 153, 241, 263
All, Ashley, 133–134
alliteration, 192–193
American University, 7, 302
Angelou, Maya, 208
Anheuser-Busch, 130
Ansari, Zubair, 68
Anthony, Susan B., 233
anxiety, how to deal with, 271–275,
    282, 297
Aristotle, 84, 140, 145
artificial intelligence (AI), xvii–
    xviii, 27, 46. *see also* chatbots
asking for input, 68–69
Athens, Obama's visit to, 227–230
attire, 278–279, 296–297
audiences
  attention span of, 260–261
  challenging, 230
  emotions of, 144–145
  expectations of, 25
  experience of, 43
  inspiring, 27–28
  involving, 290–291
  mingling with, 279, 297

questions to ask about before a
    speech, 58–60
  reactions of, 300–301
  respecting, 73, 87–88
  uniting, 99–100
authenticity, 25, 44–46
Axelrod, David, 5–6, 15, 269

Baldwin, James, 22
Bartoloni, Kristen, 209
BBQ Rule, 168–169, 170, 177
Beginning of a speech, 76–77,
    82–91, 97–98
Benioff, Lynne, 277–278
Benioff, Marc, 126–130, 277
Berger, Jonah, 111, 145–146
Berra, Yogi, 55
Biblical Responsible Investing
    (BRI), 127
Biden, Jill, 231
Biden, Joe, 16, 89–90, 107–108, 239
bin Laden, Osama, 85, 204
Black Americans, 107, 143
blemishing effect, 210
body language, 287–290, 298
Bonker, Elizabeth, 291–294,
    302–303
Boorstin, Bob, 180
Boston
  Boston Marathon memorial
    speech, 152–155
  Szuplat born in, 6
Braver Angels, 122
breathing exercises, 283
breaths, while speaking, 188–189
brevity, 261–262

Brinker, Nancy, 28–30, 224
Brooks, Mel, 94
Bud Light, 129
Bush, George W., 101–102

cadence, 180–181
calls to action, 224–227, 230, 237,
    301
Cape Cod, 3, 6, 8, 152
Capitol, attack on, 107–108, 202
Carroll, Lewis, 163
Caslen, Robert, 204, 222
Cavell, Dave, 168
Celentano, Adriano, 179, 181
challenges, shared, 100–108, 117
character, attacks on, 105
Charleston shooting, 186, 209
chatbots
    for avoiding jargon, 169
    for core messages, 65
    for editing, 268
    for elegant words, 186
    for finding quotes, 70
    generic voice of, 46
    rise of, xvii–xviii
    unoriginality of, 27
Chavez, Cesar, 233–234
cheat sheets, 282–283
Chenault, Kenneth, 128
chiasmus, xviin
Chick-fil-A, 127, 129
Childs, Edith, xx
Chobani, 127
Chouinard, Yvon, 127
climate change, 46, 96, 103, 127, 129,
    139–140, 146, 230, 242, 248
Clinton, Bill, 5, 180, 184n
Clinton, Hillary, 147, 249
The Clothesline for Arlington
    Kids, 171–172

cognitive dissonance, 141
Cohen, William, 183–184, 184n
Coleridge, Samuel Taylor, 179
Communication 4 ALL, 302–303
Confederate flag, 209
confidence, 3, 8, 20, 26
confirmation bias, 141
Conner, Alana, 105
contractions, 173–174, 178
conversations, speeches as, 11, 14,
    66, 168, 279, 286
core messages, 63–65
corrections, 279–280, 297
credibility, 26, 45, 84, 167, 204,
    205, 212, 218
Crowther, Welles, 86
Cuomo, Mario, 181
Curry, Steph, 277
Curse of Knowledge, 165, 169, 177

Daqneesh, Omran, 158–161, 295,
    301
data
    dangers of relying on, 140–142
    using statistics to tell a story,
        142–143
Davies, Alphonso, 33–35, 224, 251,
    278, 289
Davis, Miles, 193
Dean, Laura, 165
Declaration of Independence, 233
dehumanizing language, 106–107
delivery, 284–287
demagoguery, 103–108, 241
demands for action, 225–227
Democratic convention (2004), xvii,
    13–15, 23, 35, 46–47, 123–124,
    152, 241, 265, 269, 282, 300
demonizing language, 106–107
Denhollander, Rachael, 216–218

Disney, 129, 130
Double negatives, 174, 178
the Download, 20, 63–64

earbashing, 260–261
Ebola epidemic, 141
ecopreneurs, 113
editing, how to, 263–268, 275,
    280–281, 297
elegant language, 183–186, 195
Eminem, 284
emotional reappraisal, 283
emotions. *See* feelings and emotions
empathy, 155–157, 158
Endings for a speech, 76–77, 243,
    254–255, 298
enunciation, 287
Erler, Rebekeh and Ben, 191
ethos (character, authority), 84
eulogies, 25, 38, 62, 69, 82, 100,
    157, 161, 182, 224, 254, 284
Everett, Edward, 262
excitement, how to channel it,
    283–284
experiences
  of audiences, 43, 59–60
  speaking to, 155–157, 162
  speeches as communal, 46–48,
    52–54, 145, 295
eye contact, 285, 297

fact-checking, 203, 205–208, 218
failure, fear of, 76
Falmouth, 3, 6
fans (sports), 89, 98
Favreau, Jon, 74, 168, 182, 266,
    269
fear
  dangers of appealing to, 241–243
  facts and, 141

of failure, 76
of public speaking, 4–5, 5n,
    271–272
feedback, 266–268, 276
feelings and emotions
  language of, 145–146, 161
  showing, 147–149, 161
  speaking from the heart, 144–145,
    161
Feinberg, Matthew, 120
FIFA World Cup, 33–35
50–25–25 Rule, 56–57, 78, 259–
    260, 275, 302
filler words, 287
financial crisis, 220
Finkbeiner, Felix, 235–236
firsts, historic, 89, 98
Floyd, George, 36–37, 109, 128
foods, local, 89, 98
Frankel, Adam, 85
Frazier, Ken, 128
Freedom to Marry, 131–133

Geithner, Timothy, 220–221
Gelfand, Michele, 101, 102,
    221–222
Gettysburg Address, 26, 262
Gibran, Kahlil, 139
Goebbels, Joseph, 202
Golden Rule of Public Speaking, 45
Golden State Warriors, 89
Gorillaz, 181
Green, Christina-Taylor, 72
Greenspan, Alan, 164–165
greenwashing, 128
Gwinn, Casey, 247

Habitat for Humanity, 234
Haley, Nikki, 209
"happy talk," 210–211, 219

Harrington, Brayden, 15–18, 83, 262, 303
Hartz, Tim, 61
Harvard Law Review, 12, 270
Hasson, Uri, 48
hate crimes, 107
hateful rhetoric, 106–107
Haugen, Frances, 84
Health care reform, 131, 203
Hellman, Chan, 247
"Hello!", starting with, 82–83, 90–91, 97, 284
Hendriksen, Ellen, 4–5, 272–273, 282–283
Hispanic Americans, 107, 143
Hobby Lobby, 127, 129
Holmes, Oliver Wendell, Jr., 184
Holzer, Ben, 203
home crowd shout-outs, 83
honesty. *See* truth-telling
hope
  and action, 245–247
  after setbacks, 249
  contagious nature of, 249–253
  humans hardwired for, 244–245
  power of, 243–244
  as predictor of success, 247–248
  the only way to end a speech, 238
Hope Rising (Gwinn & Hellman), 247
House of Pain, 284
How to Lie with Statistics (Huff), 141
human-centered stories, 157–161, 162
humility, 210, 218
humor, 91–95, 98
Hurwitz, Sarah, 36
Hussain, Rashad, 68
hype songs, 284

ideas
  challenging, 113–114
  defending, 114–117
  shared, 112–113
identifiable victim effect, 158–159
identity, shared, 108–112, 117
illusion of transparency, 273
illusory truth effect, 202
imagery, 71
inclusivity, 67–68, 87, 110–111
interoceptive exposure, 272
introductions, 83–84, 97
ISIS, 199–200

Jacob, Susannah, 70
jargon, 163–167
jazz, 193
Jewish Americans, 87, 107
job interviews, xix, 38, 260, 261
Jobs, Steve, 234
jokes, 91–95
Jones, Amanda, 114–117, 248, 303
Jordan, Michael, 262

Kansans for Constitutional Freedom, 134
Karlin-Neumann, Zev, 125
Keenan, Cody, 74, 166, 176, 190–191, 193
Keep It Simple rule, 169
Kelce, Jason, 148
Keller, Helen, 293
Kennedy, John F., xviin, 221, 234, 265
keynotes, 62
Khan Academy, 234
King, Martin Luther, Jr., 49, 66, 70, 113, 234
Komen, Susan, 28–30
Krupin, Stephen, 71

language
  absolutist, 213–214, 219
  elegant, 183–186, 195
  emotional, 145–146, 161
  empowering, 221–222
  hateful, 106–107
  local greetings, 90–91
  lofty, 175–177, 178
  Obama's straightforward, xviin
  violent, 107–108
leading by example, 231–233, 237
learning from others, 66–67
Lechtenberg, Tyler, 144–145
legalese, 175, 178
Lehman, Alisa, 5n
lengths of speeches, 62–63
lessons, sharing yours, 222–223, 237
Lewis, John, 12
LGBTQ community, 95, 107, 114, 129–130, 131–133
lies and lying, 201–202, 205, 218
Lincoln, Abraham, 26, 176, 192, 208, 262
Lippmann, Walter, 184
listening, importance of, 11, 67
Litt, David, 92
Livingston, Donovan, 49–52, 270, 278, 290
local languages, greetings in, 90–91
lofty language, 175–177, 178
Logan, Kate, 278
logos (logic), 140, 148
Lovett, Jon, 92
Ludacris, 284
Lyoya, Patrick, 36–38

Maathai, Wangari, 235
"many," multiple meanings of, 214
marginalized communities, xvi, xvii, 36–38, 271, 302

Marine One, xv
marriage equality, 131–133
Mata-Rubio, Kimberly, 225–227, 262
Mata-Rubio, Lexi, 225–227
McCain, John, 215–216
McChrystal, Stanley, 74
McCullough, David, Jr., 113
McRaven, William, 204, 222–223
Mellencamp, John, 191
mellifluous words, 185, 195
memorization, 270–271
Meta, 127–128
Michigan State University, 217
Middle of a speech, 76–77
Milkman, Katherine, 145–146
moral empathy gap, 120
moral foundations, 120–121, 135
moral framing, 130–131
Moricz, Zander, 95–97, 302
Moy, Ellen, 171–172, 224
Murat, Ziba, 90
Murrow, Edward R., 199
Muslim Americans, 67–68, 87, 107, 200, 233, 238–239
Mustakallio, Antti, xiv, 19, 274–275
Myers, Sophia, 233
Myteberi, Alex, 159–161, 262, 295, 301

narrative arc, 76–77
Nassar, Larry, 217
nerves, how to overcome, 272–275, 282, 297
Netanyahu, Benjamin, 64
neural coupling, 48
Newtown shooting, 148
Nicholson, Marvin, 280, 281
Nike, 234

nonverbal communication, 287–290
nuance, 214–215, 219

Obama, Barack
  as a community organizer, 9–11
  confidence of, 9
  evolution as a speaker, xvii, 10–15
  "biggest mistake," 124
  greetings in local languages,
     90–91
  on his best speeches, 300
  international popularity of, xv
  McCain's defense of, 215–216
  nuances acknowledged by,
     214–215
  political campaigns, 13
  racial identity struggles, 9
  speaking to values, 123–125, 131
  speeches of. *see* Obama, Barack–
     speeches
  straightforward language of, xviin
  teaching career, 12, 47
  use of humor, 93
  verbosity of, 165–166
Obama, Barack–speeches
  in Australia, 68–69
  Boston Marathon bombing
     memorial, 152–155
  in Cairo, 216
  to Canadian Parliament, 124–125
  Charleston, SC eulogy, 186
  in Cuba, 155
  on cybersecurity, 40–41
  in Greece, on democracy, 227–230
  Democratic convention (2004),
     xvii, 13–15, 46–47, 123–124
  farewell address, 124, 240–241
  Fort Hood shooting memorial, 87
  Greenwood, SC campaign stop,
     xx

Harvard Law Review dinner, 12,
     270
  in Hiroshima, 155
  inaugural address, 191–193
  in Indonesia, 22–23
  on ISIS, 200–201
  Joplin, MO tornado aftermath,
     102
  in Laos, 156
  Middle East policy, 63–64
  MLK Jr. Memorial, 70
  to Muslim-Americans, 67–68
  New Hampshire primary (2008),
     186–190, 192, 194–195
  Newtown, CT shooting briefing,
     148–149
  9/11 Memorial Museum
     dedication, 86
  Nobel Peace Prize, 66, 211–212
  post-election (2016), 239–240
  in Selma, 176
  in South Korea, 166–167
  State of the Union, 91
  Thanksgiving turkey pardoning,
     94
  Tucson shooting memorial, 72
  United Nations refugee summit,
     159–161
  U.S. Air Force Academy
     commencement, 210
  in Vietnam, 28
  Vietnam War anniversary, 71
  to Wall Street executives, 216
Obama, Michelle, xvii, 35–36, 105,
     144–145, 168, 231, 240–241
Occidental College, 8–9
O'Connor, Kyle, 71–72, 75
100% Situational Awareness,
     57–63, 78
opening lines, 84–86, 97

optimism bias, 245
originality, 25
otherizing language, 106–107
Oval Office, 19, 55, 64, 86, 190, 228, 259
oxytocin, 158–159
Ozick, Cynthia, 81

Packer, Dominic, 110–111
parts of a speech, 76–77
Patagonia, 127
Pathos (emotion), 145
pauses, importance of, 193–195, 196, 287
performances, speeches as, 42–44, 52–54
Peri, Sarada, 74–75, 147
Pericles, 184
personalization, 23–28, 38–39
persuasion
  by appealing to values, 118–121
  moral framing, 130–131
  speaking from the heart, 144–145
physiological arousal, 145–146
plagiarism, 204, 218
Plant-for-the-Planet, 235–236
Platkin, Alexandra, 205
podiums, 62
Polarization Dictionary, 106
The Power of Us (Van Bavel & Packer), 110–111
power pose, 288
practicing, 269–272, 276
preparing to speak, 278–284
Pressfield, Steven, 8
printing speeches, 269–270
psychic numbing, 142
public speaking
  fear of, 4–5, 5n, 271–272
  Golden Rule of, 45

as a skill to be learned, 18, 20
PublicSquare, 127
puns, 94

questions to ask before any speech, 57–63
quotes, how to use in a speech, 69–70, 87, 209

rallies, 38
Reagan, Ronald, 92, 234, 262
rehearsing, 269–276
rejection, fear of, 3–5
religious beliefs, 87, 233
Remsburg, Cory, 249–253
repetition, 191–192, 196
reproductive rights, 133–134
research, how to, 66–72
Rhodes, Ben, 23, 41, 66, 228, 266
rhythm
  breathing at the right time, 188–189
  loosening up, 190–191, 196
  via alliteration, 192–193
  via pauses, 193–195, 196
  via repetition, 191–192, 196
  via sentence structure, 189–190, 196
  writing speeches like scripts for, 186–188, 195
Rilke, Rainer Maria, 3
Roosevelt Room, 67
Rose Garden, 239
Rubio, Felix, 225–227
Rule of Three, 192, 196
Ryan, Paul, 57–58

Salesforce, 126–130, 277
Sanchez, Robert, 252
Santos, George, 205

Saujani, Reshma, 113–114
Schwan, Severin, 249
scripts, writing speeches like, 186–188, 195
Scripture, quoting from, 87
second opinions, 266–268
Selma, civil rights marches, 110, 176, 193
Seneca Falls convention, 193
sentence structure, 189–190, 196
Sermon on the Mount, 233
7-38-55 rule, 288
Shakespeare, William, 40
Sharot, Tali, 142, 244–245, 248
shocking facts, 90
"show don't tell," 71
shower effect, 75
Sia, 284
Simon & Garfunkel, 141
Small, Deborah, 142
smiling, importance of, 284–285, 297
Smith, Robert F., 232
Social Equity and Education Initiative, 302
social rejection, fears of, 5
Sorensen, Ted, 221, 265
source citation, 208–209, 218
Southey, Robert, 259
speaking human
   avoid acronyms, 172–173, 177
   avoid legalese, 175, 178
   avoid lofty language, 175–177, 178
   banish double negatives, 174, 178
   BBQ rule, 168–169, 170, 177
   get real, 169, 171–172, 177
   use of contractions, 173–174, 178
statistics, 90, 142–143
Stockdale, James, 244, 246
Stonewall Inn, 193

stories
   articulating, 30–33
   beginning with, 86–87
   heart-touching, 71–72
   personal, 18–19, 20–21, 23–28, 38–39
   power of, 28
   sacred, 11–15
   telling with statistics, 143
structure, 76–77
subject matter, knowing, 65
succinctness, 260–261
Sweet, Julie, 127
Szuplat, Claire, 5
Szuplat, Erica, 8
Szuplat, Jack, 5
Szuplat, Katherine, 116
Szuplat, Peggy, 6, 7, 18
Szuplat, Stach, 6, 7, 18

Tamminga, Naiara, 36–38, 83–84, 248, 262, 301
Target, 129, 130
Ted Lasso, 238
Tesla, 234
thought leaders, 39
Threat Dictionary, 101
Three Fs, 89, 98
Thunberg, Greta, 139–140, 144, 248
time allotments, 62–63
Toastmasters International, 4
toasts, xiii, 25, 27, 38, 57, 63, 73, 92, 100, 161, 182, 224, 254
Tori, Ed, 68
tributes, 38, 254
Trump, Donald, 33, 107–108, 199–200, 227–228, 238–239, 249
trust, crisis of, 201–202

Truth, Sojourner, 261–262
truth-telling
  about the past, 209–210, 218
  as a choice, 202–204
  hard truths, 215–218, 219
  importance of, 199–202
  Ten Commandments of, 218–219
23andMe, 5n
Tyson, Neil deGrasse, 141

Ulukaya, Hamdi, 127
Underwood, Carrie, 284
unexpected statements, 90
United Bid, 33–35
unity
  shared challenges, 100–108, 117
  shared ideas, 112–117
  shared identity, 108–112, 117
  shared values, 120–121
University of Chicago Law School,
  12
unpredictability, 181–183, 195
USA Gymnastics, 217

values
  appealing to, 118–120
  in business, 126–130
  moral foundations, 120–121, 135
  shared, 121–123
  universal, 123–125
Van Bavel, Jay, 109, 110–111
Vargas, Jose Antonio, 99
Vella, Olivia, 149–152, 248, 270,
  301–302
violent language, 107–108
vision, importance of, 233–236,
    237, 247, 255
visualization, 273–274, 276
voice
  authentic, 44–46
  modulation, 285–287, 297–298
Voice of Doubt, xi, 8, 20, 74, 296,
    302
vulnerability, 149–152, 161–162

"war" metaphors, 102n
The War of Art (Pressfield), 8
"we," power of, 110–111
White House Correspondents'
    Dinners, 92
Whitman, Walt, 109
will.i.am, 195
Williams, Jamal, 147–148
Winthrop, John, 234
Wiz Khalifa, 284
Wolfson, Evan, 131–133
Wood Brooks, Alison, 283
Woolf, Virginia, 118
word salad, 163–167
writer's block, how to overcome,
    74–75
writing out your remarks, 72–77, 78

X (formerly Twitter), 127–128, 146

"Yes We Can," 86, 110, 186–189,
    192, 194–195
Yoda, 243

Zak, Paul, 158
Zoom presentations, xvii, 43,
    53–54, 285n

About the Author

TERRY SZUPLAT is a sought-after speaker and trainer whose keynote presentations and workshops empower audiences with the communication skills he learned as a White House speechwriter during the eight years of Barack Obama's presidency. From 2009 to 2017, he served as a special assistant to the president and a member of the National Security Council staff, and from 2013 to 2017 he was the deputy director of the White House Speechwriting Office. Today Terry runs his own speechwriting firm, Global Voices Communications, and he teaches speechwriting at his alma mater, American University's School of Public Affairs. His essays have appeared in major publications, including the *New Yorker*, *New York Magazine*, and the *Washington Post*. Originally from East Falmouth, Massachusetts, he now lives outside Washington, D.C., with his wife and two children.